"A how-to book that offers a clear and comp
and inspiring performing arts boards in the U.

—Olympia Dukakis

"Board members—not just of performing arts organizations, but of any not-for-profit—will benefit from reading *The Art of Governance*. The chapters are thorough and intelligent and they add up to a book which provides important insights and advice about governing organizations wisely and effectively."

—Jay W. Lorsch
Professor, Harvard Business School and author of
Back to the Drawing Board: Designing Boards for a Complex World

"A breath of fresh air. Written for (and by) board members, *The Art of Governance* is an essential guide filled with valuable insights and learning shared by the field's leading practitioners. It offers a compelling look at the state of the contemporary American theater and provides detailed information on the operational aspects of running a theater company. An excellent tool for building an enlightened and inspired board."

—Angie Kim
Director of Programs, Arts and Conservation, Flintridge Foundation

"*The Art of Governance* is an extremely important publication. The editors have compiled contributions from some of the finest thinkers of our time to explore the complex issues surrounding arts boards, and the result is a thorough compendium of pragmatic suggestions and stimulating thinking. Anyone involved with the board of a performing arts organization will be a better trustee for having read it."

—Henry Fogel
President, American Symphony Orchestra League

"*The Art of Governance* is a great resource for all who are involved in the not-for-profit sector. Although focused on theater organizations, the principles and questions raised by the various articles are applicable to any not-for-profit organization. This thoughtful compilation will be invaluable to those who seek to identify, engage and motivate board members to be effective and to give them a rewarding experience working for the public good. As a 'professional' board member of many local, regional and national organizations, I will use this book to remind me of my responsibilities, how I can honor my commitments and how I can work more meaningfully with other board members and staffs."

—Abel Lopez
Associate Producing Director, GALA Hispanic Theatre

THE ART OF GOVERNANCE

THE ART OF GOVERNANCE

BOARDS IN THE PERFORMING ARTS

Edited by
Nancy Roche and Jaan Whitehead

THEATRE COMMUNICATIONS GROUP
NEW YORK
2005

The Art of Governance: Boards in the Performing Arts is published by
Theatre Communications Group, Inc., 520 Eighth Avenue, 24th Floor,
New York, NY 10018–4156

This publication is made possible in part with public funds from the New York State Council on the Arts, a State Agency.

TCG books are exclusively distributed to the book trade by Consortium Book Sales and Distribution, 1045 Westgate Drive, St. Paul, MN 55114.

Library of Congress Cataloging-in-Publication Data

The art of governance : boards in the performing arts / edited by Nancy Roche
and Jaan Whitehead.— 1st ed.
p. cm.
ISBN-13: 978-1-55936-259-7
ISBN-10: 1-55936-259-6
(alk. paper)
1. Performing arts—management. 2. Boards of directors.
I. Roche, Nancy. II. Whitehead, Jaan Walther.
PN1584.A78 2005
791'.068—dc22 2005012826

Text design by Lisa Govan
Cover design by Kitty Suen
Cover illustration by David Diaz
Editor photos by Jinsey Dauk

First Printing, June 2005

The Art of Governance *is dedicated to all the trustees who so generously give their time, resources and passion to sustain the vitality of the performing arts in this country.*

TABLE OF CONTENTS

FOREWORD

OVER THE YEARS, I have served on a wide range of boards, and now for the past four years have served a board as Artistic Director of the Westport Country Playhouse. In my view, a strong, mutually supportive working relationship between board members and artists and management is vital to the success of our not-for-profit theaters. For me, this means board members not only being successful in fundraising, planning and finance, but also understanding the deeper nature of the art—how it is created, who creates it, what the risks and rewards are. As an artist myself, I know the difference when trustees understand my world and my work. It changes how they fulfill their governance role and how they work with me as their artistic director. And, as a board member, I appreciate how important it is for artists to understand boards—what their responsibilities are, how they work, and how the essential work of the board complements the work of the staff.

This is the first book I have seen that captures this important dimension of governing, that not only gives a solid presentation of the practical work of a board but also provides the artistic context in which that work takes place. And it is the first book I have seen that is presented through a multitude of voices—in it we hear from trustees, managers, artists and consultants, all with their own perspectives on governing. *The Art of Governance* is a real contribution to all of us who work in the arts.

Joanne Woodward
Artistic Director and member of the Board of Directors,
Westport Country Playhouse, Westport, Connecticut
May 2005

PREFACE

I LOVE BOARDS.

One of the great pleasures of my time at TCG has been the opportunity to travel around the country, meeting with boards of directors at our member theaters. Clearly, with such full lives, their decision to devote their time, energy and resources to our field is always deeply inspiring and moving to me.

I am perhaps even more moved in the last several years, given the seismic shifts in philanthropic patterns and audience behavior that our field is currently experiencing. Never have the challenges been more daunting, never has the future felt more uncertain—and never have the imperatives for effective board participation been greater. The future calls on trustees, not only to give time and resources in increasing amounts, but to provide counsel, imagination and rigorous guidance in new ways.

This book is both for them and of them.

It is for those trustees I most admire—the ones inevitably passionate about the theater, anxious to understand its inner workings and logic, and committed not only to optimizing their own performance but to improving the reach of their theater and the lives of the artists, administrators and technicians who bring the work to life.

The articles that follow are assembled in that spirit—not only in exploring the spirit of governance but in mining the "nuts and bolts" of effective practice. This book attempts to fill the terrain that lies between those books on governance that at one end offer a general introduction to life on a board, or at the other observe patterns of governance from the proverbial 30,000-foot view of research and academia. Those books are clearly indispensable ones: This one, however, tries to speak in tangible, sophisticated terms from where "the rubber meets the road."

And this book is of trustees, of course, because it is curated by Nancy Roche and Jaan Whitehead, two of our field's great trustees—trustees who have brought extraordinary passion, insight and rigor to their work on boards in Baltimore; Washington, D.C.; and New York, including our own TCG board. Their combined experience guides this book on every page; resonant with the issues not that we in the field think boards struggle to address, but that board members themselves know confound and absorb them. Added to the work Nancy and Jaan have done to date, this contribution now ratchets their legacy up yet another level by the extraordinary service they have done in bringing this book to life. All of us here are honored that they would bring it to us.

The real test, of course, will come in how the book is used. It is our hope that this book is digested, studied, debated and explored not only in every theater—but with every arts board. Boards in all disciplines will find this book informative and powerful. These discussions—and how they translate into action—will determine not only the health of organizations but the health of the field as a whole.

And so to reading—and to work.

Ben Cameron
Executive Director, Theatre Communications Group,
New York,
May 2005

ACKNOWLEDGMENTS

We are deeply grateful to our authors and contributors, all of whom essentially volunteered their time because they believed in the value of this book. Their collective contributions, we believe, advance the field of governance. Noted authorities in their fields, these trustees, managing directors, artistic directors, artists, staff and consultants are the fabric of the book, and their talent and eloquence speak for themselves. We appreciate their generosity and good will.

We consulted many people as the project evolved, quite a few of whom became our authors. In addition to our authors, we would like to thank Mary Ann de Barbieri, Gigi Bolt, Fran Kumin, Vicki Nolan, Marie Nugent-Head, Ted Rogers, Michael Ross, Richard Tickton and Elspeth Udvarhelyi for their advice and council. James Houghton and Dara Petransky were indispensable in organizing our artists' roundtable.

We are grateful to our colleagues at Theatre Communications Group, who supported our initial concept, thoughtfully advised us in its development and became our publisher. Under the leadership of Executive Director Ben Cameron, TCG is committed to the collaboration between trustees and theater leaders and has developed programs supporting that collaboration, which have become a model for the arts. We also thank Ben for the time he spent reading and editing our book. In addition, Joan Channick, Deputy Director; Christopher Shuff, Director of Management Programs and Laurie Baskin, Director of Government and Education Programs, were all especially generous in sharing their time and ideas.

We have been fortunate in our publishing team at TCG, particularly Kitty Suen, who designed the cover; Lisa Govan, who designed the text; Leigh Zona, who marketed it and Mollie Wilson, who assisted in the editorial process. Our greatest thanks go to our editors Terry Nemeth and Kathy Sova for their patience, intelligence and unstinting professional expertise. As friends and partners, they are, to a great extent, responsible for the pride we take in the book.

We also appreciate the ongoing support and encouragement of our families, particularly our daughters Kate, Anne and Sarah, who so strongly share our love of the performing arts. And, finally, we extend our heartfelt thanks to each other for the affection and patience that allowed two different minds and talents to create this book in a partnership that not only maintained but enriched an already enduring friendship.

THE ART OF GOVERNANCE: BOARDS IN THE PERFORMING ARTS

An Introduction

The Art of Governance is for trustees in the performing arts and for the artists, managers and community leaders who work with them. Although there are many excellent resources available to trustees today, few of them address the particular needs of boards in the performing arts. Our own years of experience have convinced us that the performing arts are different and that, for trustees, these differences matter.

The book is divided into two parts. The first part, "The Framework of Governance," provides the larger context in which trustees govern: the art, artists, history, institutions and national policies of the performing arts. The second part, "The Practice of Governance," explores more practical issues, such as board development, planning, finance and fundraising. The two parts of the book complement each other by placing the everyday work of the board within its artistic and institutional framework. We believe that this approach brings a new and fuller perspective to what makes boards successful in the performing arts.

The Art of Governance was specifically conceived as a book of readings because we wanted the book to be one of many voices, reflecting the collaborative nature of the arts themselves. Written by a group of distinguished artists, trustees, managers and consultants, these articles present a wide range of experiences and perspectives. Together they create a rich dialogue about the role of boards in the performing arts, while providing readers with a wealth of information and advice.

Because of the range of material it covers, the book can be used in many ways. It is an excellent orientation tool for new trustees as well as a sophisticated resource for more experienced trustees. It can also serve as a guide to managers and artists who work with boards and seek to understand them better, and as a handbook for students in arts management programs. Although the book is written primarily by practitioners from the theater world, its philosophy and practical information are applicable to all the performing arts as well as to other organizations that want to challenge their own understanding of governance. A Resource Guide is included at the end of the book for those who want to read further about general issues of governance or about the particular topics covered in each chapter.

Why the Performing Arts Are Different

In his chapter, "The Art of Theater," Todd London describes the process that takes place as a group of artists creates a play:

> Every moment of this group journey invites discovery and dares disaster. An actor may read a line in a way that brings out meanings the author never understood, and he may interpret a scene in a way the author never intended. A design choice may look beautiful on paper and distracting in practice, or it may seem drab until inhabited by three-dimensional bodies on an actual stage. One director may understand the play's themes and structure brilliantly but fail to create living, breathing events in the rehearsal room. Another director may remain silent on the play as a work of ideas or literature and yet know how to catalyze actors and designers to ignite whatever explosions of life lie latent in the text. Every moment . . . is a moment of artistic choice (this way or that way?) and human interaction (your way or mine?).

As Todd's description so eloquently shows, the process of creating art is a series of uncertain steps, and not even the most talented and experienced artists can know in advance where these steps will lead. For trustees, this creates a unique kind of risk that makes traditional approaches to governance too simplistic. All organizations—for-profit and not-for-profit—operate under conditions of uncertainty but, in the performing arts, there is a difference. In the performing arts, uncertainty comes not only from the external environment in which any organization operates; it comes from within the production process itself. It is the creative process itself that causes the uncertainty. Whether an organization produces a well-known classic or a new work, it never knows how successful the production will be.

It is not surprising that being a trustee in the performing arts is both exhilarating and stressful. Of course, it is exhilarating when a production goes well, thrilling the audience and the artists who created it. But it is also stressful living with the constant risk of mounting new productions, while also being ultimately responsible for the financial health of the organization. And when funding is harder and harder to attain, it is no wonder that trustees often feel a natural, even compelling, instinct to try to reduce risk by standardizing seasons with better known and more entertaining offerings. Pleasing audiences and critics in order to meet budget goals can easily become an overriding concern.

But trying to reduce risk by controlling programming is finally self-defeating. Not only do performing arts organizations operate under conditions of risk all the time, it is how they must operate. The creation of original productions is what the arts do; it is their lifeblood, the source of their artistry and accomplishment. In any live art form, an inherent tension exists between the need for artists to court uncertainty and the need for trustees to contain it. Finding the balance between the two—the balance between artistic creativity and fiscal stability—is the paradox trustees in the performing arts constantly face. Leaning too much toward artistic risk can undermine the financial foundations of the organization, but leaning too much toward fiscal stability can undermine the artistic process that is its very reason for existence. The challenge for trustees is to understand the nature of the trade-off and to learn to live productively—if not always comfortably—in this environment of risk.

Another unique aspect of the performing arts that affects governance is the role that artists play in the institutional life of arts organizations. Most obvious is the addition of an artistic director to the management structure. In most not-for-profits, boards create a partnership with an executive director who is the staff leader of the organization; it is a two-way partnership. But in the performing arts, in addition to maintaining a relationship with an executive director, boards also need to build a relationship of support and trust with an artistic director who leads the artistic side of the organization. It is a three-way partnership. Creating and maintaining healthy relationships in this three-way partnership becomes another challenge for trustees.

The writers, composers, performers, designers and directors in the performing arts also have an unusual role in the arts organizations where they work. Rather than being full-time employees, most of these artists are freelance and are jobbed in for individual productions. Since these artists are removed from the daily life of the organization, it is difficult for trustees to know them and understand the nature of their lives. What is it like to be a freelance artist? What pay do you receive and what health benefits? What is it like to live on the road? If trustees are not familiar with artists and how they work, it is hard for them to understand conflicts over programming and budgets when they arise. It is also hard for trustees to work effectively in an environment of risk if they don't know the artists who are at the center of that risk. Good governance in the performing arts needs to be grounded in an astute and creative understanding not only of the art but also of the artists who make it. This belief forms the philosophical heart of the book and shapes its structure and content.

The Framework of Governance

THE ART

The first part of the book, "The Framework of Governance," begins with three articles that explore the artistic and institutional framework in which trustees work. In the opening article, "The Art of Theater," Todd London brings alive the power of art: What can happen when we gather together in rooms as actors and audiences; how varied these rooms can be from warehouses to palaces to open fields; and how thrilling—and dangerous—it can be when, through the eyes of a Shakespeare, a Chekhov or a Tony Kushner, we see ourselves or our society in new ways. It is the art that underlies all that we do as trustees, and we are reminded how fragile this art can be and why we, as trustees, are so important to its stewardship.

As arts trustees, we are also part of a seminal movement that originated in the 1960s when a generation of activist artists and funders produced a flowering of the performing arts that spread theater, dance and music all across the country. Although today our environment is much less hospitable to the arts, and organizations have moved on to new generations of leadership, most of our values, ways of working and expectations come from this founding era. In "Going National," Jim O'Quinn shows us this heritage, and reminds us of the vitality of the pioneering spirit and dreams of our founders. Zelda Fichandler, one of those founders and still our most articulate writer and storyteller, then takes us to the present and the seemingly eternal conflicts that occur when art is created within the context—and confines—of an institution. She astutely argues, not for "either/or" but rather for "both/and" as we balance the ever-present tension between art and money.

Arts Advocacy and the Changing Legal Environment

Next we turn to the wider political, social and economic environment in which trustees work. Although there are many aspects of this environment that affect governing, we focus on two that are of growing importance to trustees: arts advocacy and the changing legal environment of the arts.

The role of advocacy is becoming an essential part of governance. In addressing an audience of trustees, Ben Cameron, Executive Director of TCG, candidly said: "It's no longer enough to be a supporter in order to warrant a place on an arts board. Now arts board service means being an activist on behalf of the organization . . . I would challenge every board to embrace, without reservation, its role in advocacy—to recognize that they have the power to speak and to make the cultivation of relationships with legislators and potential legislators a serious priority."

To be effective advocates, trustees first need to understand the byzantine network of public and private funding that supports the arts in this country. In "National Arts Policy," Gigi Bradford describes the complex nature of public funding in the United States, and positions this funding in the broader context of arts funding in other countries, especially those of western Europe. She clarifies the economic reasons why the arts need outside support in the first place and explores our philosophical and historical attitudes toward such support.

No one has championed public advocacy of our nation's patchwork quilt of public funding more effectively than Roche Schulfer, activist manager of The Goodman Theatre in Chicago. In "The Role of Advocacy in Trustee Governance," Roche challenges trustees to become activists, explaining what this means and why it is so important. In doing so, he dispels many of the myths that often deter trustees from becoming involved and offers practical steps that trustees can follow to become strong and effective champions of the arts.

A part of the external environment that is usually left to experts but is now becoming important to all trustees is the changing legal demands being placed on not-for-profit organizations. As the scandals and resulting board reforms in the corporate world increasingly affect the not-for-profit world, trustees and their institutions face new interpretations of their legal and fiduciary responsibilities. In her chapter, "The Changing Legal Environment for the Arts," Joan Channick explores the changes taking place in the legal environment, including the implications of the Sarbanes-Oxley Act, and details steps arts institutions can take to adjust to these changes.

THE SPIRIT OF GOVERNING

The first half of the book concludes with two discussions of multiple voices. First, a roundtable of distinguished theater artists talk about their own experiences with boards and about what they would like boards to know about them, their work and their lives. What does the itinerant artist need in order to create an "artistic home" at our theaters? What opportunities can we create to get to know our artists better and why does this matter? The voices of these artists bring a fullness to the book that is too often missing from discussions of governance.

The next article, "The Spirit of Governance," brings together the reflections of six distinctive people with long service in the arts: two trustees who have served as board presidents, two former managing directors, an expert on diversity issues and an accomplished artist. From their own experiences, these knowledgeable experts share what they think distinguishes good governance. In so doing, each recognizes that there is a "spirit" of governance that goes beyond a board's fiduciary responsibilities. Whether it is how power is shared, how board-staff relationships are handled or how trust is established, it is often the quality of this spirit that determines how successful trustees can be.

The Practice of Governance

BOARD STRUCTURE AND OPERATIONS

The second half of the book turns to the more practical work of the board and begins with an article on board development by co-editor Nancy

Roche. Most boards have a nominating or board development committee whose function is to recruit the next generation of trustees. If the board is lucky, the tenure of new trustees will be smooth. They will take their job seriously, fundraise, be responsible as fiduciary agents and contribute their time, financial resources and expertise. But if the organization stumbles or is tested by any number of possibilities—an unexpected deficit, the sudden departure of an artistic or managing leader, a public relations crisis, a season of unexpectedly low ticket sales—the ability of these new trustees will be seriously tested. Only then does a board really appreciate the more comprehensive work of this committee: not only cultivating and recruiting trustees, but also orienting, educating and continually evaluating them.

Taylor, Chait and Holland's article, "The New Work of the Nonprofit Board," reprinted from the *Harvard Business Review*, is a seminal essay for not-for-profit trustees. Describing "new work" as work that really matters, the authors argue that many not-for-profit boards do not utilize the time, talent and resources of their board members wisely. Instead of focusing in an informed way on clearly defined and important issues, many boards are mired in traditional committee structures and board/staff divisions that dissipate the ability of boards to genuinely help institutions fulfill their missions. With a thoughtful list of criteria complemented by a wide range of examples, the authors show how boards can change the way they operate and achieve more institutional and personal success.

STRATEGIC PLANNING AND UNDERSTANDING FINANCIAL STATEMENTS

In our rapidly changing world, good strategic planning has become essential for arts organizations, whether they want to undertake a capital campaign, recruit a new artistic or managing director or develop a stronger board of trustees. But planning is never easy. Some trustees find the planning process stimulating and are eager to be involved but others find it intimidating and shy away from it. And some organizations understand how to use planning effectively while others create voluminous paperwork that languishes on a shelf. In "A Guide to Strategic Planning," Ronnie Brooks offers a thoughtful and thorough approach to strategic planning. Her focus on key questions and a logical, commonsense process affords any organization a clear, sequential map.

CENTERSTAGE's veteran managing director, Peter Culman, tells the story of a new trustee, an accountant, who joined the board and was assigned to the finance committee: "At the first finance committee meeting he sat there very quietly until just before the end of the meeting when he said, 'I have a couple of questions. This number here. I'd like to understand the story this number is telling.' And we began to answer, and I thought, This is the first time I've ever been with someone who sees numbers as a means of revealing a story. After everyone left I sat down with him and said, 'I want you to tell me what happens to you when you look at a set of numbers.' And he said, 'I try to translate what they're telling me so that I can begin to understand the story of what's going on. That way I'll begin to understand the organization. The only truly comprehensive statement that a theater makes about itself, year in, year out, is its budget, because the budget reveals, for better or worse, its priorities." Pat Egan and Nancy Sasser demonstrate in "Understanding Financial Statements" how numbers tell their story. Although equipping the beginner with an accounting primer, they also provide the more advanced reader with sophisticated ways to analyze not-for-profit financial statements and track their organization's financial health. As Lloyd Richards, former artistic director of the Yale Repertory Theatre and the O'Neill Playwrights Conference, succinctly commented, "Every dollar is attached to a human life."

FUNDRAISING

As trustees know all too well, fundraising is the bottom line of their work. Without enough contributed income, the financial and artistic health of their organization is at risk. In "The Annual Fund," the first of two articles on fundraising, development director Dawn Rains provides trustees with a basic understanding of what they need to know about the annual fund, the foundation of every theater's support. She describes the different components of the fund and explains the various roles it can play in the life of an arts organization. She discusses why people give, how a case for support is developed and what methods of fundraising are most effective. And she discusses in detail why the involvement of trustees is so important.

Successful capital campaigns are like painting a room: Meticulous preparation is fifty percent of the work. In the second fundraising article, "Capital and Endowment Campaigns," veteran fundraiser Christine O'Connor carefully describes the groundwork that precedes a campaign, including the importance of asking the right questions: Why are we doing this? Is this the right time? Is a new building really the best use of potential dollars? She then discusses the different stages of a capital campaign: the feasibility study, the so-called "quiet stage," the public stage and, finally, the celebratory activities that complete the campaign. Included in her discussion is a wealth of advice on the roles trustees play as leaders, donors and solicitors in any successful campaign.

LEADERSHIP TRANSITIONS AND ADDITIONAL PERSPECTIVES

The choice of a new artistic or administrative leader is the most important decision a board makes. No other decision is so sensitive or has such ongoing reverberations for the health and vitality of an organization's future. "Leadership Succession in Not-for-Profit Organizations" is taken from an excellent study on leadership transitions by the Illinois Arts Alliance Foundation. In it, author Prudence R. Beidler takes us on a journey through a typical leadership transition, from procedures for early planning to the details of the search itself to the ongoing follow-up with the new leader. She lays out the hopes and fears that accompany leadership change in any institution and points out the most common pitfalls. And she shows how a leadership transition offers an organization a unique opportunity to think deeply about where it is and where it wants to go and then to re-present itself and its new leader to the community.

In the book's final article, "Additional Perspectives," co-editor Jaan Whitehead reaches out to small and alternative theaters whose needs are rarely addressed in books on governance. She discusses many of the challenges facing small theaters that, at a different stage of their life cycle, face different governing needs than more established theaters. She explores how artists can—and do—serve on the boards of theater organizations and what they can contribute to these organizations. And she looks at some alternative models of governance that suggest a greater range of choices for how theaters think about and construct their boards.

All arts institutions are under duress today. Whether it is inadequate funding, political pressures or the lure of commercialization, artists and institutions feel threatened. More than ever before, trustees can make a difference in how well—or whether—their institutions flourish. For those who believe in the essential value of the arts, making such a difference can be a genuine contribution to our culture as well as a source of deep personal satisfaction.

Nancy Roche and Jaan Whitehead, Editors
May 2005

Part I

THE FRAMEWORK OF GOVERNANCE

THE ART OF THEATER

Todd London

WE ARE IN A ROOM TOGETHER.

We are in a room with black walls, or maybe in a warehouse room with sides of corrugated steel. It might be a beautiful, gilded hall from an earlier century, plush draperies and portraits, the light from chandeliers crystalling off plaster friezes running along the base of a vaulted ceiling. How about an actual living room, where the hostess rings a little bell for the performance to begin? Perhaps we are seated around a fire or on stone benches embedded in the side of a hill, a sacred place rife with our shared history; this isn't what you think of as a room, but the open world has rooms, too, and our presence here circumscribes one. Maybe we're arranged on folding chairs in a raw barn or even in front of a painting of a barn on canvas hung at the back of an old Masonic Lodge; a young man from town, dressed as a cowboy, steps out from the side of the painted barn and begins to sing, "Oh, what a beautiful mornin' . . ."

What is the first place you imagine when you read the word "theater"? Whatever you imagine, wherever we are, the important thing is this: We are in a room together.

Think about it: You read a book, this book, alone. The authors speak to you, through the medium of printed words, soundless speech, their private thoughts entering yours. Think about a movie or television. You can watch it alone or with others, but the people who created it and performed it have moved on. Their past endeavor is your present. Likewise a painting or sculpture: You can enjoy either in solitude. Creation has already occurred; your experience follows.

Everything about the theater, though, depends on its live-ness and presence: At least one person must perform and at least one must watch. Everything depends on a real moment in time, a real shared space. Why is the theater transporting when it works, and excruciating when it fails? How can something so thrilling be so boring, something so rousing be so embarrassing? The answers lie in its very essence, this double nature: the immediate and the intimate.

What exactly happens in these rooms, these theaters, when we are together? Sometimes we witness, as has been said of the plays of Ibsen, "great reckonings in small rooms." Sometimes these reckonings play out against a vast expanse, and all the world seems to be a stage, or a stage appears to hold all the world. We might attend the recreation of a familiar ritual—a passion play, a retelling of the birth of our community, the annual production of *A Christmas Carol*. We may even participate, may clap along. By contrast, we might witness something entirely unfamiliar, an oddity from another world played out strangely. Or we could be ushered, one person at a time, into a tiny space of almost unbearable proximity, and in those confines another single soul will tell us a story.

These are lists: possible theater spaces, possible happenings in those spaces. I make these lists because I believe that the art of theater is an art of possibility and that every possible place or use for theater suggests more. Each vision of the theater adds to the art; each version alters the way we see ourselves, our community, our nation.

The theater is a town hall, in which citizens gather to debate issues of great moment. You might have seen how this works: In 1953, at the height of the House Committee on Un-American Activity hearings—the "witch hunt" for Communists in America, spearheaded by Senator Joseph McCarthy—Arthur Miller wrote *The Crucible*, a play that uses the allegory of that *ur* American witch hunt, the Salem witch trials of the 1690s, to explore issues of societal hysteria and individual responsibility. When called before the committee several years later, Miller would refuse to name names; in the meantime, he used the stage as a different kind of witness stand by dramatizing "the handing over of conscience to another, be it woman, the state or a terror, and the realization that with conscience goes the person, the soul immortal, and the 'name.'" Miller challenges audiences to place themselves in the action, to cross-examine and judge themselves. This challenge to (or even implication of) the spectator, still powerful today, was all the more unsettling when McCarthyism was at its height and "the gale from the Right was blowing at its fullest fury," in Miller's words.

From Ancient Greece to here and now, such theater serves as a civic forum. Anna Deveare Smith's documentary epics—*Twilight: Los Angeles, 1992* and *Fires in the Mirror: Crown Heights, Brooklyn and Other Identities*, most famously—provide more recent and equally breathtaking illustrations. In them, the African American Smith uses monologues drawn verbatim from interviews to portray a range of characters from every walk of life in the community that is her subject: men, women, blacks, whites, Asians, religious leaders, activists, cops, politicians, social workers and social outcasts—all in their own words. These one-woman shows, performed by the many-voiced Smith, play more like huge ensemble pieces than solo performances. Through the medium of her living presence, Smith serves up the knotty contradictions of racial and ethnic unrest, confronting us with a complex "we," a choral debate of ourselves right before our own eyes.

The theater is a democratic meeting place, and it's much more too. It's also a place of extremity, madness, cruelty and violence of image. There are poor theaters, holy theaters, dream theaters, bawdy theaters, boulevard theaters, activist theaters, story theaters, dance theaters, migrant farmer theaters, classical theaters of many traditions, epic puppet theaters, community theaters, laugh theaters and cry theaters. Some are classical, some avant-garde, others improvisational, comical-tragical-historical-pastoral. There are theaters that zero in on the visible—behavior, mannerism, affect; and those that grope toward the invisible—the animating spirit behind the everyday.

Whatever your definition, whatever your reason for making theater part of your life, it's almost certainly reflective of a vision or need you share with others. A theater is a house into which the spirit of its time, place and people is invited to dwell. In this way, all theater is local. What is that spirit for you and your colleagues; what is the genius of your theater?

So many possibilities, audiences, communities. I think about the upper classes of England in 1660, after the restoration of the king. Women appear onstage for the first time, decked in costumes designed to display their legs and breasts, flirting with the crowd. People eat and talk, some sell oranges, some throw them. Sexual energy electrifies the house—a vibrant licentiousness unleashed after years of Puritan rule. And then I imagine villagers in Bali, watching a puppet play; young New Yorkers carrying their beers into a cramped storefront on the Lower East Side; tourists in Ashland, Oregon, who've traveled a day or more to take in *Richard II* or *Richard III*. How do Shakespeare's histories look to them? How did the same plays look to a Polish audience under Soviet rule or township blacks under South African apartheid? How does August Wilson play in the Pittsburgh he writes about, and how does he play in Nairobi? I have a friend whose play about Cambodian genocide premiered in West Virginia, after she'd created performances in Phnom Penh with survivors of the Khmer Rouge out of their own stories; how did each audience engage with the event unfolding before them? Did they see themselves or did they see "the other"?

I remember seeing a brilliant, searing version of Anton Chekhov's *Uncle Vanya* in the early 1990s, performed in New York by a Lithuanian theater from Vilna. Two images from this production have stayed with me all this time, personal examples of the immediacy of theater. The crisis in *Vanya* begins when an old, ailing professor returns to the rural estate of his deceased wife, accompanied by his new wife, the beautiful, indolent Yelena. The visit takes the most profound toll on the professor's daughter, Sonya, and on Sonya's uncle, Vanya, brother to her mother (the professor's dead wife). The house is turned upside down by the professor's demands and by Yelena's magnetism, the lure of her idleness. Everything goes to pot, as the static nature of their lives—the equilibrium Vanya and Sonya had long maintained, running the farm to fund the professor's big-city lifestyle—gets called into question. Their usual behavior begins to feel foolish as the professor himself appears foolish; their desires for something different, long denied—repressed by routine—begin to feel unbearable.

The Lithuanian production, coming soon after the fall of the Berlin Wall and the breakup of the Soviet empire, recast this tension between stasis and change in historical terms without ever losing sight of the intense personal anguish of Chekhov's characters. The most powerful instances of this involved another character, Dr. Astrov, the province's most cultured man—a thinker and environmentalist—who begins to spend more time at the estate, tending to the despotic professor and dallying with the enchanting Yelena. Astrov's life, too, is going to pot. He becomes lazy, drinks too much vodka, loses his sense of purpose. In this rethinking of the play, Astrov's drunkenness—which escalated with astonishing extremity throughout the evening—came to stand in for the alcoholism of a devastated Eastern Europe, a hopeless wasteland left by years of totalitarianism and vodka. "Stop drinking," Sonya shouts at him as the stumbling doctor reaches again for the bottle. And in their struggle, a vodka bottle is knocked over on a high shelf and, for what seems like minutes, a waterfall of vodka cascades five feet to the floor. This simple image was terrifying in the execution—one bottle, an almost bottomless gush of anguish. When, at the play's end, the professor (whom we've come to see as the U.S.S.R. itself) and his entourage depart, they leave the rest of the family wasted. Their faith in any kind of future happiness is gone, too. Astrov takes his leave as well, but by this time he's so drunk that he must literally crawl to his horse-drawn carriage. Coatless and hatless, he grabs the rug off the floor for warmth—a bear rug—and lumbers off under it, the human image of the Soviet bear, skulking drunkenly off, leaving a ravaged world behind.

Every play that is written, every event that is staged, has a different relationship to its moment, to its place. I flash back through things I've seen: outdoor folk pageants in the woods of North Carolina; a toy-theater play for an audience of twelve, written in childhood by a playwright who died at thirty-four; a sadomasochistic sex farce about Israelis and Palestinians, performed on the night we started bombing Iraq; a Long Island teen theater production of *Damn Yankees*; Moliére's *Tartuffe*, directed by a Romanian auteur in our nation's capitol during the Reagan years; a piece created by an acting company from rural Pennsylvania, based on a hundred years of letters to the editors of local papers; an antiwar parade led by towering puppets and performers in masks; and three minstrel shows (one enacted by an all-white, twenty-five-year-old experimental ensemble; another written by an African American playwright, descended from a traveling minstrel; and a third performed by male Ghanaians, as part of a traditional comic performance inherited from British colonists).

What they have in common: They happen in a communal context, when everyone's together in a room. This communality is reflected in the very process of making theater, which is collaborative to the root. The playwright may compose a play in the privacy of her own writing space, but the play won't be complete before her creative impetus is joined by the interpretive energies of actors, designers, a director, technicians, and even composers, choreographers, puppeteers, fight directors and others. Plays are written by a writer with a "voice," but because that voice is dispersed—into the mouths and dialogue of many—it can't be heard until its music is captured by others. A play is a partial thing until it's brought into real time and space by a company of artists.

Every moment of this group journey invites discovery and dares disaster. An actor may read a line in a way that brings out meanings the author never understood, and he may interpret a scene in a way the author never intended. A design choice may look beautiful on paper and distracting in practice, or it may seem drab until inhabited by three-dimensional bodies on an actual stage. One director may understand the play's themes and structure brilliantly but fail to create living, breathing events in the rehearsal room. Another director may remain silent on the play as a work of ideas or literature and yet know how to catalyze actors and designers to ignite whatever explosions of life lie latent in the text. Every moment of rehearsal—from the initial conceptual discussions, drawings, models, readings around a table, to the final technical and dress rehearsals where lights are focused, sound is cued, and costumes are paraded and altered—is a moment of artistic choice (this way or that way?) and human interaction (your way or mine?).

The most interactive of arts, theater is also the most integrative. Everything comes together in the theater—music, movement and dance, visual and spatial design, text, politics, history. It's the art that leaves nothing out.

This rough motley points to another, more important integration: The theater, to a greater extent than any art form I can think of, brings together body, mind, heart and spirit—the mind of the playwright, the body of the actor, the heart of each of them and of the audience, and the spirit of all of us *together*. Alive together in a room. This is what I look for in the theater and, speaking personally, it's what I want from my life. I can think of no better definition of living fully than this combination of the physical, mental, emotional and spiritual. Nor can I think of any better place to find it.

This profound wholeness of the theater, its essential connectivity, has an added urgency in the contemporary, technological world. Not only does the theater aim to connect us to ourselves and to each other, but it does so in a uniquely unmediated way. Increasingly, we are capable of staying virtually connected and actually isolated. We can attend meetings by phone and video, hold lengthy instant conversations by email, and travel great mental and visual distances without leaving our homes. The theater is the antithesis of the virtual, and it's the antidote. The theater demands our physical presence and our communal proximity. It forces us to breathe the same air, face the same action, process the same emotional information in a public space at the same time. It is, I repeat, the natural antidote to everything that keeps us apart, drives us to our corners, tells us where to focus and how to feel, mediates, manipulates and spins our experience of the real.

Even the most synthetic theatrical event can't hide the sweat, the dust motes in the lights, the smell of musty curtains or new carpet. The danger of the immediate is always with us in the theater: a chair might break; an actor might flub his lines, fall into the orchestra pit or spit into the first row on his big soliloquy; the woman next to you might shout at the stage. And when it goes well, you can hold its liveness close to your heart: You were there, you saw it, there was no second take, no stunt double, no close-up shot through gauze for effect.

We are all keepers of the spirit of the theater—from the artists who identify and articulate our core human impulses, to the administrators who make homes for art; from the trustees who secure those homes and create the bonds between artists and the larger community, to the audiences, without whom there can be nothing called theater. Sometimes shouldering the responsibility for this most consistently endangered, ever-ephemeral endeavor can feel like carrying burning embers wrapped in leaves through a rainforest. If the necessary spark goes out, how will we light the fire around which we gather, night after night, place after place? That spark is what we have; it's the art of the theater, your theater, any theater. And so we carry and protect it, fan it to flame, watch it die down to a faint glow, wrap it up and carry it again, always hopeful, always together.

GOING NATIONAL:
A Nutshell History of the Regional Theater Movement

Jim O'Quinn

WHEN THE AMERICAN REGIONAL THEATER MOVEMENT took off in earnest in the early 1960s, it was traveling alongside some heady companion movements: civil rights, feminism, environmentalism, sexual liberation. The upstart effort to foster resident professional theater companies in cities, towns and communities across the nation hardly rates, on the Richter scale of social and political consequence, with those broader categories of revolutionary impulse; but a revolution it was—one more finite and focused than those larger societal movements, and with consequences that can be documented and quantified as well as debated for their impact on the art form itself.

Numbers tell part of the story.

In December 1961, when the Ford Foundation approved an initial grant of nine million dollars to begin "strengthening the position of resident theater in the United States," the term itself was newfangled and obscure: foundation staff helpfully referred in early grant documents to "what Europe knows as 'repertory theaters.'" While an array of educational and amateur theaters kept stage activity alive outside New York City, the professional theater landscape at the time was limited (with rare exceptions) to the Broadway commercial theater, New York–based touring companies and a smattering of summer stock companies. As Zelda Fichandler capsulized it: "There was Broadway and the Road."

Fichandler was only slightly exaggerating. A few significant theater companies with professional aspirations had put down roots in the early part of the century—the venerable Cleveland Play House opened in 1915, and Chicago's Goodman Theatre was founded as a school in 1925—and others predated the Ford initiative by little more than a decade: most notably, Nina Vance's Alley Theatre in Houston, founded in 1947; Margo Jones's Theatre 47 in Dallas, launched in the same year; and Fichandler's own Arena Stage in Washington, D.C., initially organized in 1950 as a commercial venture. A number of festival theaters (usually meaning summer seasons only) devoted to Shakespeare were also in operation, including the Oregon Shakespeare Festival in Ashland (founded in 1955), Joseph Papp's New York Shakespeare Festival (founded in 1954) and The Old Globe in San Diego (founded in 1957). These and a handful of other professionally oriented companies were poised—alongside those hundreds of others about to be kindled into existence—to benefit from what turned out to be Ford's visionary largesse.

The growth came fast and furious, in a kind of perfect storm—a convergence of money and legitimacy with passionate interest on the part of young theater artists (fueled in no small part by daredevil work being done Off-Broadway and the anti-establishment tenor of the times) in alternatives to the economics and aesthetics of the commercial theater, and in new repertoires the commercial sector had ignored (the classics, cutting-edge new work, forgotten masterpieces). The money and legitimacy were to come from Ford's philanthropy to theater companies, which would eventually total an astonishing $287 million. Then, the establishment of a membership support organization, Theatre Communications Group (TCG), and the founding in 1965 of the National Endowment for the Arts (the first program of designated federal subsidy for arts institutions in U.S. history), sealed the case for an unprecedented national expansion of theater art.

Why was this expansion of theater in the U.S. so essential to the viability of the art form in American cultural life? The question has any number of answers, depending on your perspective. "The idea that artists could create a life in the theater in Providence or Louisville was inconceivable in 1961," pointed out Peter Zeisler, a cofounder of the movement's exemplary institution, the landmark Guthrie Theater of Minneapolis, speaking, as he often did, as an advocate for individual artists and their creative independence. Building a theater career before the '60s was indeed synonymous with living in New York City; and, to the detriment of artists and audiences alike, Broadway had devolved after World War II into an upscale retailer of popular musicals and boulevard comedies, virtually devoid of the classics and equally shy of risky new plays (the occasional Miller or Williams or O'Neill excepted). From the perspective of the larger American public, theater was geographically and economically inaccessible—and essentially off the radar.

All that was to change significantly in the first five years after Ford's initiative was announced, as some twenty-six major new theater companies (not counting burgeoning Off-Off-Broadway groups) were established in far-flung U.S. cities, large and small. Suddenly, for millions who thought of theater as a distant and esoteric experience, live performance was becoming a local affair, an alternative to movies or television, even a bonding community experience (when theaters played their cards right). Within the same period, more Equity actors began working in not-for-profit companies than on Broadway and the road combined.

In 2005, forty-four years later, the numbers are off the charts: more than 1,200 U.S. not-for-profit theaters are currently alive and more-or-less well (the number is based on TCG's annual fiscal research, though neither TCG nor the Endowment ventures an exact count), mounting some 13,000 productions a year and having an estimated economic impact on the U.S. economy of more than $1.4 billion.

Such tallies show the enormous scale of the regional theater movement, but its impetus can only be understood in terms of the outsized personalities who led the charge. Along with Guthrie pioneer Zeisler, who continued to spur the movement on from his post as executive director of TCG from 1972 to 1995, and the trio of visionary women whose names are attached above to theaters they inaugurated (of the Alley, the indomitable Nina Vance was fond of saying, "I clawed this theater out of the ground"), those personalities include the man who conceived the Ford Foundation initiative that started the ball rolling: W. McNeil Lowry. Lowry was only three-and-a-half years into what would become a distinguished twenty-three-year career at the foundation when a new, national-scale philanthropic program in support of the arts was placed under his direction in 1957. Ford's aim in nurturing the theater was, in Lowry's own words, "to offer American artists a clean slate, to encourage them to build companies devoted to process; in other words, to foster the coming together of American directors, actors, designers, playwrights and others beyond a single production and beyond commercial sanction."

Lowry—soon to be known as "Mac" to the theater people he advised—launched a series of field studies; staged a planning session in Cleveland in 1958 attended by such key movement personalities as stage director Alan Schneider, impresario Joseph Papp and producer Roger L. Stevens (who was destined to become the first chairman of the NEA); followed up with a landmark 1959 conference in New York, where, Lowry said, "the first planks in the resident theater movement were laid down"; and, a year later, drafted a grant for a four-year program to establish TCG. This essential groundwork, and the continuing flow of foundation support to theaters through the '60s and '70s, carefully overseen by Lowry—including backing for the seminal experimental work of such groups as Joseph Chaikin's Open Theatre and Ellen Stewart's struggling La MaMa E.T.C., and the controversial underwriting of the creation of the Negro Ensemble Company (which resulted in charges from civil rights leaders that Ford had retreated from its integrationist policies)—gave the movement its backbone.

That backbone undergirded the network of professional resident theaters that came into being or solidified their identities during this era of proliferation—basically, the array of companies that today belong to, or aspire to the standards of, the League of Resident Theatres (LORT), the national association representing the interests of larger-budget organizations. The imprimatur of the newly formed Arts Endowment—and the important legislative provision that twenty percent of the NEA's total budget was to "pass through" directly to the states, resulting in the establishment of state arts councils as well—put theaters, along with museums, symphonies and other arts organizations, on a new and more public footing.

The single event that became the most potent symbol of this simultaneous burgeoning and decentralization of the American theater, and that defined both the movement's dearest goals and some of its shortcomings, was the establishment of the flagship Guthrie Theater in Minneapolis.

While most regional theaters originated locally, carefully molded and tended by their organizers, the Guthrie (first known as the Minnesota Theater Company) sprang full-grown from its creators' heads in

1963. Zeisler, who had been working as a Broadway stage manager, and his fellow New Yorker Oliver Rea, a scenic designer, wanted to find a hospitable American city in which to begin a regional repertory theater devoted to the classics. They enlisted the aid of the eminent British director Tyrone Guthrie, who joined as a partner in the enterprise, and after four-and-a-half years of fundraising, planning and meetings in seven U.S. cities, the triumvirate settled in the Twin Cities to bring forth what Guthrie called "an institution, something more permanent and more serious in aim than a commercial theater can ever be."

The Guthrie's dazzling first season, with George Grizzard, Hume Cronyn and Jessica Tandy as part of a forty-seven-member company playing in rotating rep on designer Tanya Moiseiwitsch's distinctive thrust stage, was greeted with national fanfare. *Life* magazine called it "the miracle in Minneapolis." "Planting the Guthrie full-blown in a Midwest landscape, for many corporate and lay patrons, gave credibility to new efforts in other communities," wrote Lowry, whose foundation provided funds to insure the theater against loss in its first three years. Lowry was right: The advent of the nation's most fully realized not-for-profit professional company, complete with its own brand of Equity acting contract negotiated by the newly formed LORT, stimulated popular support for both existing institutions and for the start-up of new ones.

The Guthrie was an enduring success (as this book is being written, an expansive new $125-million complex to house the much-celebrated company is under construction), but its operations over the years serve as a textbook case for the regional theater's thwarted ambitions as well as its accomplishments. Size matters, and the Guthrie's vast, 1,437-seat auditorium was often hard to fill. The ideal of a permanent acting company playing in rotating repertory (one of director Guthrie's key principles) got a great run in the company's early years, but was unable to take permanent hold there—or, indeed, anywhere in the American theater system, despite the best efforts of such determined rep-company advocates as William Ball, at San Francisco's American Conservatory Theater; Robert Brustein, at Yale Repertory Theatre in New Haven, Connecticut, and later at American Repertory Theatre in Cambridge, Massachusetts; and Ellis Rabb, at his short-lived APA Phoenix in New York. Similarly, the frequently articulated aim of developing an original, genuinely American classical acting style, free of the stiffness and histrionics of English traditions (at one extreme) and the mumbly hyper-naturalism attributed to the Method (on the other), got lost in the shuffle of artistic leadership after Tyrone

Guthrie's departure, and was pursued elsewhere only in fits and starts. On the plus side, as Zeisler has written, "Once the Guthrie and a few other theaters started to examine the classic repertoire, actor training changed radically in this country. Suddenly, enormous physical demands were being made on actors. It became necessary to have voice work and movement work in the training programs that there'd never been before."

Many other changes were afoot, including a concurrent and equally vital wave of theater activity only tangentially affected by the economics and mechanics of Ford and TCG. This initiative came from artist-activists, a rich array of politicos, experimentalists, collectives and rebels of various stripes who were less interested in theater per se than in the proud traditions of social organizing, labor issues and identity movements. They seized the historical moment—its free-wheeling ethos, its radical sense of possibility—to put theater to work in passionate service to their causes: racial or ethnic equality, the anti-war and antipoverty movements, gay liberation.

On this front, the San Francisco Mime Troupe redefined American street theater with its sharp satires opposing the war in Vietnam; Luis Valdez, with the support of protest leader Cesar Chavez, founded El Teatro Campesino as a company dedicated to the heritage and lives of Hispanic farm workers; Bread and Puppet Theatre's peace pageants, with their craggy, monumental puppets, inspired thousands; budding experimentalists like Sam Shepard and Lanford Wilson plied their trade at Off-Off-Broadway's Cafe Cino; John O'Neal's Free Southern Theatre championed civil rights in the Deep South; acclaim for the Negro Ensemble Company enlivened the Black Arts movement and fostered the New Lafayette and New Federal theaters in New York City; some years later, Roadside Theater sprang up in Appalachia; and East West Players took up the cause of Asian American artists in Los Angeles. The list is as long as it is inspiring.

This mushrooming theatrical activity, grassroots and otherwise, was part of the larger arts renaissance of the era, and it fed variously upon the new energies being unleashed in the worlds of dance, literature and the visual arts (via "happenings," for example, and, more generally, the minimalist impulse that gave rise to what we refer to today as performance or performance art). Another important outgrowth of this general artistic ferment was the formation of collective theaters, alternative troupes or, in National Endowment for the Arts parlance, circa 1984, "ongoing ensembles," dozens of which burst onto the scene in the '60s and '70s, and many of which continue to endure today despite the odds against them. Such artistically original groups as New York City's Wooster Group and Mabou Mines, northern California's Dell'Arte International, Milwaukee's Theatre X and the traveling Cornerstone Theater Company based their work on longstanding partnerships, democratic decision-making and collective creation by communities of artists whose bonds were deepened by time. The NEA's eventual addition of its IntraArts and Expansion Arts programs bolstered those who did not recognize themselves in the more traditional trappings of the theater establishment.

The decentralization and diversification of the American theater did change university and conservatory training for designers and directors as well as actors, much as it reconfigured the economics and the locus of the theater business in America. The stage became tempting again to writers, as playwriting shed its esoteric status and gained prestige as a literary form; new plays, freed of the hit-or-miss constraints of the commercial system, were touted by many theaters as leading attractions. Audiences, it goes without saying, changed and grew as well (today's arts advocates are fond of citing the statistic that more people now attend live performances than sports events in the U.S.).

Zeisler again: "Perhaps the most stunning thing of all—and one of which we need to constantly remind ourselves—is that the not-for-profit professional theater was created with no precedents, no role models. It was learning to fly by the seats of many pairs of pants; textbooks didn't exist. Has there ever been such a radical change in the form and structure of the theater in so short a period of time?"

That rhetorical question's answer—"Undoubtedly not!"—may be taken as both admonition and affirmation. The speed with which changes in the system occurred meant that expectations and reality were sometimes out of sync. The aforementioned ideal of permanent acting companies, for example, was abandoned for a host of reasons, artistic and economic. Such an arrangement put limitations on casting; actors were not willing to commit themselves long-term, especially in geographically isolated areas of the country; and the maintenance of full companies proved prohibitively costly. Still, other manifestations of the company model emerged in cities like Chicago, Philadelphia and Washington, D.C., where clusters of not-for-profit theaters offered regular employment to a local talent pool, and it became possible for designers and directors to engineer satisfactory, regionally based careers as well. In the same spirit, a great success of the movement has been the affirmation and nurturing of the American playwright, not only in terms of production but of writer development.

Recent decades have seen playwriting in this country advance from the status of an adjunct literary genre to that of a viable career. Theaters in the regions have become the showcase of America's best theatrical writing—of the past thirty-four winners of the Pulitzer Prize for Drama, thirty-two have premiered at not-for-profit companies.

As the years passed and founders of theaters inevitably turned leadership over to a new generation, the character of the work on some regional stages underwent changes. In the less charitable view, many once-vital wellsprings of theater art grew into management-heavy institutions, supporting a vast array of artists, but missing the spark of visionary intensity that was the movement's animating impulse. While such criticism may have been valid in some places and at some times, the fact remains that the movement's larger goal of making it possible for theater professionals to make a living in communities throughout the nation has been by and large achieved—the regional theater movement has provided America's theater workers with an "artistic home."

Once upon a time, professional theater in America operated centrifugally: from the creative crucible of New York City, theater spun out, via the touring circuit or the scattered outposts of resident stages, to the nation at large. Today that dynamic is precisely reversed. Theater in America is centripetal: its creative fires burn in hundreds of cities and communities, and that energy flows from the regions to New York City, where the commercial sector has grown dependent upon its sprawling not-for-profit counterpart for virtually every aspect of its well-being. Broadway is still the place where talents are validated and economic prospects escalated, but it is no longer the singular, or even the primary, font of the nation's theatrical creativity. That distinction belongs to the array of not-for-profit professional theaters that has blossomed into being over the past forty-five years in every nook and cranny of this country: the diverse, still-evolving network that must be acknowledged for what it is—America's national theater.

WHITHER (OR WITHER) ART?

Zelda Fichandler

The following article was written by Zelda Fichandler as part of a sometimes-heated dialogue taking place at the time about the state of the American theater spurred by a series of critical articles in American Theatre *magazine in the fall of 2002. These articles challenged whether theaters had failed their original purpose and become too institutionalized to maintain a healthy balance between creative art and fiscal responsibility—between art and money—and whether established theaters remained sufficiently open to new artists and new work. Zelda's article was a response to these sharp challenges and reflected her role as a founder of the regional theater movement and one of its most thoughtful and articulate spokespersons. Citations for the other articles in the debate are listed at the end of this essay.*

OT THIS OR THAT, but this *and* that. Because one thing is true, it doesn't necessarily follow that the opposite is not also true. Up and down, back and forth, move ahead and drop back, no straight staircase to the sky but growth in a kind of spiral: success, success, success, then failure and disappointment, then the struggle to get unstuck and push ahead, to keep on keeping on, and the one who finishes last wins. Brecht has Galileo say, "As much of the truth gets through as we push through; we crawl by inches."

Over the holidays, I had time to catch up with the October, November and December 2002 issues of *American Theatre* magazine and was astounded by the thought-provoking riches I found in them. Every theater worker in the land appreciates and needs Ben Cameron's recurrent: "Cheers!" Which is not to say that the TCG constituencies are not always encouraged to think outside the box but here was something else again, something new, I believe—challenges to and warnings about the box itself. Serious questions were posed about the very form and nature of what we have come to know as the "institutional theater"—a kind of theater that in the past half century has transformed the way we pro-duce (bring forth) our art. We are pushed to think about whether these institutions do or do not, did but now don't, nurture the art and the artists. Since those who challenged and warned are our friends and colleagues and raised their voices not only out of anger, disappointment and frustration, but also out of love and a sense of responsibility, I took their queries very seriously. I hope we can avoid being defensive and can listen up. Here are some personal ruminations.

I co-founded Arena Stage in Washington, D.C., in 1950 and was its producing artistic director for forty years. I left Arena in 1991, and I know that much has changed since then. It has become increasingly difficult to keep a theater pressing forward in a creative way. In my several years with The Acting Company, Margot Harley's spirited young ensemble that tours the country with classics and new work, I continued to learn about the aspirations of young talent and about the amazing audience across America that is hungry for theater. Now chairing an intense actor training program in the Tisch School of the Arts at New York University, I've been taught how the weight of a highly structured, top-down institution actually feels; I have a deeper empathy with the artist's sense that the largest issues are decided above. I speak in this essay as a representative of what has come to be called the "institutional theater," now under scrutiny, if not attack.

My six-year-old grandson is wont to ask me how things were in the olden days (starting with the Age of the Dinosaurs, followed by an unimaginably long historical period pre-TV and baseball computer games, followed thereupon by the more hospitable present, which he very much enjoys). My point being that I may be able to bring some information from my experience with the dinosaurs that others of you may not have.

What are the critics saying to us? What do they suggest as the next crusade? What have they misperceived, and what enlightens us? What is feasible and what is pie-in-the-sky? And the big issues: A new generation of founders? Challenge the power of our boards? No longer an alternative theater as we were founded to be, pass the torch to the new alternatives? Fold up our expensive tents and silently steal away? Out with the old, on with the new and every dog has his day? These are provocative questions, indeed! How do we respond to them? One critic acknowledges that not every theater or board or mission statement is like every other, but feels that the pressure of institutional art (with the emphasis on "institution" rather than "art") is widespread enough to warrant sounding the alarm.

What does she mean by "institutional art"? The following, I think: Art that is made with the right eye on the dollar, the left eye on the stage, with the right eye dominant. Art that doesn't fly because it's tethered to the bottom line. Formulaic art—this was a hit in Cleveland (Boston, Milwaukee, on or Off Broadway), this could attract a star, this one got a Tony, this one would be great for group sales or students or at Christmas or for spring vacation or for St. Patrick's Day or around Rosh Hashanah, etc., etc.; too many lows and not enough highs—a sense of uniformity, predictability, a sense of low-grade depression. Where is astonishment, derring-do, originality, hoopla? Is it one from Column A and one from Column B, or does it all add up to something intentional and brave? Does what we think the subscribers want or what quickens the theater's artistic heart come first?

Ah, what the subscribers want! The circle the critic traces really exists. I've felt the clutch of that circle closing around me, and it's a circle from hell. To stave off death, the maw of the box office must be fed. We count on the subscribers who make up one-half (or one-third or two-thirds or ninety percent) of our audience to feed it. Indeed, if we appear plump and chipper, other sources of nourishment may open up; no foundation or corporation wants to feed a dying theater. If things work well and we give our subscribers what they want (and, of course, what we can afford), they'll be back next year and we'll be set for another season on a full stomach. And while there's life, there's hope.

This looks like a fair exchange, almost too good to be true, but we become suspicious and look around. Aha! it's the audience who is running the theater! No, the box office is running the theater! No, the board and the executive director and his PR and marketing colleagues are running the theater! No, the institution in general is running the theater! That's it, we've abdicated our creative freedom—that which defines us and for which we struggled to be born—so as not to bite the hands that feed us. And where does that get us? What might be the unintended consequences? The criticism serves to open up thoughts that we have probably thought before and pushed aside, for where do these thoughts lead?

A theater gets the audience it signals to and deserves, and repertory is destiny. As in any real-life relationship, the response we get springs from what we send out, give off, invite. Are we underrating our subscribers? Why should their taste, curiosity and capacity to chew hard on some tough thoughts or forgive a well-intentioned miss be less than ours? Presumably, deep down they're very much like us despite differences in ethnicity, age, range of income. They come to the theater to be awakened emotionally, psychologically, even intellectually and politically, and to have an adventure, to identify with a life that's similar enough to theirs so they can recognize it but that plays out in different circumstances. Maybe their numbers would increase if we shared our own personal tastes more fully, opened ourselves up through our work to our own deepest concerns. And how do we know what *they* want if we don't offer what *we* want? And how do they know what they want when they haven't seen it yet? This is a better line of speculation; we should think further.

And what if the real audience, the one we must have to complete our work, drifts away and another audience replaces it who is satisfied with less? Audiences are not interchangeable integers, after all. Do we think that when the world turns—which it will—and the economy recovers—which it will—and a new president (maybe John Kerry?) stimulates a change in the Zeitgeist, do we think that *then* we can return to what we really want to do? And recover the audience we've lost? The future grows out of the present while the present seeps up out of the past. The choices we make today describe the theater we'll have tomorrow. Process is everything, and the outcome can't be predicted. It's possible for a theater to die of starvation, and that, of course, is very sad. It's also possible for it to wither away, and that is sadder.

So how should we consider the relationship between institution and art? I think of an institution as a cradle and the thing we call art as the baby. There is reciprocal need: the baby needs the cradle, but the cradle is an empty, useless piece of wood without the baby. Baby Eugene O'Neill didn't have a cradle: he slept in a dresser drawer on the road with his actor-father and mother, but he created anyway, or perhaps because of. The institution can be as lean and simple as that dresser drawer or as elaborate and multileveled as money will buy; the sturdier-yet-flexible it can be, the more support it can offer. The cradle's/institution's function is to provide a continuity of comfort and stability, an opportunity for growth, an empathetic, responsive face, a respect for organic creative process, tolerance for behavioral slip-ups (like flops!) and pride in the baby's hijinks. The institution accepts that the baby will develop according to its own internal laws and dedicates itself to providing the environment to encourage that.

Or this metaphor: The main event is not the institution. The main event is under the Big Top where the performers with their feats of magic and daring and the audience with its imaginative belief and its empathy get together and all breathe the same air at the same moment. All of them are grateful to the management for seeing to it that everyone has been paid, the lights are on, the event has come in on budget, the seats are filled and that the tent doesn't leak. The president of the board and other board members have the best seats, as they deserve, and will later throw a party in appreciation of the extraordinarily audacious circus troupe. The clarity of this relationship is harder to maintain in threatening times because the board has the responsibility for the survival of the institution and can become excessively interested in what goes on in the tent as well as how much it cost to put it there. Tensions are to be expected and worked through, always remembering that while theater is a business, its business is art, not business.

Because one thing is true it doesn't necessarily follow that the opposite is not also true. The artist must have freedom to be playful, to work from internal impulses. But he also shares responsibility for the fiscal health of the institution; it may surprise the board to hear that, but I've always found it to be so. The various production departments struggle to stay on budget and are proud when they do and actors extend themselves in many ways to build audiences. As an artistic director, I have always celebrated the box office. The dollar that came to us through it was twice-blessed: once for what it could buy in goods and services and twice as a vote of confidence that bought us freedom. The first law of the theater is success—without success there can be no theater. That thought wraps around everything else one can say about what's right or wrong about our institutions. It's the iron-framework of fact. Since the norm of theater is failure, not success, and since times are generally out of joint, the box office has come to be a place of special honor. Looked at in this way, the link between creativity and fiduciary responsibility is unbreakable.

Here's one from the Dinosaur Age that just surfaced in my memory, all of a piece down to what I was wearing and where I sat. President Eisenhower had moved into the White House and the Republicans moved into Washington with him, buying the houses from the Democrats who were moving out. Our audience at Arena dwindled, and it would take several years to cultivate another one. In that Republican year, we lost $10,000 at the box office—a large amount on such a small budget. My teacher and the co-founder of Arena Stage, Edward Mangum, had moved on, so that fingers pointed only at me at the final board meeting of the season where the loss was to be explained and justified. I did my best. The board members were my friends, handpicked by Ed and me and Tom Fichandler, the executive director, for their love of theater and their willingness to put in $1,000 each to get this idea off the ground. And they were pleased enough with the season. After I spoke, there was a fraught silence and then the chairman spoke up—heavily. This was the gist of it: "Of course we're committed here to a balanced budget and no red ink and so we regret the $10,000 that was lost in this year's operations. Zelda has explained to us how this happened. In the expectation that this was a one-time circumstance and that she will be able to guide us to a balanced budget next year and the years following, we accept the explanation and the loss." And then the chairman asked that the board give me a vote of confidence, which they did. This was very sweet of them, and I appreciated it. But I chiefly remember the gesture as a moment of profound and unexpected learning. For I had not for a minute anticipated that a vote of *no*-confidence was anywhere in the cards.

What I learned was that while I was entitled to enjoy the freedom to fail, it was anticipated that I would not indulge in it too frequently. Further, that it would be much more comfortable for me if the failure could be attributed to some outside power—the Republicans, the snow, a parade, a flood in the Potomac River—and not to my own bad judgment or creative misstep. The vision thing was mine to have as long as whatever that vision generated by way of art could pay for itself by way of money. When the Ford Foundation and W. McNeil Lowry entered the field toward the end of the '50s, Arena became not-for-profit in order to qualify for gifts and grants. But the same implicit understanding applied over the successive decades (and I never signed a contract; we would both know when it was time to part). Boards have become more sophisticated since the '50s—through experience, they've learned the ways of a creative enterprise (up and down, back and forth). But I lived through my long tenure at Arena Stage in a state of not this *or* that but this *and* that—Money *and* Art, Art *and* Money. In later days, the unresolved dialectic was not even imposed by the institution; it had become internalized because that's how things had to be. Since the late '80s, the balance has become even more difficult for the artistic leaders to maintain as financial support has dwindled.

These critical voices ask us to cease looking outside and turn our gaze inward, to the inside of our institutions for the source of our sense of oppression and ways we might free ourselves from it. And, indeed, we must do that. But the *outside* is the primary dimension within which our theaters live. A theater is an organism, an artwork in and of itself, and the person who holds the vision is its primary artist. It's her angle-of-viewing that, like the super-objective of a play, animates all the rest. (Ralph Waldo Emerson was wise to note that "an institution is the lengthened shadow of a man." For "man," read "person.") It's as she confronts the sounds, sights, political conflicts, rhythms, scientific achievements, timbre of human relationships, status of minorities and women, contemporary forms of theater and other art forms, and especially the economic support systems of her time that her vision for a theater forms itself. An artistic director belongs to both worlds—one foot inside the institution, one outside. Consciously or unconsciously, a personal vision is born in reaction to a world.

Just imagine how the artistic director's vision would expand and her heart lighten if suddenly there were a generous infusion of funds and she could pay for everything that she and the artists gathered around her had ever dreamed of. Then the tension between art and money could resolve. Then the relationship between institution and art could become crystal clear, unclouded by the pressures of survival. To think this way is to play with fantasy of course, for the Great Benefactor has retired and departed on a long tour of the universe and we don't expect him back. But it's a good bit of fantasy for it helps us to perceive the difficulty of artistic freedom in a culture defined by success in the marketplace. "He who pays the piper calls the tune" may be an overstatement of our situation, but that notion does now thread through all aspects of our institutional life.

But let us imagine that the Great Benefactor does, indeed, return with a new perspective on the Good and the Beautiful and, particularly, on those needy arts institutions that are impeded in their flowering. Could he lull our anxieties (Am I talented enough? Was that the right decision? Is this play going to make it?) or endow us with the talent and wisdom that isn't already ours? Of course not. Take away our headaches, help us to sleep more soundly, provide more time with our families? Not a chance. Attract collaborators who will stake their creative fate with us? Show us how to build acting companies and use them well? Teach us how to be effective diplomats, fundraisers, problem-solvers, writers, speakers, psychiatrists, and still be prepared for rehearsals? No way. Reveal to us how to treat Molière and Chekhov as old friends we would never betray, yet move their texts into a contemporary world, or how to read a new script in an unfamiliar form and be able to imagine it living on the stage? Strengthen our will so that we can take the hills and valleys and not flee? Endow us with humor, tact, wisdom, patience and the capacity to affect others with our exhilaration in the work? Make clear to us the language of budgets and balance sheets so that we know how to match expenditures to a value system and spend money without wasting it? Sharpen our judgment and broaden our taste? Awaken our capacity for collegiality and our teacher's warmth so that we may give our personal attention and support to all the work, not just our own, and to all the people doing it? Keep us on the pulse of our community so we can fathom our neighbors' deepest thoughts maybe even before they themselves are aware of them? And keep us in touch with our world so its preoccupations can be reflected on our stages? No, he can't. Of course he can't.

I've just set down a job description for artistic leadership—the artistic director and his comrades who share the vision and contribute to it with their own skills. And that was the short form! So what *can* Mr. Great Benefactor do for us where it is suggested that we are remiss? First, he would allow us to use the planning process as a way to fulfill our artistic dreams. Planning for the future would cease to be merely a function of budgeting and become one of dreaming. We would be able to plan out of the images in our minds rather than within the vise of this year's (reduced?) budget and/or the nagging weight of accumulated debt. What else? He could lift from us the fears that repress the creative spirit. For it's fear, I suggest, rather than lack of talent or imagination or good will that leads to making what the outside voice calls institutional art. Which one of us wants to be the one to fold up the tent?

Fear encourages caution and conformity, and caution and conformity are antithetical to what we refer to as art, since art is always a personal and original way of knowing the world. Creativity is born out of the capacity to play, and it's the very capacity for meaningful play that defines us as human beings. We can play with political ideas, with scientific hypotheses, with new forms in literature, with bodies in space; we call a theater production a play and we play the piano and the violin. The notion of play is indissolubly connected to the idea of freedom, and I left something out of the job description. It's the artistic leader's role to create a quiet and concentrated and nonjudgmental environment so that the entire community can play within it without fear. Benefaction can help her with that. I emphasize the organic connection between funding and fear, for I'm not sure that it's fully understood by those several who are pointing to our lapses, unfulfilled commitments, seeming inhospitality to artists, etc.

One of these bravely opts for a new generation of artistic directors and a new generation of theaters and, for the companies and playwrights within them, not just a place at the table but the table itself. "Where is a new generation of writer-founders, of playwright-managers?" he asks. That's a rousing manifesto, and certainly anything conceived in the imagination has the potential to be born into reality. Let some talented, courageous new leaders come forward and hitch themselves to the wagon. They will be warmly welcomed into the field—and gently warned. For founding today is very different from founding yesterday.

News from the dinosaurs: Beginning in the '50s there was but a blank slate, and only a few of us were scratching on it. No models, just us, hanging onto skyhooks. An almost primitive instinct for improvisation and testing of reality was released. "What is to be done?" (by chance, the title of Lenin's revolutionary pamphlet!) and "*How* is it to be done?" were the subtexts of our daily lives. The sands take lines unknown, as the poet said, even as a painter lays down on his canvas a random sketch that will define the painting to follow. At Arena, we sketched as we went, rapidly producing one thing after the other (seventeen shows in the first year because the audience was very small and we had to turn productions over quickly). Poor, so poor! Tireless—no, tired!—we lived play to play, and all there was of the future was right now. Modestly, slowly, the audience grew. Unexpectedly, the foundations (circa 1957) and the NEA (1965) and, later, corporations and our own community found us. They gave us money, but better than that, they gave us respect. Respect: "to look more at, to give attention to, to regard." We felt important to more than this tiny unit on this tiny budget; we seemed to matter to the culture of our country. It was a heady ascent during those middle decades.

A kind of promise was made to us, not in so many words, but a promise: These agencies would continue to be there for us and would participate in our future, caring that we survive. The promise was kept over many years, deepening as time went on and as we evolved artistically. We enjoyed the sense that if we came up with an innovative idea—artistic or organizational (organization was also considered creation)—it stood a chance of being funded. Then, for reasons you know, the promise was broken; the official culture turned its back. The final signal for me, theatrical in its communicative power, was that during her term as chairman of the NEA, Jane Alexander was able to pin down only one private meeting with Bill Clinton, which lasted just twenty minutes and offered no assurances (as noted in her book, *Command Performance*). There was no longer any political capital to be gained for a sitting president to support the arts. And nothing has happened since then to suggest that the climate has changed.

The need, it is suggested, is to "move out from under institutional shadows" and that the time is ripe to look for "a new age of pioneers." Pioneers will come or not come without our intervention and will always be welcome, and our theaters cast far more light than shadows—just imagine the American theater without them! I salute the work of avant-garde theaters, community-based theaters, ethnically diverse theaters, ensembles of form-seekers, playwriting collectives and all forms of socially based theaters. I admire their creativity and freedom. I've watched them proliferate since the '60s—often out of a singular aesthetic vision, the product of a single mind, or in response or antithesis to the institutional theater. But while we come from the same line, the same root, these theaters are not "an alternative" but "a parallel" to the institutional theater; they will neither replace nor inherit it, nor do we need to choose one form over the other. We are on different paths, with different tasks and structures that reflect them. Variants of the same species, each of us is a vital and essential part of the wonderful variety-within-unity that is the American Theater. These parallel theaters are in great need of increased funding, which their flexibility and very variety make it hard for conservative funding agencies to categorize and, therefore, to support. That's a great injustice that won't be set right, I fear, until we have the seven years of plenty due us. We should work together to discover and elect a president with an affinity for the arts. We should write and disseminate broadsides making the case for a New Deal for the arts in America. We should make immediate contact with Dana Gioia, the new chairman of the NEA, who promises to restore grants to individual artists and to find a way to increase federal funding. We should take inspiration from and look for another Helen Clark, elected prime minister of New Zealand in 1999, who promptly declared herself minister of arts, culture and heritage and within months injected tens of millions of dollars into a "cultural recovery package." Something like this grand boost could happen to us; hope is a thing with feathers.

This isn't the time, I suggest, to man the barricades and whip up an assault against a form of theater that in the past half century has become so imbedded in our theatrical way of life as to now be its dominant form, and which at the same time finds itself in the same position as many solo artists, locked outside and knocking at the gates. But is it not the time to listen hard with our inner ear and ask again as we asked before, in that Age of the Dinosaur, "What is to be done?" And "How?"

There is an old Russian saying: "Circumstances alter cases," which I take to mean: "Depending on where you sit, is how you see it," or: "A thing changes depending on who's looking at it." It's about relativism and the subjective nature of truth. Institutions feel betrayed by this spate of critical articles in *American Theatre*, kicked when they're down—"After all we've done for you!"—while the artists are frustrated and angry and prod the institutions to set new imaginative goals that will include them.

The feelings of the institutions are justified. Since the mid-twentieth century, they've been the primary developer of talent for the American theater—for stage as well as film and TV. Go to a movie, turn on the tube, get tickets to a Broadway or Off-Broadway show, there our artists are. "We promised opportunity for artistic development, we delivered on that promise; there are more jobs for artists outside of New York than in it, the so-called center," the institutions say. Taken all together, our theaters constitute a kind of national bazaar where Broadway producers shop for next year's product and next year's Pulitzer playwright. Where else can our new playwrights and their plays be developed but with us?

And we've created the possibility of a new way of life for those who want it. Actors, directors, designers, playwrights can move from theater to theater, using themselves creatively in dialogue with intelligent audiences, often evolving a sense of belonging with one or several theaters where they can count on coming back. What with these "theater gigs"—plus film, TV soaps and commercials, voice-overs, designing or directing for opera, teaching—an artist can have a respected, even fulfilling life while building funds for retirement. Besides, say the institutions, artists don't really want a home, they prefer moving along from choice to choice, it's hard to pin them down even for one project; their agents stand in the way of long commitments out of town.

So what's wrong with this picture? Nothing, if everybody's satisfied with it. Don't institutions tell it the way it is? Yes, but there are other voices, speaking up now loud and clear. They ask for involvement, a kind of permanence and continuity, the sort of emotional security and ebullience you feel in a personal relationship. They want their work to add to the overall work of the place, to build something with others and watch it grow. They want to belong to an idea they believe in and can serve with their creativity. They want to have a sense of self-determination and a role in defining the destiny of their institution.

Transient, temporary work sometimes feels as nothing but a high form of what the manufacturing industry calls "piecework"—you get paid for the number of "pieces of work" you turn out and how many you turn out is the measure of things, not you yourself. On a rainy day, "jobbing-in"—our word for piecework—can make one feel devalued: a "gig" can only be followed by another "gig." You may be moving along but only from here to there—moving, but not evolving.

If an actor is always cast because he's "right for the role" with no consideration for the development of his own range and versatility, if with each role he starts over again with a group of strangers who have no collective experience to draw upon, if he sometimes gets the sense of himself as a kind of commodity—paid to fill a need—and then "time's up and thanks," what is it we're saying to him? That "theater's a precarious profession, we always knew that, be glad you're working"? Is that okay? Is that enough?

Of all the artists, the playwright gets the most focused attention from the institution, and never more so than right now. That's been my experience and it's what I observe and read about. But the number of productions the playwright receives may not be the main point to her. To have her voice mingle with the voice of others in a collective consciousness as the play is evolved from within itself into production; to know that even if this one fails, the next time she knocks, with a telephone book of pages in her hands, they have to let her in, might weigh more than any number of exposures of her work produced out of any number of disparate motives in any number of theaters.

There's a tendency to romanticize our beginnings, as if we were an early Ideal Community. The beginnings weren't romantic—they were exhausting, impoverished and full of anxiety, but, yes, there was a specialness about that time because our intention was so clear and unconflicted. Each of the small band of beginners, flying blind in our separate air spaces, was struggling to create an artistic home: a company, an artistic collective, living and working in one place over a period of time, all of us with the same notion of why it was important to be doing that, having compatible skills and talents and a view of our world and the role of art within it, all of us together engaged in an ongoing dialogue with our audience via theatrical means. It didn't seem very complicated, it seemed entirely natural, inevitable, not even requiring elaboration in a manifesto or a mission statement. What else could a theater be? How could you call it a theater if it wasn't a *place*? Who else could define the culture of a theater but its artists? Define its style? Didn't a collective art form require a collective? Weren't we here to protest and even replace the put-it-up, smash-it-down, one-shot system of Broadway?

Our earliest banners were emblazoned with: "Not a Hotel for Theater, but a Home!" and a few of us held onto these (and still have them!), but not very many of us. As years went by, other slogans came into style: "Professionalism! You Can Count on Us!" or "Good Plays Well Done, That's the Ticket!" or even "Eight-for the-Price-of-Six!" And until I picked up my October, November and December issues of *American Theatre*, I had come to think that no one objected to the way things had become except some of my professional friends and my students, who want to be in companies, having been trained and proselytized for that kind of a life in art, but have not been able to find them.

The fact that artists are angry, frustrated and disappointed is not necessarily bad news. The other side of these feelings is that artists are insistent, energized, geared up to make larger commitments; they want in. Artists have become eager to become part of the warp and woof of institutional life and even take responsibility at its center (or as one of our commentators puts it, *occupy* that center) but find institutions inhospitable or simply closed to them. Is this perception an illusion? How many artists have these thoughts and feelings? Six? Six hundred? Six thousand? If we were to throw a party, would they come? And is it true that the institutions are inhospitable or closed to artists? Is it too much of an ongoing responsibility to nurture a group of artists, drawing them into the center of the work? These questions are, of course, no use in a theoretical way, they need to be answered in practice. And the theaters would need to make the first move.

For starters, I suggest an effusive display of understanding that audiences come to the theater to witness and partake of the work the artists have made—that it's art that makes the money and not the other way around. "Imagination is the nose of the public," wrote Edgar Allan Poe, "by this at any time it may be quietly led." What else? Pay those who are mature and committed artists the top salaries within the institution, at least equal to that of any (other) fundraiser or audience-builder. This gesture more than any other will signal where the artist stands as to recognition and power. In the deepest sense, artists are teachers—out of the darkness, they bring light—and their salary should be pegged to what a full professor makes at the university in the theater's community. In some smaller communities, that may still not be enough, so that allowances should be made for commercial Time-Outs. (Time-Outs for creative refreshment need to be possible as well.)

Artists should be invited to become involved in the total life of the institution in order to provide it with their special knowledge and point-of-view and to have their say. I read that while Ingmar Bergman was heading the Swedish National Theatre, he established a five-member artists' council that he consulted about repertory, company membership, casting and the like. I don't know how this idea would play out in America, though I wish I'd tried it myself. And a proportion of board positions should be set aside in the theater's bylaws or be established by common understanding for artists to occupy. This would be a very important change in the way we have operated, but it must be pressed for.

The presence of artists at board meetings would necessitate a transposition in vocabulary from a bottom-line, market-share, brand-conscious, focus-group lingo brought into the boardroom from a for-profit culture to a language of emotional meanings, thus bringing the board closer to the heartbeat of the theater and unifying everyone around the real ideas that underlie the theater. Significant issues do come up at board meetings, but are presented in such a way as to disconnect them from the life of the theater as it's experienced by those living it. The artists' presence will focus these issues in a more appropriate way. Remember that artists are smart; planning is the strategy by which they bring art into the world; the artist's ability to juggle the animating idea along with time, money and materials is an aspect of her talent. Artists have much to contribute to the deliberations of a board.

To keep the artist outside the business of the institution (with which he's engaged, at any rate) is to romanticize him ("artists are above business") at the same time that it miniaturizes him ("artists just don't have the head for it, they're fanciful, unworldly creatures, we need to take care of them"). Why has it taken so long to see this?

The creative courage of the artistic director will inspire artists; they, in turn, will support the risks she takes on their behalf whether or not they succeed. The transparency she fosters so that information—whether good news or bad—is available to all, up and down and around the building, will deepen the sense of mutual respect and a communal destiny. And she will see to it that no one is made to feel intimidated to speak up; in story and myth, the figure of Death is always silent. The artistic director's acknowledgment of ambiguity, relativism, second thoughts and struggle that exist behind difficult decisions will draw the artists even closer to her, revealing her as worthy of having, using and sharing power. The blinding glare of certainty always reduces intimacy and trust.

And so on. There are myriad ways for the institution to build an interactive relationship with its artists that will create the sense of a home where each can be for himself and also for the other and where all are for the work. Eventually, all of us must come to a much deeper understanding of the nature of the organism that we call a theater. I hold close Aristotle's statement: "What a thing can be, it must be, whether it be a horse or a man." Or a theater, he might have added. At some point in the future, we'll want to define ourselves by whether we insisted strongly enough on becoming what we can be, and therefore have become it. We will have come to consensus that artists *are* the theater, not a separate tribe bussed in for the performances. The artists *are* the theater, but administrators who protect and advance the artists' work are also the theater. And the theater is also its board, volunteers of time, money and caring on behalf of a profession that must sometimes seem to them a total mystery, operating as it does on hunches, gambles, the unknown. What else is the theater? The repertory is the theater, its very flesh and bones. Its ticket prices, its brochures and ads and newsletters, its spaces, even if they're humble, the intimacy of people pulling for the same thing, its respect for the intelligence of its audience, its restlessness and unceasing workload and so on and so on, and even the way the very air that hangs off the walls tells a stranger what kind of a place it is—all these are the theater.

Everything both tangible and intangible is what a theater is, and every thing is a part of everything else. A theater is a refracted image of life itself and Life is All One, as Barbara exultantly discovers in the last act of Shaw's most revolutionary play. Being All One, a theater must organize itself in circles—concentric circles, not vertically as in Enron, but rather like the rings of a tree trunk, with the artistic director and her artists in the center, yes, but what's a center without a circumference? It's the outer border of the cell that guarantees the integrity of the nucleus.

Since theater is both art and money, money and art, how will we pay for our ultimate epiphany? "How?" The question hovers and Aristotle is silent. Margo Jones, who had the original idea of professional theater outside of New York and with her small, 198-seat theater in Dallas, Texas, began the long revolution in which we are still engaged, would say, "If you have a million-dollar idea, you can raise a million dollars." She said this in the late '40s, however, and I don't know how many millions it would take to pay for that idea today. It might be that the roughly hundred million (plus or minus) that seems to be the price of a new theater building could just as well be raised as endowment to support the idea of an artists theater. Or if the building is a must-have, then a half of what is raised, or if not a half, then a third or even a quarter, but no less, could be set aside for an artistic leap forward. What is a building but the enclosing of an Idea?

In the November 2002 issue of *American Theatre*, there is a National Call for Manifestoes concerning the American theater. It's sponsored by Polly Carl, Executive Director, Playwrights' Center and the Guthrie Theater, Joe Dowling, Artistic Director, with other distinguished associates: Anna Deavere Smith's Institute on the Arts and Civic Dialogue, the Literary Managers and Dramaturgs of the Americas, Actors Theatre of Louisville and Vanderbilt University Theatre. The Call asks for Manifestoes "to imagine new possibilities for the future, engage in the idealism of the past, step forward and define our changing times, address the needs and necessity for the creation of new work of the theater today." Among the judges of the winning Manifesto are Morgan Jenness, Tony Kushner and Diana Son.

The engine of the Call seems to be "the need and necessity for the creation of new work" and the search for a contemporary American theater that will define itself by responding to that thought. It's of note that the Guthrie, one of America's most esteemed theaters, whose artistic director is committed to developing new work, and the Actors Theatre of Louisville, with its long history of important new plays and playwrights, will be involved in bringing the chosen Manifesto to life. I hope that the negative perception of "our behemoth institutions with their repressive powers" will want to be abandoned and that the rhetorical cry: "Where are the theaters worthy of these artists?" will come to seem hyperbolic, since the glass that seems only half full holds the half that promises well-equipped stages, experienced staffs, practiced audiences, in-place administrative systems—the protection of an institution able and interested to embrace new thought.

While our institutions may not currently be satisfying all the needs and expectations of artists, it's only through and with them that there's any hope for growth. In both a Marxist sense and a practical, theatrical one, only the institutional theaters possess the "means of production" necessary to carry the work forward. Acquiring these took labor, love, grit and guts, as well as an act of large imagination sustained over a long period of time. There is accumulated wisdom within the institutional theater. Suspecting or undervaluing these theaters as partners would be more than foolhardy and would demonstrate to the world an unfortunate lack of historical perspective. All of us have to listen up, not just the institutions.

Nothing is so irresistible as a good example. If the time is right, one or two examples can become two or four, two and four can become eight or twelve, and so on. Transformation via contagion is the evolutionary pattern of the resident theater movement.

The only way to begin something is to begin it. The only way to change something is to go yourself, not send someone else. You may not want to grab hold of your destiny; you may want someone to hand your destiny to you, while meanwhile you can keep on railing against your unjust fate. That would be too bad; there's so much future in the present moment.

I, too, send out a Call. It's not as resonant as the other Call and won't reach as far, but it could evoke an immediate response, and it's achievable within current circumstances. I call out to a leading American playwright whom the world admires and trusts to step up to the plate and to take on the responsibilities of artistic directorship of the next theater that's looking for one and wants to devote three-quarters of its repertory to new work.

Our playwrights seem to be the most angry; the sense of exclusion, of disempowerment, seems strongest among them. Since their art is seminal to all the other arts, if it can be empowered to flourish, the other arts will bloom along with it. Beneath "the rage of powerlessness," noted in one of the articles can lie a deep and rich source of creative power, but it can be released only by opportunity. A director, designer or actor as artistic leader can surely provide this opportunity and each has done so. But a playwright-leader is one of their own and could serve them with a special understanding. The playwright whose authenticity is already established and whose empathy is assured carries a natural authority with other playwrights. Is it to be an impromptu table reading, a workshop, a lab production in an informal space, a full production? Which is best for the playwright? The "workshopped-to-death" syndrome will be resolved by someone who has already been there, done that. The act of "auditioning" will have a different intention; from a test, a judgment, it will become an exploration, part of the overall process.

A number of our theaters focus very successfully on new work, but their relationship to the world's classics is casual, if they produce them at all. I would hope that a playwright's theater would find the classics essential to its lab/teaching component: No playwright, no artist, was born yesterday; every artist stands on the shoulders of other artists working in other forms in other times. Classics in new adaptations and translations *are* new works and, representing profound excavations of the human spirit, belong in any theater that claims to be contemporary.

In the work of a theater, the playwright provides the scaffold of meaning and intention to which all the other arts attach. In performance, the actor is at the center; theater as a performing art is an art of experience. Through the flesh and blood of the actor, the playwright comes alive, no matter when she lived. Playwrights and actors are natural companions, creating in a different way but always symbiotically. Anton Chekhov wrote to the company of the Moscow Art Theatre: "Never be afraid of an author. An actor is a free artist. You must create an image different from the author's. When the two images—the author's and the actor's—fuse into one, then an artistic work is created." There are soft rustles in the air; the idea of acting companies is blowing in again (and, of course, in a few theaters the idea has never left). Could it be that the playwright, actor, director could come together in a place in such a way as to form a dreamed-of golden triangle?

There will be a board who will understand the precarious nature of the undertaking and yet find it irresistible. The notion of research and development will be familiar to them; they will understand that it takes a lot of chaff to yield the wheat, that without bad plays there's no field from which the good ones can emerge. One doesn't know if the idea rates as a million-dollar idea that could raise a million (or whatever that is in current) dollars, but it's not beyond imagining that it could. The budget has to be large enough to support the goals, otherwise fear will take over from imagination yet another time. "Art requires luxury, even abundance," wrote Tolstoy. Indeed!

There is a level of fantasy to my line of thought, for is there an established playwright who would set aside his own writing for the arduous, time-consuming life of an artistic director? A playwright is the most solo of all theater artists, while the artistic director belongs to the entire society of the theater, last to herself. But there needs to be but one of you who hears the call. *Sui generis*, the example that occurs only once. And what follows is up to the others.

I was given for Christmas Mel Gussow's book *Conversations with Miller* [Applause Books, New York, 2002]. Here, from a conversation in 1986, is Arthur Miller's response to a question from Gussow about his use of time:

> If I had a theater that I was connected to, a theater of my peers, a working theater with a good group of actors, I probably would have written a number of more plays. I had one experience like that and that was before Lincoln Center collapsed. I had done *After the Fall*, and Harold Clurman came to me and said, "Look, we've got to have another play. Do you have anything else? And I wrote *Incident at Vichy*. And it worked out magically; there was a part for every actor in the company. That never occurred to me. There was an excitement about it. You didn't have to run around finding producers . . . It's very important. It's a defense against the outside. "We're all in this together."

Yes, we are.

Referenced Articles

Lenora Inez Brown, "The Real World," *American Theatre* magazine, TCG, New York, November 2002.

Polly Carl, "Creating the Swell," *American Theatre* magazine, TCG, New York, November 2002.

Todd London, "The Shape of Plays to Come," *American Theatre* magazine, TCG, New York, November 2002.

Cynthia Mayeda, moderator, "Is Art the Bottom Line?" *American Theatre* magazine, TCG, New York, May/June 2003.

Jaan Whitehead, "Art Will Out," *American Theatre* magazine, TCG, New York, October 2002.

NATIONAL ARTS POLICY:
What Trustees Need to Know

Gigi Bradford

> I look forward to an America which will reward achievement in the arts as we reward achievements in business or statecraft. I look forward to an America which will steadily raise the standards of artistic accomplishment and which will steadily enlarge cultural opportunities for all our citizens. And I look forward to an America which commands respect throughout the world not only for its strength but for its civilization as well.
>
> —JOHN FITZGERALD KENNEDY

S THE GOVERNING TRUSTEE of a not-for-profit arts organization, what do you need to know when thinking about the relationship of your organization's mission, operations and finances to national and international arts policies? How does the big picture affect daily operations? Why does it matter?

Arts Policy in the U.S.: What Is It and What Makes It Distinctive?

National arts policy in the U.S. is based on the premise that democratic expression occurs from the ground up. Unlike many other countries with a top-down Ministry of Culture, the U.S. government does not sustain particular cultural organizations that reflect national identity. In fact, some observers say that the U.S. has no national arts policy, and this is true if one defines "policy" as a consistently applied, primarily federal role in defining, regulating and funding the arts. In fact, we do have a national arts policy: It is a hybrid system of public and private support in which government is designed to be the minority partner. Public funds are generally intended to be the smallest piece of the "giving pie," with most of the support coming from the private sector donations of engaged individuals, corporations and local and national foundations. National arts policy in the U.S. supports an environment or ecology in which diverse, individual expression can flourish. As a result, our arts policy is varied, complex and fluid.

According to calculations published in the Foundation Center's 2003 *Arts Funding Watch*, government support at all levels—national, state, local and municipal—to all not-for-profit arts (institutions and individuals) constitutes just over ten percent of their revenues. Earned income comprises almost fifty percent of the total, and private sector contributions make up the remaining forty percent. In other words, private contributions to all the arts are almost four times greater than public funds. The myriad individual decisions of private citizens throughout the country collectively become America's "arts policy."

In this respect, the U.S. differs significantly from countries that actively work to bolster and shield their culture by defining it as expressive nationalism. These countries support organizations and sectors they feel to be culturally significant. They not only directly support important national organizations (the Louvre, the British Museum); they also manipulate domestic markets to support their own culture. France subsidizes its film industry; German cities boast multiple publicly funded opera companies; the Netherlands has at times bought all the artwork that its citizens produce; and through its Public Lending Right, the Canadian government pays its authors a residual fee each time their books are borrowed from a library. In all these cases, the government decides which art is eligible for support, and that art reflects the culture of the country. As such, government-subsidized art can play a defined role in the contemporary nationalism of other countries in a way that it does not in the U.S.

Here it's neither so simple nor so directive. As a nation of immigrants, it's fair to ask what our defining culture might be. Is it the varied indigenous Native American art that was here before Columbus? Does our culture reflect the northern European heritage of many early settlers on the east coast? Is it the customs and traditions that slaves brought to this country centuries ago? Maybe it's the diverse Hispanic legacy of what will soon be the majority ethnic group in this country. When the United States became a country, it did not have one primary culture. Unlike countries where political boundaries are drawn to reflect ethnic and cultural homogeneity, the U.S. is a truly multicultural and multiethnic society, and the ways we support our arts reflect this.

The Commercial Arts: Why Are They Important?

Another way the arts in the U.S. differ from many other countries is the impact the commercial arts sector has on how we think about the arts. In our country, art is divided into two camps: the commercial and the not-for-profit. Some art lives squarely in the commercial realm—think of Disney and Madonna. This art is primarily entertainment-oriented and earns significant profits, not only in this country, but throughout the world. (One of the most popular TV shows on the globe is *Baywatch*.) Some art, on the other hand, will always operate in the not-for-profit world—think of the Guarneri Quartet and the Shakespeare Theatre in Washington, D.C. Organizations in the not-for-profit world operate of necessity as hybrids, finding support wherever they can. Groups such as theaters and opera companies that can earn only about half of their operating costs must rely on grants, donations and dedicated, underpaid labor to balance their budgets.

During the postwar period in America, commercial art for mass consumption grew into an economic powerhouse. For the first time, some kinds of theater, film, music and publishing became identified not as privately experienced and supported high art, but as profitable, commercial, public entertainment. The differences between commercial and noncommercial models in the arts became unclear, and many people conflated some not-for-profit art forms with the commercial standards of their more entertainment-oriented cousins. Independent filmmakers now operate within the shadow of Hollywood; poets are held to the profit standards of global media giants like Time Warner;

chamber musicians are compared to The Rolling Stones; and not-for-profit productions like *Lackawanna Blues* or *I Am My Own Wife* are judged in the same way as Disney's Broadway production of *Beauty and the Beast*.

Under these conditions, it is not surprising that people ask why the not-for-profit arts can't support themselves. Why do they need public funds and private donations? Why can't they operate as commercial enterprises like Disney or DreamWorks? Isn't it true that not-for-profit organizations are just badly run companies? Couldn't they run in the black if they improved their administration? The answers to these questions are complex, and to understand them we first need a fuller understanding of the economics of the not-for-profit arts.

The Not-for-Profit Arts: Why Do They Need Support?

Not-for-profit charitable and educational organizations are defined as those that exist to serve the public good. This is codified in the Internal Revenue Code as Section 501(c)(3), whose purposes are shown below. While it is interesting to note that the arts are not explicitly cited in the text, both the courts and the IRS have consistently held that artistic organizations and activities are covered by this designation, and any U. S. artistic organization that solicits grants or donations and offers a tax deduction to donors operates as a 501(c)(3). The Internal Revenue Code states:

> The exempt purposes set forth in IRC Section 501(c)(3) are charitable, religious, educational, scientific, literary, testing for public safety, fostering national or international amateur sports competition, and the prevention of cruelty to children or animals . . . The organization must not be organized or operated for the benefit of private interests, such as the creator or the creator's family, shareholders of the organization, other designated individuals, or persons controlled directly or indirectly by such private interests. No part of the net earnings of an IRC Section 501(c)(3) organization may inure to the benefit of any private shareholder or individual . . .

The U.S. government has established a policy of encouraging citizens to support organizations such as arts institutions that advance the public good. A key point to understand, though, is that arts institutions differ fundamentally from the prevailing free-market model because they are mission-driven, not profit-driven. They exist not to make money but to make art. Like libraries, schools, colleges and most hospitals, mission-driven organizations aim to improve the common wealth, not the individual bottom line. Being labor-intensive, the "product" of such organizations does not lend itself to increased efficiency and improved performance. Some activities just aren't subject to significant productivity gains and never will be. It takes the same five people to perform Mozart's String Quartet in G Minor as it did when he composed it in 1787, and it takes the same amount of time to play the music. *Hamlet* consists of the same twenty-three named dramatis personae as it did when printed in 1604, and it still has the same five acts. Wagner's *Ring Cycle* is no shorter in 2005 than it was in 1953.

The problem is that, in order to fulfill their function as public goods, the arts need to be available to a wide range of the population, and that means their price has to be accessible. But, since costs rise over time, an income gap opens up between what can be reasonably charged and the rising costs of production. Since this income gap can't be closed by gains in productivity, other sources of income are needed. Economists call this the "cost disease," and it's a way to understand why some parts of societies and economies will always need a level of subsidy.

It's not only the arts that experience the "cost disease." Lectures and sermons take as long as they ever did. It takes the same nine months to gestate babies, and tulip bulbs still bloom only in spring. Economists would say that the productivity of these things has not increased over time. The rest of the American economy, however, aims to continually become more efficient, and efficient companies strive to produce more for less. So we pay a lot less for batteries, computers and TVs than we used to, and CD-ROMs are now so cheap that they arrive unbidden in home-delivered newspapers.

Cost disease is endemic to things that don't lend themselves to market pricing, like babies and flowers and education and religion and art. Cost disease operates outside a market model. It's hard to make any of these things more efficient, which is why economists have dubbed it a "disease." Maybe it isn't really a disease, but an opportunity to think of the word "value" in a different way.

Entire segments of the cultural and artistic life we value will never earn their own way. They do not fit a commercial model. It is for this reason that other sources of support are needed.

Public Support for the Arts: A Complex System

> Legislation creating the NEA and its companion, the National Endowment for the Humanities, was probably the single most important measure ever enacted in our country in support of the life of the mind and the imagination.
>
> —JOHN BRADEMAS
> FORMER CONGRESSMAN AND
> PRESIDENT EMERITUS OF NEW YORK UNIVERSITY

Our present system of public grants for the arts is quite young. It was not until 1965, nearly two hundred years after the birth of the republic, that the government instituted a consistent federal system of direct support for the arts. The first national system of government grants began with the establishment of the National Endowment for the Arts (NEA) in 1965, which, in time, sparked the development of state and local arts agencies. At its peak level in the mid-1990s, the Arts Endowment boasted a budget of around $175 million. This appropriation was approximately one one-hundredth of one percent of the federal budget, or sixty-eight cents per taxpayer per year.

Most public funding for the arts comes from community appropriations to the nearly six thousand local arts agencies throughout the country. The fifty-six state and territorial legislatures in the U.S. provide state arts agencies with the second largest aggregate amount to the arts. Federal funding, primarily through the NEA, but also through such disparate agencies as the Defense Department, Department of Justice and Army Corps of Engineers, provides the smallest piece of the public funding pie. The public funding equation can be imagined as a pyramid, with local appropriations at the base, state contributions in the middle and federal funds at the top.

Despite its limited nature, public funding has helped to shift culture and audiences for culture away from a market model toward a more democratic national focus and public availability. It has widened the concept of culture beyond the parameters of profit-centered entertainment and mostly European-derived high art. It has made more art—and more kinds of art—available in rural areas. And it has leveraged funding from the private sector to support new areas of creativity, such as regional theaters, filmmaking and indigenous expression.

Since the late 1960s, grants from the NEA have helped to make not-for-profit theater in the U.S. more egalitarian and more geographically diverse. Without public funding, the regional theater movement that began in the 1960s would not have spread throughout the country as it did. According to Theatre Communications Group, nearly every Pulitzer Prize–winning play since 1976 originated at an NEA-funded theater.

Although we tend to think of arts policy mainly in terms of funding, by far the biggest source of support for the arts in this country is the tax code. By writing into law the individual tax deduction and the organizational tax exemption, the U.S. government forgoes significant revenue and signals the importance of diverse individual choice. Gifts of appreciated property, the estate tax and the ability of artists to deduct the fair-market value of their work are tax policies that also directly affect the income of artists and artistic organizations.

Other federal policies affect the arts as well. Postal rates include a not-for-profit designation that substantially benefits the arts. Visas for foreign artists to tour the U.S. have recently become increasingly important to cultural groups, because new restrictions on their availability have made it more difficult for foreign dance companies, musicians and actors to tour our country, and for our artists to travel abroad.

Copyright and intellectual property issues directly affect individual artists and those who work primarily in the not-for-profit sector. Legislation, such as the Digital Millennium Copyright Act and the Copyright Term Extension Act, has restricted the public domain and benefited established commercial interests more than it has helped emerging artists. Government research and development invented the internet, and government regulation of technology directly affects the content industries. While not all federal arts policy is directed toward funding issues, all federal policies that touch the arts affect the bottom line of artists and arts organizations.

Public support of the arts is complex and, as mentioned earlier, accounts for about ten percent of public funding when state and local funding are included. The balance of contributed support comes from individual gifts and from foundation and corporate donations. But there is one other source of financial support for the arts that is almost always overlooked, yet is an important part of the funding picture: the underpaid labor of its professional work force.

According to Dance/USA, dancers usually work on contract for a thirty- to thirty-five-week season each year and earn $400 to $600 for those weeks in the season. Actors Equity rates for not-for-profit theaters range from about $250 to $850 a week, depending on the size of the theater, and most actors do not have steady year-round work. Visual artists are dependent on the sale of their work, and usually carry other jobs to support themselves. And many artists in all fields have to leave their work as they become older and have families and homes to support. Because so many artists work for the love of their art, they are caught in an economic system that discounts their labor; they themselves become a major source of subsidy for the arts. Artists and the administrators who work alongside them in the not-for-profit world embody the phrase "labor of love," and are the hidden funders of the arts. Without this source of subsidy, the public and private financial needs of the arts would be much more acute.

Public Support and the NEA: A Changing Landscape

Within this complex system of arts support, it is the National Endowment for the Arts that has attracted the most attention and has been at the heart of most of the public dissension and debate about arts funding. So a closer look at the NEA—how it operates and how it is changing—is helpful in understanding today's political climate.

Roughly speaking, NEA funding can be divided into two eras: 1965 to 1995 and 1995 to the present. The "culture wars" of the 1980s and 1990s and their repercussions resulted in Congressional changes to and restrictions on the way federal funds can be allocated. Although they were indicative of much larger social and political currents, the Mapplethorpe and Serrano "scandals," which questioned the appropriate use of public dollars, ultimately resulted in a sea change in the way federal funds support the arts.

Before 1995, the NEA was organized into programs that mirrored generally recognized art forms. There was the Theater Program, the Dance Program, the Literature Program, the Opera Program, etc. This system gave art forms their own internal budgets, a highly trained staff with specific discipline expertise and an unparalleled national overview of organizations, activities and people in each artistic field.

The Director of each NEA discipline program was a respected professional who helped target appropriate federal funding to successful applicants throughout the country. He or she, in accordance with Congressional mandates, would carefully put together panels of peers from across the country that would come together to read, assess and adjudicate grant applications. A typical discipline program, such as Theater, would utilize nearly one hundred different citizens each year to help it make funding decisions.

Panels consisted of working experts in the field and of laypeople knowledgeable about the discipline but with no professional affiliation. All panels were carefully screened for conflicts of interest, and in some cases applicants applied anonymously. Grants were by no means assured; some fellowship programs were able to award funds to only four percent of eligible applicants. At their best, NEA grants came to be seen by applicants themselves, by private foundations and corporations and by individuals as a "seal of approval" indicating that the applicant had passed rigorous peer review and adhered to federal organizational standards.

Most NEA funding is structured to require matching funds as a means of increasing the impact of government support. NEA funds must be matched on a one-to-one basis, and presently the agency cites figures showing that each federal dollar is matched by $3.50 in private funds. These federal matching requirements became an important lever for developing state funding through state arts agencies. Only six state arts agencies existed before the NEA was established. Seeking to work with partners at the state level, in its early years, the NEA helped to establish many more state arts agencies by giving them their first grants. Indeed, an increasing percentage of the NEA's program budget is allocated to the states; at this writing it is a full forty percent.

The federal matching requirements also were important in developing the NEA's Challenge Program, one of its most successful initiatives. The Challenge Program utilized the concept of the three-to-one funding match. Designed to stabilize arts organizations, this program provided funds not just for artistic programming but for organizational development as well. Successful applicants were required to match each public dollar with three dollars in private donations. This program helped organizations to become more effective administratively and to knit themselves more tightly into their communities. Often, a public grant assured potential private donors that an organization and a proposed project had met the highest professional standards.

In 1995, when Congress slashed the NEA's budget by almost fifty percent, the agency was forced to reorganize both conceptually and administratively, and specific discipline programs were eliminated. The Theater Program, for example, went from eleven full-time professional staff members to three. It no longer had a discrete budget within the agency; it could fund only projects and not organizational seasons; and it did not have its own panels of theater experts, but instead awarded grants along with other disciplines in functional areas such as "Heritage and Preservation" or "Creation and Presentation." Panels consisted of experts and laypeople with expertise in different art forms, not only the specific art form under review. Several years later the NEA inaugurated its Challenge America program, designed to spread federal funding more evenly throughout the country. Challenge America grants were typically much smaller (around $5,000) project-based funds—a world away from the former Challenge Program, which offered a few highly competitive awards in the six-figure range.

With a decline in federal funding and increased localized grant-making, observers have noticed:

- More instrumental grant-making, focused primarily on how applicants contribute to community need
- Smaller grants requiring fewer private sector matching contributors
- A shift in funding from unrestricted, organizational support to restricted project grants
- Less money for touring and for projects that cross state lines or community boundaries
- Fewer innovative and cutting-edge grants
- A drastic decline in grants to individual artists
- More time between grants
- Increasingly stringent eligibility requirements.

However, by setting federal standards; defining eligible application areas (dramaturgs, directors and playwrights come to mind); supporting service organizations such as Theatre Communications Group; and establishing a locus for national information about specific artistic disciplines, the NEA has been able to leverage a small public investment to help assure private contributors that the organizations and projects to which they donate are worthy of their support. The NEA has also been particularly important in giving credibility and visibility to less institutionalized fields like dance and folk art.

Cultural Policy Today: Where Are We?

Over the course of the twentieth century, the telegraph, the telephone, photography, films, commercial publishing, broadcasting and the internet—new systems to disseminate ideas—utterly changed how quickly thoughts and images move around the globe. In the past fifty years, the world's Gross Domestic Product increased fivefold, but trade across national borders increased fourteen times. In his remarks at the Massachusetts Alliance for the Commonwealth's 1999 Conference on International Business, Federal Reserve Chairman Alan Greenspan attributed the surge in international trade to technological innovation and "the substitution of ideas—new insights—for material bulk and brute human effort."

Three centuries ago, a nation's wealth was measured in its raw materials—its land, water, lumber and coal. During the Industrial Revolution, nations became rich through commerce, industry and trade. But in the global information and knowledge revolution, economies are increasingly based on ideas and culture. The internet makes ideas and cultural products readily accessible. The worldwide web was born a decade ago, and has revised the information equation. Suddenly, anyone with a few simple tools and easily acquired techniques can become not only a "content provider" but a distributor of ideas and cultural products. The distinct economic character of information and ideas has changed how we view national wealth, which is increasingly measured by the vitality, energy and dynamism of a country's culture. In the present economy, countries that do not promote policies to allow their citizens and their cultures to be creative and innovative will be left behind. A nation needs a vibrant labor force of artists, actors, writers, designers, painters, musicians, architects, engineers and scientists—and the policies and regulations to support them.

As a result of these changes, we are redefining what we mean by the "cultural sector"—what is included in it and how big it is. Today most people agree that the term applies to industries, goods or services that combine the creation, production and distribution of intangibles protected by copyright. Under this broad definition, the arts are just one part of the cultural sector, and a rather small part at that. But, using this more inclusive approach, culture's economic contribution becomes substantial. In 1996, cultural products (films, music, television, books, journals and computer software) became the largest U.S. export, surpassing all other traditional export categories, including automobiles, agriculture, aerospace and defense. In the United States, the copyright industries generate roughly five percent of the Gross Domestic Product and contribute nearly eighty billion dollars in global sales. An estimated 7.6 million people work in these fields, and their numbers are growing at three times the rate of the rest of the economy. The movie industry has a surplus trade balance with every country in the world.

What we have learned to call globalization has both extended the reach of commercial American cultural products and multiplied their profits. Much of the rest of the world views the U.S. through the lens of its cultural exports: movies, television, music, computer software, books, etc. The domestic "culture wars" of the 1990s, in which the halls of Congress, government agencies, museums, symphonies and theaters rumbled with controversies over cultural content, public funding for artists, censorship and freedom of expression, are being superseded by today's international "cultural wars," which focus on the impact of our commercial entertainment on other cultures much more than on the specifics of the not-for-profit arts. In this more complex cultural world, it may become more difficult to articulate and advocate for the particular needs of our traditional arts.

> In Canada (as in many European nations), culture is an expression of national identity, and as such is to be promoted and protected as a public responsibility. To the degree to which culture for Americans is about the profit-making entertainment industry and for Canadians about the politics of national identity, there should be little doubt about the propensity for mutual misunderstanding.
>
> —KEVIN MULCAHY
> "CULTURAL PROTECTIONISM V. CULTURAL IMPERIALISM: U.S.-CANADIAN RELATIONS,"
> CENTER FOR ART AND CULTURE

The Role of Trustees: Now More Important Than Ever

Art is becoming both more important and more difficult to fund. The work your theater performs stands a better chance of affecting more people across the globe than at any time in human history. But its global reach and human story are becoming harder to sustain. Shrinking public and private dollars cannot be made up for by increased administrative efficiencies. The "cost disease" persists. Arts organizations will continue to be judged by the standards—both high and low—of their commercial counterparts. The hybrid U.S. system of support is straining to sustain a not-for-profit sector increasingly dominated by commercial expectations.

Policy does make a difference. Establishing and supporting a not-for-profit arts sector is a crucial element of American policy. The principle of minority public support has been a cornerstone in the growth of the arts in this country over the last half century. State, city and local funding provides invaluable financial support and community connection. Private donations from individuals, corporations and foundations—a key component in the complicated funding performance piece that every arts organization continually mounts—often complement as well as augment public funds.

Trustees are more important than ever to the success of the not-for-profit arts. They work with local and national officials, national service organizations and government agencies of all types. They collaborate with community leaders, individuals, foundations and corporations. They stabilize finances and support professional staff. They inform others about how the arts operate and how important they are to our national well-being.

Not only can trustees support the specific organization of which they are an integral component, they can also support the not-for-profit sector as a whole. If the estate tax is repealed, for instance, fewer donors will leave bequests to regional theaters. If federal funding through the NEA is cut off, the leveraging power of public funds at the state and local level will disappear as well. Trustees can raise awareness for these and other issues.

The arts help to nourish the environment in which creativity and innovation can flourish in the twenty-first century. Their health depends on their artistic and financial strength *and* on the ability of trustees to spark and sustain an environment that will ensure their future.

THE ROLE OF ADVOCACY IN TRUSTEE GOVERNANCE

Roche Schulfer

O TRUSTEES HAVE A ROLE in arts advocacy? If so, what is it? To answer these questions we must first understand what advocacy is and what it takes to become an effective arts advocate.

What Is Advocacy?

> Advocacy—active verbal support for a cause or position.
>
> —ENCARTA COLLEGE DICTIONARY

Arts advocates are individuals who can articulate and promote the case for support for the arts to the public. Although advocacy is often linked to lobbying, the work of arts advocates goes beyond seeking government support. It includes promoting the case for support to audiences, funding sources and other constituents. Everyone involved with an arts organization should be an advocate for the arts—from the chairman of the board to the front-of-house staff. Since trustees are both dedicated to the arts and have an important profile in their community, they have a key role to play as arts advocates.

How Do You Become an Effective Arts Advocate?

> The healthiest relationships . . . exist between board and staff members who genuinely respect each other. This is obviously easier if the board member from the business world has some real understanding of the fields served by the not-for-profit organization.
>
> —WILLIAM BOWEN

Creating effective advocates involves leadership and commitment from the artists, staff and trustees of an arts organization. Arts advocates must be able to articulate clearly and concisely the mission of their organization as well as the role the arts play in society. Understanding the mission, goals and values of your organization is at the heart of becoming an effective arts advocate.

The organization's mission must be developed through collaboration among the artists, trustees and staff—a process that can generate tension unless it occurs in an atmosphere of mutual respect and trust. Since most trustees work in the for-profit world, it is crucial that they familiarize themselves with the unique characteristics of a not-for-profit corporation—both the legal structure and the field to be served. Trustees should recognize that there are two bottom lines in the arts—artistic and financial—and that the artistic vision is key to this mission.

> The main event is not the institution. The main event is under the Big Top where the performers with their feats of magic and daring and the audience with its imaginative belief and its empathy get together and all breathe the same air at the same moment . . . The clarity of this relationship is harder to maintain in threatening times because the board has the responsibility for the survival of the institution and can become excessively interested in what goes on in the tent as well as how much it cost to put it there. Tensions are to be expected and worked through, always remembering that while theater is a business, its business is art, not business.
>
> —ZELDA FICHANDLER

At the same time, arts professionals must understand the importance of determining the institutional values of the organization. In any established arts organization, artists, staff and trustees must determine the long-term values of the institution. This must be done without limiting the possibilities for the current and future artistic direction. Creating institutional values does not mean selecting plays, concerts or exhibitions. It does involve reaching a consensus on what motivates the key stakeholders of the institution—for example, a commitment to quality, a belief in the importance of diversity and/or a desire for involvement with the community. While institutional values are essential, they should not be chiseled in stone—they must be reviewed and evolve as the organization evolves.

Trustees and arts professionals also need to understand the complex measures of success in a not-for-profit arts organization. What defines success: attendance, reviews, new work, classics, funding level, operating surplus, educational programs, endowment size, etc.? There is no easy answer since many factors play a role in defining success. Artists, trustees and staff must resist the urge to define the ultimate success of their organization in simple terms such as reviews or the financial bottom line. The dynamic process of balancing artistic objectives with institutional values is essential to developing a mission that has the support of the artists, trustees and staff. And it is the only way to create effective arts advocates.

Government Support for the Arts: Fact and Fiction

Through political advocacy we articulate the case for arts support to our government representatives and the public. The goal is to increase direct government funding as well as to pass legislation that is favorable to the arts in areas such as education, tax policy and immigration.

In order to make the case for arts support, we must first separate fact from fiction. Misconceptions have surrounded government support for the arts, particularly support from the National Endowment for the Arts (NEA), for many years. We have been told that government funding of the arts:

- Distorts the mission of art organizations
- Is so small that it is irrelevant
- Supports excellence instead of access to the arts

- Supports access to the arts instead of excellence
- Promotes overly conservative works of art
- Promotes primarily obscene works of art.

The misconceptions are not only numerous, they are often contradictory! The facts indicate that by any reasonable standard government support for the arts has been a great success since the creation of the NEA in 1965:

- The NEA has been a model public-private partnership in which a small amount of federal support leverages a large amount of private support. This is because almost all NEA grants are matching grants that require each organization to generate significant local support.
- The NEA has been an effective federal-state partnership in which forty percent of the NEA budget goes to state arts councils. This has stimulated the creation of state and local arts agencies and greatly increased access to the arts around the country.
- NEA grants are allocated almost exclusively through theme-based peer panels, providing the best opportunity for recognizing artistic excellence.
- In forty years, only a handful of NEA grants have generated major public controversy. During the same time, NEA support has stimulated the growth and development of thousands of artists and organizations, including some of our most acclaimed museums, theaters, operas, orchestras, dance companies and presenting groups.
- While overall government support is generally less than five percent of an arts organization's budget, the NEA and state arts councils together represent the largest funding source for the arts in the country.

The partnership between the NEA and state arts agencies has been essential in linking our society together in a completely new way. Government support has helped create the cultural equivalent of the interstate highway system in our country—and for only a fraction of the cost! In fact, if the federal government ran as economically and effectively as our arts agencies, the national budget would be in much better shape.

The Political Base

If government support for the arts has been so successful, why do arts advocates have to battle to preserve funding for the NEA and state and local arts agencies? Some argue that the arts are ultimately elitist and lack a large political base of support. Without a broad political base, arts advocates cannot be successful in making the case for support to society. To get a better sense of the political base, let us examine one segment of the arts in more detail: not-for-profit theater.

Over the past forty years, the not-for-profit theater has grown at an extraordinary pace, thanks in large part to the stimulus provided by government support. From a handful of theaters in 1965, there are now more than 450 members of Theatre Communications Group (the national service organization for the not-for-profit theater), plus several hundred more who are not TCG members. In the city of Chicago alone, the League of Chicago Theatres (LCT) has grown from approximately a dozen members in 1979 to more than 150 today. Millions of people around the country participate in not-for-profit theater as artists, staff, trustees, audiences and contributors. In addition, the theater has a tremendous economic impact on communities across the nation. Figures compiled by the LCT and the Illinois Arts Alliance indicate that in 2002 direct spending by Chicago theaters exceeded $147 million, and related spending (restaurants, suppliers, etc.) added another $200 million. In addition, more than 6,000 full- or part-time jobs were created.

Professional and public participation in the not-for-profit theater in this country is enormous. When combined with participation in the other arts, the figures are staggering. Clearly, the arts have a huge potential grassroots political base. If these individuals and organizations were to become active advocates for the arts, the results would be extraordinary.

The Case for Government Support

> If men and women of capacity refuse to take part in politics and government, they condemn themselves, as well as the people, to the punishment of living under bad government.
>
> —SENATOR SAM J. ERVIN

There are already many dedicated individuals and arts advocacy organizations that have created a network of support throughout the country. They have developed extensive materials to bolster the case for arts support, both on a local and federal level. To be effective as an arts advocate, it is essential that you become a part of this network. At the end of this book is a list of advocacy groups and discipline-based service organizations. Contact them for more information.

Why advocate for government support of the arts? Because government support can help:

- Support artists in their pursuit of excellence
- Provide institutional stability to arts organizations
- Ensure access to the arts for underserved audiences
- Enhance the education of young people through the arts
- Stimulate the economic impact of the arts
- Leverage arts support from private sources
- Promote the cultural life of our nation to the world.

The U.S. has developed the most broad-based system for arts support in the world. Through the not-for-profit, tax-exempt model, we can provide a wide range of support for the arts that gives artists the opportunity to do their best possible work. With support from audiences, individuals, foundations, corporations and the government, we can avoid a situation in which one source of funding becomes dominant, thereby having an explicit or implicit impact on content.

This system of broad-based support has led to enormous accomplishments over the past four decades, but has not yet come close to reaching its potential. The low level of government support is a prime reason for this. No thoughtful arts advocate argues for a system in which the government becomes the primary source of support. But if government support were to rise to ten percent of the average arts organization's budget, it would have an enormous impact on arts groups, most of which are small and undercapitalized businesses. Increased government support plus leveraged private support would pump millions of new dollars to artists and organizations. This infusion of funds would lead to greater resources for artists plus greater access to the arts for audiences. And because government arts support is so economical and efficient, the total cost to federal, state and local governments would be nominal compared to federal commitments to health care, education and public safety.

Perhaps the most important reason to advocate for increased government support of the arts is that our cultural life ultimately defines us as a nation. In a very small and troubled world, it is critical that the values of our nation be clearly communicated to other countries. While American popular culture has an enormous impact on the world, it presents a largely distorted view of our society, one dominated by money, violence and sex.

Through the arts, however, we can ultimately promote the core values of our nation, including freedom, equality and justice. The arts can provide answers to complicated moral questions—but the answers are unlikely to be simple. This, of course, has made the arts a primary target in the "culture wars."

Through the arts, we can communicate the core values of our nation to the rest of the world. In order to achieve that goal, artists and institutions must have the resources to do their best possible work. This may ultimately be the most important reason to advocate for increased government support of the arts.

What Can Trustees (and Others) Do?

> Democracy is measured not by its leaders doing extraordinary things, but by its citizens doing ordinary things extraordinarily well.
>
> —John Gardner

1. Be an active citizen. As citizens we have a responsibility to be aware of the issues confronting our community and country. Furthermore, it is our duty to work to improve the quality of life in our society. You cannot be an effective advocate for the arts unless you are an active citizen. By participating in the life of the community, you can articulate the impact that the arts have on critical issues such as education, community development and support for creativity.
2. Make advocacy part of your overall development plan. As discussed earlier, the NEA and state councils represent the largest source of support for the arts in the country. Yet many arts groups do not devote appropriate time and effort to cultivating this support. Make advocacy part of your overall fundraising strategy by allocating the appropriate resources. Trustees should make sure that advocacy is integrated into their organization's overall development plan.

3. Work the grassroots. All politics are local—arts advocacy starts in your organization and community. Make sure your local, state and national government representatives are aware of your programs, and invite them to tour your facility, take part in an educational or outreach program or event, or a luncheon/dinner, and honor them with an award. Make sure that during these events you create photo opportunities and then publish the photos in your publications. As community leaders, trustees play a crucial role in helping to make support for the arts a core value of their community.
4. Identify your representatives and know which committees they sit on. Start by writing to your representatives on the local, state and federal levels. State and national organizations are making it increasingly easy to contact representatives using automated email. If you are on their list, you will be sent an action alert when important issues arise, and then provided with simple instructions to make your voice heard. Remember: In politics, every letter counts, literally.
5. Attend National Arts Day in Washington. Schedule a visit with your congressman (or one of his staff). Bring a packet of materials about your organization. Say thank you! If you can't say thank you, make the case for support of your organization. If your senator or representative sits on an appropriations committee, this visit becomes more important. Even if you talk to a staff member, your visit will be recorded. Does your state arts association sponsor a state arts day? If so, represent your organization there and schedule visits with key representatives.
6. Get personal. When you have a funding proposal pending on the state or local level (e.g., a bond bill), your physical presence at hearings is important. Make contact with your city council; get yourself to the state capital. Then, whenever and as often as possible, introduce yourself, name your organization and ask for support.
7. Network, network, network. Through advocacy you are "selling" the case for arts support to the public. Create a trustee advocacy committee and look for new ways to promote the value of the arts in society. Be proactive—don't wait for a crisis. Build coalitions by working with other not-for-profit arts groups or other local organizations. For example, since most arts groups are small businesses, you might find opportunities to collaborate with your local small business association. Trustees should par-

ticipate in the networking process to help build relationships that strengthen arts advocacy efforts in the community.

8. NETWORK SOME MORE. There is a very strong arts advocacy network that has been developed in this country through the efforts of individuals and organizations on a local, state and national level. Learn more about this network and become an active participant in the local and national organizations involved in arts advocacy. If there isn't a local coalition of arts groups devoted to advocacy in your community, organize one. Make sure that trustees are aware of the opportunities they have to participate in these advocacy groups. The arts have not fully realized the potential of their political base because not enough artists, staff and trustees have become involved with the advocacy groups and efforts that already exist. Review the list of organizations at the end of this book and participate.
9. COMMUNICATE WITH YOUR AUDIENCE. A director of a political advocacy group once observed that the arts community has a great opportunity to be effective advocates because its biggest supporters (our audience) walk right into museums, theaters and concert halls. Yet we rarely communicate with our audience about government support and the value of the arts in our society unless there is a crisis. While arts groups cannot endorse candidates, we can spend considerable time and resources promoting the value of the arts to our constituents. Trustees should make sure that their organization knows the guidelines for arts advocacy and takes full advantage of the opportunities for communicating with their audience.
10. COMMIT FOR THE LONG HAUL. Political advocacy is not glamorous—it is a slow and deliberate process. It is also often frustrating and grueling. Our system of government was designed to make sure that nothing happens without considerable debate, reflection and compromise. It took almost two hundred years for our nation to acknowledge that the arts should be on the national agenda of priorities. It may take another two hundred years to achieve an appropriate level of funding! Since trustees are concerned with the long-range vitality and stability of the arts, a commitment to advocacy should be a key responsibility of trustee governance.

A Success Story

One of the most successful state arts advocacy organizations is the Illinois Arts Alliance and Foundation, led by executive director Alene Valkanas and a dedicated board of directors. The IAA has become a truly statewide organization, bridging the gap that can exist between urban and rural communities. The IAA was formed in 1982 in the midst of a budget crisis in the state of Illinois. The governor at the time proposed eliminating the budget for the Illinois Arts Council. This caused a group of concerned citizens and arts professionals, led by Fred Fine, Mort Kaplan and Doug Donenfield, to convene a group that became the IAA. This new group of arts advocates, representing a wide range of arts professionals, launched a grassroots campaign that led to the saving of the Illinois Arts Council. Now, for more than twenty years, the IAA has been a tremendously effective advocate for the arts throughout the state, helping to increase the Illinois Arts Council budgets to record levels.

In 2004, Illinois, like many states across the country, faced a budget crisis. Once again, an Illinois governor was facing difficult decisions as states drastically cut or attempted to eliminate arts budgets. But in Illinois, the governor proposed only a five percent cut in the arts budget. This was due to more than twenty years of work by the IAA.

How did the IAA do it? By communicating the tangible and intangible benefits of the arts to every legislative district and every politician in the state. This included the first comprehensive study of the economic impact of the arts industry in the state of Illinois. The study was made available as a CD-ROM presentation that the IAA delivered to communities and legislators throughout the state. The IAA made sure that every legislator was aware of the impact the arts have on the local economy, education and community development.

In addition, the IAA supported the initiative developed by the Illinois Arts Council under the direction of Shirley Madigan to create a new category of support, the Established Regional Arts Institution (ERAI). Previously, the major cultural institution category included only a dozen or so of the well-established Chicago area institutions. With the creation of the ERAI category, the number of established major institutions tripled and extended to the entire state. This brought a greater awareness of the importance of the arts to many communities. It increased the awareness of each legislator about local activity. And it brought appropriate recognition and a sense of pride to many outstanding organizations outside the major metropolitan area.

These efforts have created a climate in Illinois in which the value of the arts is understood by elected representatives and the public at large. While it has certainly not made arts advocacy easy, the work of the IAA over the past twenty years has permanently changed the political climate for arts support in Illinois.

Another Success Story

The continued existence of the NEA throughout the "culture wars" is a tribute to the thousands of individuals and arts advocacy groups who worked to preserve federal arts support throughout the 1990s. The arts faced many powerful opponents who had made elimination of the NEA a key part of the "culture wars" agenda. They spent millions of dollars to end federal support for the arts. Given the size and dedication of the opposition, it seemed unlikely that federal arts support would survive. In response, however, advocacy groups, service organizations and arts advocates organized a grassroots campaign and an effective Washington, D.C., advocacy effort. The American Arts Alliance, Americans for the Arts and the other arts advocacy and service organizations worked in collaboration to build a case for support for the arts in Congress. The work of these arts advocates has resulted in a different climate for government support of the arts. In recent years we have seen increases in the budget for the NEA, something that was unthinkable a decade ago. Now, with a stronger and more coordinated national advocacy network, arts advocates have the opportunity to activate our broad political base. This could be the beginning of a new era in federal, state and local support for the arts.

Politics and Art

Arts professionals are often uncomfortable with any connection between art and politics. Since politics always play a part in government support for the arts, this becomes reason enough not to want to participate in arts advocacy efforts. At the same time, no federal, state or local government support for the arts has ever been free from political considerations, even if the connection has not always been obvious. Politics have always been a part of the NEA since its establishment in 1965. It is unlikely, however, given the diversified funding base for the arts, that government support could have a significant impact on an organization's mission, even at two or three times the current level. Furthermore, if the baseline level of government support increases, our system of government will balance the political considerations in the long run. Administrations and individuals will come and go, but support for the arts should be a bipartisan constant. In addition, at a time when there is increasing pressure to limit the size of the federal government, maintaining a national arts agency indicates that the arts are important in this country. Arts advocates should recognize that politics are a part of government support for the arts, and they need to continually work to keep the arts on the national agenda of priorities.

A Note of Caution

A final and perhaps obvious note of caution: Freedom of expression is not pretty. Controversy is inevitable in the arts; it cannot be eliminated. As an arts advocate you will eventually have to support or defend an artist or work of art that you personally find objectionable. This is not easy for anyone to do. It is often particularly hard for trustees. It requires the recognition that freedom of expression is what makes this country extraordinary. This is the only nation in the world in which an incredibly large and diverse population confronts the challenge of living together in a fair, equitable and free society. Nothing communicates this more clearly than our belief in freedom of expression. This is why arts advocates must be prepared to fight for the right of artists to express unpopular and controversial points of view in their work.

What Is the Role of Advocacy in Trustee Governance?

While everyone involved in the arts should be an arts advocate, trustees play a critical role in this effort. Here is a review of some key concepts:

- Understand the mission, goals and values of your organization
- Commit to being an advocate for the arts on behalf of all of your constituents
- Learn the true facts about government support and the arts' political base
- Work to make the arts a core value of your community

- Make arts advocacy a key part of your organization's development plan
- Network, network, network—on a local and national level
- Make sure your organization communicates with your audience
- Accept the relationship between government support and politics
- Become an advocate for freedom of expression.

The arts foster creativity, enhance the educational experience, build communities and stimulate economic development. For these reasons alone, arts advocates can make the case that the arts are an essential part of the fabric of American society. There is an advocacy network in place and an enormous political base to be tapped. We can create a bright future for artists and audiences in this country. All it will take is effort.

> And perhaps, just perhaps, we'll begin to build a consciousness of our own role in civic life—a role we claim, but too rarely present convincingly . . . We will see genuine warmth and recognition of arts organizations as true partners in working towards a healthier civic society—a force to be reckoned with and not a party to be dismissed.
>
> —BEN CAMERON
> EXECUTIVE DIRECTOR, TCG

I would like to thank Mary Beth Fisher for editorial consultation, and Laurie Baskin for providing the information on arts advocacy organizations at the end of this book.

THE CHANGING LEGAL ENVIRONMENT FOR THE ARTS

Joan Channick

NOT-FOR-PROFIT ARTS ORGANIZATIONS operate in a complex and frequently changing legal environment. They are incorporated under state laws, given tax exemption under both federal and state law, and subject to the same array of federal, state and local employment and other laws that govern all businesses. As such, not-for-profit arts organizations are subject to regulatory scrutiny by the Internal Revenue Service, state Attorneys General and a host of other governmental bodies. While boards often pay considerable attention to internal governance—the relationship between board and staff leaders that ensures the organization's mission is fulfilled effectively—equal attention should be focused on what might be deemed "external governance": oversight by and accountability to the government and the public.

The Not-for-Profit Sector

The not-for-profit sector represents a significant part of the American economy and plays an important role in American society, attempting to fill gaps left by the market economy and government in meeting social needs. According to a March 1, 2005, report by the Independent Sector's Panel on the Nonprofit Sector:

> The number of public charities and private foundations in America has nearly doubled over the last twenty years. Designated by the Internal Revenue Service as section 501(c)(3) organizations, they currently employ approximately 11.5 million people. The sector is predominantly composed of small organizations, with sixty-four percent of all 501(c)(3) nonprofits operating with budgets of under $500,000 per year. Only six percent of nonprofit organizations have annual budgets larger than $10 million, though this group accounts for a considerably larger portion of the sector's overall activity. The American people contribute over $201 billion annually directly to charitable institutions, and the country's 65,000 private foundations and corporate giving programs provide an additional $40 billion toward charitable endeavors. A number of nonprofits also serve as the instruments through which government discharges some of its obligations, and are partially funded through public dollars.

A rash of high-profile financial scandals in recent years has focused public and regulatory attention on egregious failures of corporate governance. These corporate scandals, combined with memories harkening back to a less recent but much-publicized 1992 scandal involving the United Way and concerns about the American Red Cross's fundraising practices following the September 11, 2001, World Trade Center attack, have unfortunately created an atmosphere of mistrust for not-for-profit organizations as well.

It is inevitable that, in a climate of public skepticism about corporate finance, governance and ethics, not-for-profit organizations and their practices are coming under increasing scrutiny. Although the ultimate legislative scheme is still evolving, not-for-profit arts organizations can and should familiarize themselves with the developing legal principles, and should review and, if necessary, adapt their own practices accordingly.

Fiduciary Duty of Not-for-Profit Boards

Board members typically join not-for-profit arts organization boards as volunteers, motivated by their desire to support worthwhile artistic endeavors and, perhaps, as a counterpoint to their everyday responsibilities in their own professions. Even such a voluntary commitment, however, brings with it significant legal responsibilities that the board as a whole, as well as each individual member, must understand.

Board members of not-for-profit arts organizations have a fiduciary duty to that organization, the highest level of legal duty that can be owed. Benjamin Cardozo, who later became a Supreme Court Justice, characterized it this way in a famous New York Court of Appeals decision: "Many forms of conduct permissible in a workaday world for those acting at arm's length are forbidden to those bound by fiduciary ties. A trustee is held to something stricter than the morals of the marketplace. Not honesty alone, but the punctilio of an honor the most sensitive, is then the standard of behavior." *Meinhard v. Salmon*, 249 N.Y. 458 (1928). Understanding and fulfilling their fiduciary duty is the central obligation of any board member.

In legal terms, a board member's fiduciary obligation encompasses three duties: a duty of loyalty, a duty of care and a duty of obedience.

Duty of Loyalty

Board members owe a duty of loyalty, meaning that they must act in a manner they reasonably believe to be in the best interests of the organization. Board members must put the organization's needs before their own or any other party's, may not appropriate organizational opportunities for themselves, should avoid or disclose conflicts of interest, must maintain appropriate confidentiality regarding the organization's business and should see that the organization fulfills its not-for-profit purposes.

Duty of Care

While different states may formulate the duty of care in slightly different ways, the essential elements of the duty of care are that board members must carry out their duties in good faith, with the care that an ordinarily prudent person in a like position would exercise under similar circumstances. In practical terms, the duty of care means that board members must keep themselves informed about the organization's programs, practices and policies; prepare for and attend board and committee meetings; and exercise independent judgment in making decisions regarding the organization.

Duty of Obedience

The duty of obedience means that trustees will comply with all federal, state and local laws that apply to their organization, including meeting all reporting requirements and making sure that the reports submitted for their organization are accurate. The duty of obedience also includes the commitment by trustees to oversee how well its organization is fulfilling its stated mission.

Although these legal obligations seem straightforward, like all legal concepts, they are open to a range of interpretations, which can become the foundation for litigation against boards or individual trustees. The "business judgment rule" is a legal principle which holds that board members cannot be held liable for the consequences of decisions they make on behalf of an organization—even if those decisions turn out badly—as long as the board members exercised reasonable business judgment, i.e., they acted in good faith and reasonably believed the decision to be in the best interests of the organization, in accordance with their fiduciary duty. Not-for-profits generally indemnify board members against liability arising out of their board functions, provided that there is no breach of fiduciary duty.

Oversight of the legal activities of not-for-profit organizations is shared by federal and state regulators and, in today's environment, this oversight is changing.

Federal Oversight

Compensation

Oversight of executive compensation is one important aspect of a board's governance responsibilities for which there are very specific federal regulations. Section 501(c)(3) of the Internal Revenue Code provides that the assets of an exempt organization cannot inure to the benefit of individuals. Accordingly, an exempt organization must pay its executives "reasonable compensation," i.e., the amount that would be paid for comparable services by comparable businesses under comparable circumstances. An organization that pays or distributes assets to insiders in excess of the fair market value of the services can lose its exempt status.

Executive compensation is an area of increasing federal scrutiny. In August 2004, the Commissioner of the Internal Revenue Service declared that: "We are concerned that some charities and private foundations are abusing their tax-exempt status by paying exorbitant compensation to their officers and others." Accordingly, the IRS has begun an enforcement initiative that involves reviewing the compensation practices of 2,000 charities and foundations. Although it may feel ludicrous to have to consider issues of excess compensation in the not-for-profit arts field, whose challenge is more often trying to provide merely adequate salaries for staff, boards must be careful to educate themselves about compensation standards in their field and be sure that the compensation provided is fair and reasonable.

Of even greater concern than federal oversight of compensation, however, is the drive underway to create new legislation to increase regulation of not-for-profit organizations, which began with the passage of the Sarbanes-Oxley Act.

Sarbanes-Oxley

In the wake of serious financial mismanagement and accounting improprieties by corporations such as Enron and WorldCom, Congress adopted the *American Competitiveness and Corporate Accountability Act of 2002*, known as the Sarbanes-Oxley Act, which imposed new standards aimed at restoring public confidence in financial reporting by publicly traded corporations. Although this legislation is, for the most part, applicable only to publicly traded companies, not-for-profit organizations should be aware of the Sarbanes-Oxley provisions and alert to the implications for the not-for-profit sector.

The major provisions of Sarbanes-Oxley applicable to publicly traded companies are summarized below:

- Audits: Sarbanes-Oxley requires that corporations establish an audit committee to hire and oversee the outside auditors. The audit committee must be comprised of independent board members, i.e., individuals who are not members of the corporation's top management staff and who are not receiving compensation from the corporation for consulting or other professional services. Corporations must disclose whether audit committee members are financial experts; they are expected to have at least one such financial expert on the audit committee and, if not, must explain why. Moreover, the lead and reviewing partners of the audit firm the corporation hires must rotate every five years, and the audit firm cannot provide non-audit services to the corporation.

- Financial statements: The chief executive and chief financial officers must certify the accuracy of the corporation's financial statements and that there are adequate internal controls in place.
- Conflicts of interest: Loans to insiders, i.e., officers and directors of corporations, are prohibited.

Two other provisions of Sarbanes-Oxley are applicable to both publicly traded companies and to not-for-profit organizations, so these are of particular importance to the arts:

- Whistleblowers: Organizations may not punish whistleblowers who report suspected illegalities, and there are criminal penalties for taking such retaliatory measures.
- Document destruction: There are also criminal penalties for alteration, falsification or destruction of documents to prevent their use in government proceedings, such as investigations or litigation.

The adoption and implementation of Sarbanes-Oxley, which had only modest direct impact on not-for-profit organizations, was just the beginning step in what has become an intensive re-examination of not-for-profit governance.

THE GRASSLEY HEARINGS

During June 2004, the U.S. Senate Committee on Finance, chaired by Iowa Senator Charles Grassley, conducted an extensive series of hearings, entitled "Charity Oversight and Reform: Keeping Bad Things from Happening to Good Charities," aimed at introducing federal legislation parallel to Sarbanes-Oxley that would improve not-for-profit governance and accountability. The tenor of the Grassley hearings was quite hostile to the not-for-profit community, suggesting widespread abuse rather than isolated incidents.

In his opening statement, Senator Grassley remarked:

> Today the Finance Committee considers a very serious matter—ensuring that charities keep their trust with the American people. We will hear testimony today that is troubling. The testimony we will hear suggests that far too many charities have broken the understood covenant between the taxpayers and nonprofits—that charities are to benefit the public good, not fill the pockets of private individuals. Too many well-meaning charities have fallen prey to the charlatans' pitch about easy money. Some charities are blinded by their own mission and the need for additional dollars. These charities are willing to sign onto deals that provide dollars to promoters and insiders but only pennies to the charity. It is the taxpayers who are the losers.
>
> In addition to well-meaning charities being led astray, we also have a growing number of individuals who knowingly set up a charity to evade taxes. Finally, we have charities—even big-name charities—that seem to just have the wheels fall off. Often problems at these charities can be traced back to poor governance or failure to abide [by] best practices.

Similarly, Montana Senator Max Baucus, the ranking member of the Finance Committee, stated:

> But while many charities are focused on doing good works and preserving the public trust, there have been a number of high-profile examples of problems in this expanding sector:
>
> - Inflated salaries paid to trustees and charity executives
> - Insider deals with insufficient transparency
> - Charities engaged in abusive tax shelters
> - Charities serving as conduits to finance terrorist activities and operations.

SENATE FINANCE COMMITTEE PROPOSALS

In July 2004, following the Grassley hearings, the Senate Finance Committee released an extensive discussion draft outlining "proposals for reforms and best practices in the area of tax-exempt organizations."

The proposals include a requirement that the IRS review the status of tax-exempt organizations every five years to determine whether the organization is still operating for an exempt purpose, and would allow the IRS to revoke the tax-exempt status of any organization they concluded was no longer qualified. Failure of the organization to file the required review documents—including current articles of incorporation, bylaws, conflict of interest policies, evidence of accreditation, financial statements, management policies regarding best practices and a narrative about the organization's practices—would also result in revocation of tax-exempt status.

The proposed reforms would also require independent audits of financial statements for tax-exempt organizations with more than $250,000 in annual revenues and, like Sarbanes-Oxley, would require that a new auditor be used at least every five years. The proposal would further make changes to improve the quality and scope of the Form 990 information returns filed annually with the IRS by tax-exempt organizations. The chief executive officer would be required to sign a declaration, under penalty of perjury, that there are procedures in place to ensure that the return complies with the Internal Revenue Code and that they have reasonable assurance that the return is accurate and complete. Penalties for failure to file Forms 990 or for incomplete forms would be significantly increased. The IRS would be required to implement electronic filing of Forms 990 and to coordinate with states to encourage uniform reporting for exempt organizations.

Organizations with more than $250,000 in revenues also "would be required to include in the Form 990 a detailed description of the organization's annual performance goals and measurements for meeting those goals (to be established by the board of directors) for the past year and goals for the coming year. The purpose of this requirement would be to assist donors to better determine an organization's accomplishments and goals in deciding whether to donate, and not as a point of review for the IRS."

To allow for greater public oversight, charitable organizations would be required to make more documents available to the public and, if the organization has a website, to post on its website its application for tax exemption, its determination letter from the IRS, any return that is required to be made public and its financial statements for the past five years.

In addition, the Senate Finance Committee proposal would go beyond tax exemption issues and financial reporting to "encourage strong governance and best practices" through the imposition of specific fiduciary duties on board members of all charitable organizations: "In performing duties, a board member has to perform his or her duties in good faith; with the care an ordinarily prudent person in a like position would exercise under similar circumstances; and in a manner the director reasonably believes to be in the best interests of the mission, goals and purposes of the corporation. An individual who has special skills or expertise has a duty to use such skills or expertise."

Other board duties prescribed by the proposal include approval of compensation for all management positions annually, unless the only change is an adjustment for inflation. "Compensation arrangements must be explained and justified and publicly disclosed (with such explanation) in a manner that can be understood by an individual with a basic business background."

Additionally, board duties would be defined with great specificity:

- The board must establish basic organizational and management policies and procedures of organization and review any proposed deviations.
- The board must establish, review, and approve program objectives and performance measures, and review and approve significant transactions.
- The board must review and approve the auditing and accounting principles and practices used in preparing the organization's financial statements and must retain and replace the organization's independent auditor. An independent auditor must be hired by the board and each such auditor may be retained only five years.
- The board must review and approve the organization's budget and financial objectives as well as significant investments, joint ventures and business transactions.
- The board must oversee the conduct of the [organization's] business and evaluate whether the business is being properly managed.
- The board must establish a conflicts of interest policy (which would be required to be disclosed with the 990) and require a summary of conflicts determinations made during the 990 reporting year.
- The board must establish and oversee a compliance program to address regulatory and liability concerns.
- The board must establish procedures to address complaints and prevent retaliation against whistleblowers.

Board composition for tax-exempt organizations is also addressed by the Senate Finance Committee, which proposes limitations on board size ("no less than three members and no greater than fifteen"). Furthermore, "[n]o more than one member may be directly or indirectly compensated by the organization," and such individuals may not serve as board chair or treasurer. At least one-fifth of the board must be independent, which is defined as "free of any relationship with the [organization] or its management that may impair or appear to impair the director's ability to make independent judgments."

The IRS would have the authority to seek removal of officers, board members or employees who violate "self-dealing rules, conflicts of interest, excess benefit transaction rules, private inurement rules or charitable solicitation laws." Such individuals would be prohibited from serving on any other exempt organization for a period of years, and an organization that knowingly retained such a person could lose its tax-exempt status.

The Senate Finance Committee also proposes that the IRS create a national accreditation system for charities, and would give the IRS "the authority to base charitable status or authority of a charity to accept charitable donations on whether an organization is accredited."

The U.S. Tax Court's authority would be expanded to include the ability to rescind transactions entered into by not-for-profits.

Whistleblower provisions would give board members the right to bring derivative suits seeking action by the organization, and other individuals could file complaints with the IRS.

Finally, the Senate Finance Committee proposes that disputes regarding the valuation of property donated to charitable organizations be resolved by a mandatory "baseball arbitration" procedure under which both the IRS and the donor submit a number to the arbitrator, who must decide between the two competing valuations.

The potential implications of these Senate Finance Committee proposals are profound. Limiting the size of boards to fifteen people, for example, could have a devastating effect on not-for-profit organizations, which rely heavily on the volunteer efforts and charitable contributions of board members. The financial, administrative and personnel burdens of implementing some of the proposals are likely to be beyond the realistic capacity of some small not-for-profit organizations.

The portrayal of the not-for-profit sector in the Senate Finance Committee hearings and proposals seems extreme, predicated on an assumption that abuses are pervasive rather than isolated. Cognizant of the gathering force of these political winds, however, the not-for-profit sector has begun to respond, acknowledging the need for change but also attempting to provide a more nuanced representation of the situation.

PANEL ON THE NONPROFIT SECTOR

In September 2004, after the release of the Senate Finance Committee's draft proposals, Senator Grassley invited the Independent Sector to convene an independent panel of experts and leaders from the not-for-profit field to make recommendations "to strengthen governance, ethical conduct and accountability within public charities and private foundations." The panel on the Nonprofit Sector issued its interim report on March 1, 2005, and will complete its work in the fall of 2005.

Guiding Principles

The panel's interim report offered a different view of the context than the Senate Finance Committee:

> The vast majority of charitable organizations conduct their work in an ethical, responsible and legal manner. As in the commercial and public sectors, a small number of individuals and organizations have abused the public trust placed in them by engaging in unlawful or unethical conduct. Particularly after the corporate governance scandals that marked 2002, the national media has reported on allegations of questionable conduct by trustees and executives of public charities and private foundations. In some instances, the alleged abuses were clear violations of the law. In other cases, questions were raised about whether the practices at issue met the high ethical standards expected of the charitable sector.

The panel prefaced its recommendations with a statement of eight guiding principles:

1. A vibrant nonprofit sector is essential for a vital America
2. The nonprofit sector's effectiveness depends on its independence
3. The nonprofit sector's success depends on its integrity and credibility
4. Comprehensive and accurate information about the nonprofit sector must be available to the public
5. A viable system of self-regulation is needed for the nonprofit sector
6. Government should ensure effective enforcement of the law
7. Government regulation should deter abuse without discouraging legitimate charitable activities

8. Demonstrations of compliance with high standards of ethical conduct should be commensurate with the size, scale and resources of the organization.

Recommendations for Improving Transparency

The panel's recommendations include ensuring "that the annual [Form 990s series] information returns . . . filed by charitable organizations with the IRS provide accurate, timely information about the organization's finances, governance, operations and programs." More specifically, they would require that Forms 990 be signed under penalty of perjury by the chief executive or chief financial officer or highest-ranking officer of the organization; enforce existing penalties for failure to file or inaccuracy in filing such information returns; suspend tax-exempt status for failure to file for two or more consecutive years; make existing penalties for omission or misrepresentation by tax preparers applicable to preparers of 990 returns as well; move forward with mandatory electronic filing of Forms 990; coordinate federal and state e-filing requirements and require electronic filing of applications for tax exemption under Section 501c(3).

Additional measures are aimed at "the accuracy and completeness of financial information on charitable organizations" by requiring those organizations that file 990s to have an independent audit if their annual revenues amount to $2 million or more, or a review by an independent public accountant if their annual revenues are between $500,000 and $2 million.

And "to improve the accuracy of lists identifying organizations qualifying for tax-deductible contributions," the panel recommends that organizations falling below the $25,000 threshold for filing a 990 must file an annual notice with the IRS; failure to file the notice for three consecutive years should lead to suspension of tax-exempt status. Organizations that cease operations should be required to notify the IRS and file a final 990.

Recommendations for Enhancing Governance

The panel urged that charitable organizations take certain measures to improve their own governance practices: adopt a conflict of interest policy, include "individuals with some financial literacy" on their boards and "consider establishing a separate audit committee of the board if the organization has its financial statements independently audited." The panel also encouraged the adoption of whistleblower policies and protection for whistleblowers.

Recommendations for Strengthening Government Oversight

While making various recommendations to strengthen government oversight of not-for-profits, the panel also cautioned that such measures be carefully drawn so as to deter abuse but not discourage contributions to charitable organizations or punish inadvertent violations. The panel encouraged better collaboration between state and federal authorities, suggesting that Congress "encourage states to incorporate federal tax standards for charitable organizations into state law," provide more resources to the IRS for oversight and enforcement and allow state Attorneys General access to IRS information about charitable organizations.

The reforms suggested by the Senate Finance Committee and the Independent Sector are still proposals, subject to debate, revision and the usual lengthy legislative process. Not-for-profit organizations should be alert to these developments and take the opportunity, while new approaches are evolving, to advocate for an approach that will achieve a rational balance between curbing abuse and common sense.

State Oversight

Although at the time of this writing only California has actually adopted a not-for-profit equivalent of Sarbanes-Oxley, other states, including New York and Massachusetts, are considering such legislation, aimed at improving governance, accountability and transparency in not-for-profit organizations. These three states are often leaders in adopting new legislative approaches and are seen as models by other states, so these initial forays portend a more widespread national trend.

CALIFORNIA

California's *Nonprofit Integrity Act of 2004*, which became effective on January 1, 2005, requires charitable organizations (other than religious organizations, educational institutions, hospitals or licensed health-care plans) doing business in California with gross revenues of $2 million or more to have independently audited financial statements prepared in accordance with generally accepted accounting principles. (The $2 million threshold does not include government grants if the not-for-profit must provide an accounting of the use of the funds.) Audits must be made available for inspection by the state's Attorney General and the public within nine months of the end of the fiscal year. If the auditing firm also provides other, non-audit services, the auditors must adhere to the federal standards for auditor independence (but the state may impose different and more stringent standards).

The California law also states that any not-for-profits required to prepare audits must have an audit committee to oversee the auditor and ensure that independence is maintained. Although board members may serve on the audit committee, no staff members of the organization, including the chief executive and chief financial officers, may serve on the committee. Finance committee members may serve on (but not chair) the audit committee as long as they constitute less than half the audit committee. Members of the audit committee may not receive additional compensation for their service and may not have a material financial interest in any entity doing business with the not-for-profit.

The board must approve the compensation and benefits of the chief executive and chief financial officers, both when hired initially and whenever their employment is renewed. Significant changes at other times must also be board-approved, unless similar adjustments are being implemented for substantially all employees.

Professional out-of-house fundraisers, who previously had to register and file reports annually with the California Attorney General, are now subject to further regulation of their conduct, including record retention for ten years. Written contracts between fundraisers and charitable organizations are required, and such contracts must specify the financial terms between the two parties and ensure proper disposition of the funds raised.

New York

New York's Attorney General has proposed not-for-profit reforms that, although not adopted by the legislature in 2004, have been reintroduced in 2005 and are likely to be adopted eventually in some form.

The proposals would encourage, but not require, not-for-profits to designate executive and audit committees. Not-for-profits with boards of more than twenty-five members would be required to designate an executive committee of least three members, unless prohibited by their own certificate of incorporation or bylaws. And not-for-profits whose financial statements are audited or that have revenues of at least $2 million in any fiscal year would be required to appoint an audit committee of at least three members, unless prohibited by their certificate of incorporation or bylaws. Audit committees would be responsible for overseeing the work of the outside auditors. Audit committee members would be prohibited from accepting consulting or other fees from the not-for-profit organization and could not have participated in any transactions with the organization within the past year. Procedures for handling complaints regarding the audit or other financial matters must be established. Not-for-profits would be required to maintain internal control systems designed to ensure that their financial reports are correct and that fraud or deficiencies in financial controls are reported to the audit committee or board.

The New York Attorney General's proposals also include amendments to the already existing regulations regarding charitable solicitations, as well as amendments to the state not-for-profit law that would simplify voluntary dissolutions and allow the Attorney General to dissolve by proclamation not-for-profits that fail to file the required annual reports for five years or more.

MASSACHUSETTS

Massachusetts's Attorney General proposed *An Act to Promote the Financial Integrity of Public Charities* in 2004, similar to the California and New York approaches, further evidence of the growing urgency perceived at the state level—where oversight of not-for-profit organizations has traditionally been centered—to take action.

In a span of just a few years, the political climate has changed and the impetus for not-for-profit reform has accelerated rapidly. The corporate scandals of the 1990s gave rise to the Sarbanes-Oxley Act's imposition of new corporate governance standards, which led to the Senate Finance Committee's investigation of the not-for-profit sector and proposals to extend Sarbanes-Oxley principles to that sector, which further inspired authorities in key states to begin to implement more stringent measures regulating not-for-profit organizations in their own jurisdictions. The not-for-profit sector has also responded to these dynamics, taking action to strengthen governance by developing various voluntary standards as guideposts for not-for-profit managers and boards.

Voluntary Codes of Ethics

A number of umbrella organizations in the not-for-profit sector now promulgate standards for not-for-profit organizations in an attempt at voluntary self-regulation. Not-for-profits that meet the criteria are given seals of approval or certifications, intended to assure donors that their contributions are in good hands. Such standards can also serve as useful guidelines for not-for-profits trying to embody best practices. Not-for-profit arts organizations might consider seeking certification under one or more applicable codes or use these codes as blueprints to guide a comprehensive review of their own policies and ethical standards.

Maryland Association of Nonprofit Organizations

One of the first voluntary codes, now widely emulated, was the *Standards for Excellence: An Ethics and Accountability Code for the Nonprofit Sector,* created by the Maryland Association of Nonprofit Organizations (MANO) in 1998. MANO implemented a statewide program long before the Sarbanes-Oxley legislation and now offers its program nationally, including training and technical assistance. The standards go beyond compliance with applicable laws to define values and performance benchmarks designed to help strengthen not-for-profit organizations. The standards require clarity about, and regular evaluation of, the organization's mission and program; articulate the governing board's responsibilities, composition and conduct; require policies and procedures to avoid conflicts of interest; require adoption of human resources policies and systematic orientation and evaluation of employees and volunteers; define practices designed to ensure sound financial management and legal compliance; encourage openness and responsiveness to the public; establish fundraising guidelines; and encourage the organization's commitment to public affairs and public policy.

The Independent Sector

Similarly, in January 2004, the Independent Sector adopted a *Statement of Values and Code of Ethics for Nonprofit and Philanthropic Organizations,* intended to be used as a model for all tax-exempt charitable organizations. The Independent Sector states, "Adherence to the law is the minimum standard of expected behavior. Nonprofit and philanthropic organizations must do more, however, than simply obey the law. We must embrace the spirit of the law, often going beyond legal requirements and making sure that what we do is matched by what the public understands about what we do. Transparency, openness and responsiveness to public concerns must be integral to our behavior."

Independent Sector's formulation of values is as follows:

- Commitment to the public good
- Accountability to the public
- Commitment beyond the law
- Respect for the worth and dignity of individuals
- Inclusiveness and social justice
- Respect for pluralism and diversity
- Transparency, integrity and honesty
- Responsible stewardship of resources
- Commitment to excellence and maintaining the public trust.

The Independent Sector's code of ethics categorizes things a bit differently from MANO's, but the common threads in the topics it addresses are evident: personal and professional integrity, mission, governance, legal compliance, responsible stewardship, openness and disclosure, program evaluation, inclusiveness and diversity, fundraising and grantmaker guidelines.

BETTER BUSINESS BUREAU WISE GIVING ALLIANCE

The Better Business Bureau's (BBB) Wise Giving Alliance, like MANO, offers a seal of approval to charities meeting their *Standards for Charity Accountability*. Its goal is "to assist donors in making sound giving decisions and to foster confidence in public charitable organizations. The standards seek to encourage fair and honest solicitation practices, to promote ethical conduct by charitable organizations and to advance support of philanthropy." Tax-exempt 501(c)(3) organizations receive the seal if they meet basic standards:

- In how they govern their organization
- In the ways they spend their money
- In the truthfulness of their representations
- In their willingness to disclose basic information to the public.

While the standards address basic governance matters, much like the other voluntary standards discussed above, the Wise Giving Alliance pays particular attention to fundraising solicitations and requires that an organization spend at least sixty-five percent of its total expenses on program activities. In addition, organizations should spend no more than thirty-five percent of "related contributions," i.e., contributions received as a result of fundraising efforts, on fundraising.

Conclusion

Because legislation is continually evolving, any summary such as this is almost by definition out of date as soon as it is published. Moreover, because laws vary from state to state, arts boards should consult their own legal counsel about any relevant state legislation, review their own practices thoroughly and discuss these issues candidly among themselves and with the organization's staff. A list of the references cited in this chapter as well as suggestions for additional reading can be found in the Resource Guide at the end of this book.

There is no doubt that Sarbanes-Oxley and its progeny are widely interpreted as setting new standards for best practices in corporate governance. Prudent not-for-profit organizations are voluntarily adopting, to the extent possible and appropriate, the new federal standards established by Sarbanes-Oxley for publicly traded companies, the standards beginning to be established for not-for-profits by state Attorneys General and the model standards promulgated by not-for-profit umbrella organizations, anticipating that an extension of some version of these standards to the not-for-profit world is inevitable.

Boards of not-for-profit arts organizations should use the shifting legal environment as an opportunity to reexamine their own standards and practices with a fresh perspective. Boards should consider instituting conflict of interest policies, develop procedures for internal financial controls, consider creating a separate audit committee, adopt a code of ethics and articulate standards of conduct for the board. While the effort may be time-consuming, perhaps difficult, and even expensive, the result—a reaffirmation of confidence in the value, effectiveness and integrity of not-for-profit organizations in the eyes of government, the media, funders and audiences—is perhaps the most important function a not-for-profit arts board can undertake today to position their organization for the future.

THE ARTISTS SPEAK

In this chapter we invite the reader to hear directly from our artists. A panel of distinguished artists, each with a different perspective, tells something about who they are and what they need from boards of trustees. Although their experience with boards ranges from almost none to that of an institutional leader, and from good to indifferent to difficult, our artists share similar views on the nature and power of the arts, the sobering financial realities for artists and the ways in which they would like to work together with trustees.

A Roundtable Discussion

JIM HOUGHTON, *Moderator*: Founding Artistic Director, Signature Theatre Company

JAMES BUNDY: Dean, Yale School of Drama; Artistic Director, Yale Repertory Theatre

KATHLEEN CHALFANT: Actor

DOUG HUGHES: Director

PETER FRANCIS JAMES: Actor

CHRISTINE JONES: Scenic Designer

PAULA VOGEL: Playwright

Jim Houghton: Our goal is to come out of this discussion with some insights that will bridge communication between artists and board members. We have a good mix here of artists who have run theaters, people who have sat on boards and people who have done neither. Let's start by going around the table. I'd like each of you to give us a little background about yourselves. I'd especially like to know something about the nature of your interaction with boards. For instance, Doug, you've run a theater.

Our Own Experiences

Doug Hughes: Yes. I grew up working in institutional theaters, so for most of my theatrical life, I have worked closely with boards. My earliest job was at Manhattan Theatre Club, where I was the associate artistic director. I was also associate artistic director of Seattle Repertory Theatre for about a decade and then its acting artistic director. After that I was the director of programming at the Guthrie Theater in Minneapolis for a season. And then I became the artistic director of the Long Wharf Theatre in New Haven, Connecticut, where I served for four seasons. I resigned just at the conclusion of my fourth season, about three years ago, because of problems in the boardroom, which I'll come back to later. Now I work as a director.

James Bundy: I started in the theater as an actor, and while I was still acting, I became a trustee of Cornerstone Theater Company, which, for me, was a pretty transformative experience, because it's a company that I believed in so fervently. Cornerstone was driven exclusively by the interests of the artists for a long time, although eventually the company came to the conclusion that, in order to establish better working conditions and a better future, they needed a board that was more active. But, even as the company and the board changed, I always found their relationship was a constructive one, centered on the evolving tension between the impulses of the artists and an institutional agenda that was supportive of the artists' ultimate goals. It was a great experience for me.

After Cornerstone, I worked as the associate producing director of The Acting Company in New York, and then I became the artistic director of Great Lakes Theater Festival in Cleveland, Ohio. And now I have the altogether different experience of serving in an institution where I have no board of trustees, Yale Repertory Theatre and Yale School of Drama. I report only to the president and the provost at Yale.

CHRISTINE JONES: In stark contrast to both of these gentlemen, I believe I have probably been introduced to a board member on one or two occasions, but I could not tell you their names at this moment. I've been set-designing for about eleven years, since I graduated from New York University, and I've had very little contact with boards or trustees. I believe Signature here in New York sponsored an event last year, or two years ago, where some artists came and spoke about what we did to a group of board members. And at various opening nights I've had brief conversations about the show. And that's it. I really have very little understanding of what they do and often feel that they have very little understanding of what I do. So this is a great opportunity to build some bridges.

PETER FRANCIS JAMES: I suppose I'm more or less in Christine's position. I have been an actor for twenty-five years. In that time, other than board members that I knew for other reasons, I've had only two conversations with board members, although both were fascinating. One was twelve years ago and the other probably twelve years before that, which I can bring up as an anecdote in a moment. But that is my extent of contact with boards of directors in terms of theaters.

KATHLEEN CHALFANT: I've had a checkered career. I've been in New York for—it's difficult to believe—thirty-one years. Mostly as an actor. In the beginning I was involved with the establishment of two institutions: Playwrights Horizons, under Bob Moss's astounding leadership, and the Women's Project. Then I was asked to be on the board of New York Theatre Workshop, and I served on that board for four or five years. I was on the board of Classic Stage Company for the term of David Esbjornson's artistic directorship, and I've been on the board of Vineyard Theatre for six or seven years. In every case I was the mole, the artistic mole, and was asked because I had a personal relationship with the artistic director.

All of those boards were successful during the periods I served on them. Not that I was successful as a board member, but the boards themselves seemed to me to be successful because, in every case, they existed to move the stated agenda of the theater forward. They were all small institutions with small boards, and the work they did was almost entirely for the good of the institutions. As the institutions grew—and all these institutions grew—there got to be big issues about the bottom line, about who wanted to sit at the table with whom and whether being on the board became a social identity. And, if being on the board became a social identity, that was in some ways a good thing for the theater because it gave the board more leverage in raising money; but it was sometimes dangerous, too, because people who were powerful in the real world—I shouldn't call it the "real world," the *nontheatrical* world—got on the board and imagined that they would have artistic clout. And that can end up being dangerous.

PAULA VOGEL: I've encountered boards since working as Wynn Handman's secretary at American Place Theatre, just preparing minutes and Xeroxing things. And I had one brief, wonderful year sitting in with the Circle Repertory Theatre board when Tanya Berezin was artistic director there and they routinely had artists sitting in on board meetings. Since then, I have had a number of experiences. The best was the glorious experience of working with the Perseverance Theatre in Alaska, which I now realize was an anomaly. At Perseverance, there really was a functioning community board and they really read all the scripts and they talked and had potluck dinners and I knew where they lived and actually met them for coffee. That was some fluke that could probably only exist in this little northern-exposure town.

At the other extreme, the most difficult experience I had was realizing that I should never be an artist-in-residence in a transitional year when a theater company is changing over from one artistic director to another, which I did at Arena Stage when Molly Smith became the new artistic director. That was a very hard year for me. It was a hard transition for many people there, but I felt like I was sort of the battering ram during that change in artistic direction. And my experience with the board was not good. There were some lovely board members who understood what I was doing but there were also some board members who were definitely unsupportive. So that's the gamut, from the sublime time at Perseverance to this very strange year at Arena Stage. None of this was Molly's doing at Arena; I think perhaps departing artistic directors need to do some work with their boards when they leave institutions so that there isn't that awful hazing process for the newcomers.

My more typical experience is to be trotted out to be the advocate for new plays once a season as I travel from theater to theater, never really being introduced to people, names never sticking, never having any personal contact, just sort of a blur. But I can also say that, even if the names don't stick, I can walk into an organization and kind of feel the vibe in the lobby and know whether or not people are actually talking to each other. I mean, just by the way board members talk to me, even if I'm only there for two or three days, I know when the communication is going well.

HOUGHTON: I'll just throw in a few things to give some background on me. I started Signature Theatre here in New York and built its board over the last fourteen years, and it has been one of the healthiest experiences I've had with a board. There's been a sort of natural evolution. People serve for a time and know when it's time to move on, so the board continues to grow and blossom. I think this is much easier in a founder situation because, in my case, or in any founder's case, you're there before anybody serves on the board. So building this board has been a happy experience and continues to be a happy experience—always challenging, but always good.

I've also been involved with a place in Indiana called the New Harmony Project, which is a writers conference, a relatively small one, that brings in writers from all over the country for a two-week period. New Harmony was a very different experience for me than Signature. I was the organization's second artistic director and came in, I think, in its tenth year, after the first artistic director had been there two years. Before that it was all artist-driven, and the board had not functioned particularly well. It had struggled to find a central core value and was troubled by various agendas coming to the table without any sort of focal point or arbiter of the mission. This ultimately became the role of the artistic director. I was there for five years, and then I took over the O'Neill Playwrights Conference in Waterford, Connecticut, where I succeeded the longtime artistic director Lloyd Richards. I found the transition, with regard to my relationship with Lloyd, very smooth and well done. But my experience with the board there was that it had never been allowed to grow and organically find itself so that it could deal well with all its responsibilities. So there were problems. I served for four years and then, like Doug, I resigned, in my case because the board had made some basic artistic decisions without consulting me and the bonds of trust were broken. So I also have had a broad range of experiences with boards.

The Conversation Turns to the Role of Theater As Both Radical and Conservative

HUGHES: One of the things my experience at Long Wharf showed me is that it is in hard times that we most remember that theaters are rear-guard actions on behalf of civilizations—they're a radical thing to take part in. They are highly idealistic, perpetually undercapitalized, very risky ventures. And when you bring a group of people together to do something like theater, it runs against the dominant ethic of our society. That's what we're here to do, ladies and gentlemen. We're invoking a conspiracy here, in the purest sense of that word. *Conspirare*: We're going to breathe together to try to inject into our community—another worthwhile word that has become so tired—some antidote to the forces in the society that keep us not present, not awake, and enslaved to tiny bits of what it means to be human.

At Long Wharf, when things were very bad, when we were broke and the board felt humiliated because the reputation of the theater was in the ashbin, in some ways it was wonderful. It was wartime and we had the one-point focus of taking risks. And we did all the things that characterize times like that—lots of talking, sack lunches, board people in and out of the office—and I was thrilled by the board's generosity and tolerance of risk. I was able to say to them, "We are not going to save our way into success. We can't amputate limbs to save the patient." And that worked well. But the transition to peacetime was difficult, and I must take some responsibility for that. After the balance sheet was clean, it was like in a Shakespeare play: What do we do after the war? Like Beckett: What do we do now that we're happy? In our case, what emerged was the concern that we were tenants, that Long Wharf had never been a householder, never had its own theater. So the feeling was that we had to build a theater or this property was going to be sold out from under us. That was a fearsome challenge. My own problem with the board, which was basically a personality conflict with the board chair, ran concurrently with this big challenge. I think it's when the theater of the boardroom becomes supreme to the theater being made onstage, that you begin to be in trouble. Trusteeship should be an act of service, and we always need to be reminded of our responsibilities and that we are serving something wildly idealistic in this society. There is a sense of an adventure, something that's running against trends. It's radical, and yet sometimes it's hard to portray it that way to a board.

JAMES: I appreciate Doug's use of the word "radical" in terms of the enterprise of theater, but I think it is essentially the opposite. I think theater is the most conservative institution in human civilization—and important for that reason. There's something about putting a celebrant in the middle of a community and having that person be the voice of the entire community, to say the unsaid, to wish the illegal. That is fundamental, not an addendum. These are not amenities. This is not saving the niceties of civilization. This is saving the core of it. Of course the idea of plays really came from someone sitting down and telling a story that explained who "we" are, which is the central concept of civilization: "We." My experience is your experience. This is what we are dealing with—and without it we are nothing. It is only because we live in the society we do that theater appears to be a radical idea. But it really is the most conservative idea.

VOGEL: Yes, it's also what's been eradicated. I'm sure a lot of other people here have gone to the Texas School Book Depository. Well, I got up my courage and went. It was the first time I was going through Dallas. It was empty the day that I visited, and the thing that really wounded me wasn't looking at the window or any of that. I was in the middle of this empty display when I heard John F. Kennedy's voice giving an address on the arts. And the words "culture" and "grace" reached my ears out of his mouth and it occurred to me that, since that time, I have not heard a United States president talk about the arts in a policy address—ever. It's this that's been eradicated. And I absolutely agree with what you're saying, Peter. I think that, in small, little increments we've been adjusting to a less radical society, if you will, and it is that which makes us seem radical. We've been turning very, very gradually away from the core notion that the arts are essential—that they're a spiritual daily bread.

BUNDY: I want to add that the notion of service is one that I certainly feel is important to me as an artist—and most of the artists I know feel it's very important. When I hear Doug talk about that I get quite inspired. But I don't see it as a vision of a group of artists issuing marching orders to passionate laypeople. I see it as a point of common agreement about what it is that we're all engaged in. I've worked with Christine a lot, and I know she's not out there designing these beautiful sets simply so she can go home and pat herself on the back. And Paula hasn't become a playwright just to gratify her own ego. I think that sense of service on the part of the artists is something that really needs to be understood.

The Delicate Balance Between Fiduciary Responsibility and Artistic Mission

Hughes: The other thing that is basic here is that it is so much about the money. In this world, one feels not only the terror of an institution collapsing but, I've got to say, at times, deep shame—I felt shame when a show didn't make its money. I felt that I was there to drag the theater, push the theater, out of the red without losing my soul at the same time and, somehow, foster around the boardtable the patience for healing things financially. Otherwise you can find yourself in the situation where you're being very much encouraged to fundraise at the box office. If the institution is the primary goal, why yes, my job is to fundraise at the box office—fine. But somehow I wish we could all share the shame, or we could purge the shame. I would like a climate where the board and I were constantly mindful of the fact that, if we are in the red today, we might find ourselves in the black eighteen months from now or two years from now.

Chalfant: I think there can be an enormous difference based on the size of the institution. The larger the institution, the more everyone's interest becomes maintaining the institution, and, quite often, because there are vast amounts of money involved, the adventure, the subversive adventure that we're embarked on, is lost. Theater has to be an act of communication because, as James was saying, you don't do it for yourself. If it isn't an act of communication, it's meaningless for the artists and, in the same way, the institution ceases to move and enlighten and communicate with its community. In the end, it must be a partnership. If it's anything else, then it's pointless. It's Plays 'R' Us, and do whatever you like. The most successful artistic ventures that I've been involved in—and certainly the ones in which the institutions have flourished—have been in times when chances were taken. It's the adventure that keeps the thing alive. And even the theaters that are huge civic institutions flourish when they take chances, when they jump off the end of the diving board.

Vogel: These problems aren't as great in smaller organizations. The only times I've ever served on boards have been in tiny, maverick, fly-by-night, hole-in-the-wall kinds of places where, if you were being pragmatic in the first place, you wouldn't join the board. And the people that I meet in those institutions do accept risk. They giggle a lot. They don't stand on dignity. They realize that it's quite a strange venture that they're doing, and those are the people that I actually adore the most. So I think size does matter.

HOUGHTON: I've noticed that, too, because Signature is small to mid-range in size, and I've watched what happens when you start to grow. When you are a hole-in-the-wall theater, everyone is happy to help. But as budget demands increase, a board can get a taste for success, for a show that does well, where suddenly the money is really coming in. Then the box office does become attractive as a fundraising tool. When a board starts to get a taste for this, it can be difficult to back them off. They say, "Maybe we could do another play like that, like the one that was so successful," which, of course, prior to doing it, you had no idea would bring any sort of financial reward.

JONES: The *Shrek 2* model doesn't always work.

HOUGHTON: Exactly. It never works in theater.

BUNDY: I think people often misunderstand the idea of fiduciary responsibility, which is so fundamental to boards. Fiduciary responsibility is often taken to mean solely a financial responsibility. But, in fact, fiduciary means a responsibility of trust. Too often bottom-line thinking tends to overtake institutions, and the subjective, impassioned, fluid elements of managing a mission, which should be an important part of the conversation and of a board's responsibility, get lost. It's about keeping faith, not just about the bottom line.

The Importance of Human Capital and How Artists Subsidize Our Theaters

HUGHES: One thing I feel, sitting here with Christine and Peter and Kathy and Paula, is that the great subsidizers of the American resident theater are the people who work in them. These artists are very clever people who could make a lot more money doing other things. I wish I could say, "May I tell you what Christine's fee is? What Peter's salary is? What Paula's advance is?" Most of the time, these are laughable figures compared to what a comfortable middle-class life is in this country. There's something about the value assigned to the work that's done, even by the people who are its principal supporters—our patrons, our mensches—that is off-kilter.

Chalfant: Part of that is that it is so much easier for theaters to raise money for capital expenses than anything else. So, oddly, you can actually raise forty million dollars to put up a building or one hundred million dollars to put up a building, but you can't raise ten million dollars to invest in human capital. You can't say: "What we're going to do is raise ten million dollars and, with this ten million dollars, we will raise the salaries across the board of not only the artists but the people who work twelve to fifteen hours a day answering the phone, who are here making only entry-level or unemployment-level salaries." So I think there is a biased view of what constitutes the capital of the enterprise. The real capital of the enterprise is the human capital, and that is where the least possible investment is made.

Jones: I'd like to make a distinction between supporting the person and supporting the work. None of us is here to make money. We could all be doing something else. That's a given. I don't know how involved a board member is in my salary, but I don't expect the board to support me as a person. I've chosen to be a designer. I've chosen this life. I'm a thirty-seven-year-old woman who lives in an apartment with four guys so that I can afford to work in the theater. It would be great if I could get a wonderful salary and have a nice apartment and do all those things. But, if you asked me what makes my experience at a theater a good experience versus a bad experience, I would answer that it's when I feel my work is supported. It's having my work supported that makes me want to go back and work at a theater. And what that means for me is not so much my fee, but my assistant fee. When a theater has an assistant fee that is reasonable in scale to what I'm being paid, right away that's a big neon sign blinking, saying: "We get what you do; we understand that you're not just a draftsperson and a model builder and a technician and a craftsperson—you're a visionary. And the best thing that we can do to support your vision is to give you somebody to help you do the nuts and bolts."

James: Yes. One anecdote I wanted to tell was about being at the Guthrie Theater on a picnic with the board, sitting down next to a man and having a delightful conversation with him. He was an important person in one of the corporations there, but very easy to talk to. He said, "If you don't mind, I should know this, but I don't. Feel free not to say anything, but I'm curious as to what you're paid." And I said, "Well, this is one of the better-paying theaters in the country, fortunately." This was around twenty years ago. I said, "I'm making

$550." He said, "How many performances a week do you have?" And I said, "Well, there are eight performances scheduled because we're in real rep. I'm only in five or six of the shows. So, actually, although I'm rehearsing during the day, I have a relatively light burden in terms of the shows, only five or six shows a week." And he said, "All right, well, that, of course, cuts into your money." I looked at him curiously. He said, "$550 times six . . ."

I said, "Oh, no, no." I said, "That's a weekly salary, not per show." And he just stopped breathing. And then he said, "You must really love what you do. You're very good at it, I know that. But you must really love what you do." I said, "Well, of course." And then he said to me, "Do you know what your skills are worth in the corporate world? I hire two guys to come in to talk to my top people four times a year because I'm a bright, dependable guy but I'm not a motivator. You stand up in front of 1,400 people, and hold them spellbound. And I pay my dog-and-pony show six times what you make in a year." And you know, I thought that the next time this board member muscled up to somebody to ask him to write a check, it was going to be with a different sense of purpose. I don't know if it's a shared sacrifice or a shared commitment, but it's a sense that everybody is doing something here and everybody is in on it. It's a confederacy. There is a noble enterprise underway here in which people are not looking primarily for financial reward. They want to be able to offer the best that they have. That's very important to them and they want nothing to impede that.

Chalfant: It's about whether you can have a decent life and continue to work in the theater. And by a decent life, it only means being able to raise a child, having a place to live that is acceptable, the possibility of having some small amount of safety. It's quite a modest life that people are asking to have because, after a certain point, without it, you actually can't do your job. What is acceptable for people in their twenties becomes problematic for people in their forties.

Bundy: Yes, in so many ways artists are subsidizing the theater. But the commercial media is also subsidizing the theater because, even at my theater, we're only paying actors $750 a week. Now the fact of the matter is, I don't know an actor who would be really happy coming to work an entire season at Yale Rep, because they wouldn't be able to do the three episodes of *Law & Order* that actually make it possible for them to live in New York City.

Chalfant: And provide their health insurance.

Bundy: And provide their health insurance.

Chalfant: Because you can no longer manage a kind of regular health regime on one union's insurance policy. Now both of the major unions require contributions from the members to maintain the health insurance that they have, so that doing something commercial under Screen Actors Guild jurisdiction is almost essential—absolutely essential, if you have a family or any kind of major health problem. It's the only way you can survive.

How Our Theaters Can Support Our Artists

Hughes: So how can we make our theaters great places to work? How can we even make them fun places to work? How can that be fostered?

Bundy: How many theaters have, as part of their strategic plan: "Be the best theater to work at in our region or in our state or in the nation." Very few, I would say.

Jones: The thing is, for us, it takes so little. We're so emotionally undernourished that if a basket of fruit is in the room when you get there, suddenly you're like, "Oh my God, I feel like a movie star." Or, as I said before, in my case it's knowing I'm being supported. For instance, the McCarter Theatre is paying me and the director and a couple of the actors to do a four-day workshop of a new play this week. And then we may come back one more time and do another four-day workshop before I design the play, which will be presented next April. That kind of thing just makes me feel warm and fuzzy. It makes me want to go back and work at that theater. I also would like to say to theaters: "Could you somehow create a research budget, so I could research the location of a play if that is important?" When Jim and I did *The Last of the Thorntons* here at Signature, we flew to Wharton, Texas, and spent the weekend with Horton Foote, the playwright, and he took us to the nursing home that had inspired the play, and, man, did that make a difference—for my work, for Jim's work, and for what we were able to bring to the actors. These kinds of things matter. Nothing disheartens me more than when I go to a theater and they have just built this brand-spanking-new, shiny building, and my fee for four months of work is $1,500.

Chalfant: Quite often artists, particularly designers, are put in the position of having to subsidize their own work, particularly at smaller institutions. You look at something and say, "Well, another $500 would make this work much better. So, do I come up with the $500 or do I allow the work to suffer?" And the other thing is that we're all itinerant workers. We're visitors in these places and, in some sense, strangers. Gift baskets, somebody opening their house, the idea that the institution and the people who support the institution are welcoming us, that we're not outlanders, that we're actually being welcomed to visit—that can make such a difference.

James: In that respect, probably the most important hire a theater makes in terms of actors is the company manager, who is the actors' lifeline. When you get a good company manager, that theater's reputation soars among actors. When you get a bad one, it has a tremendously negative impact. If I were on a board, I would want to know who the company manager is. If they're good, they know everything that's needed. They can relieve an enormous burden on everyone else in the institution if they see their job as the advocate for the actor, and the scrounger in this rolling blitzkrieg campaign to get a play on in four weeks.

Chalfant: You're so right. I've just come back from a job where that person was a disaster. Every single thing she touched fell apart, and she had no gift for it. It affected everything, and it made it impossible for the people who had nowhere else to go, who didn't feel like they could call up the artistic director and say, "What's the thing about the train tickets?" And, you know, my daughter is a new designer, and she's just gone to do her first job in regional theater. She's gone to the Georgia Shakespeare Festival. She's been there two weeks after doing guerilla work in New York City. She's gone down to this apparently wonderfully run institution, and she called up the first day and said, "They've done it. They've built the thing the way I drew it." I talked to her at the end of the first week and she said, "I'm beginning to feel guilty. This is like a vacation. You know, the work's going on. Everything's being built. I show up . . . it's miraculous." She will work twenty-four hours a day anyway—but, as Christine says, she's now working twenty-four hours a day happily, not thinking that she might die.

Also, people should look into artists' living conditions because it's the thing that impacts people the most. When those living conditions are pleasant—they don't need to be vast, but they do need to be pleasant—when the living conditions are pleasant, people will do anything. Anything.

JONES: I'm sure this has happened to everybody: You show up in a town, you're given a key to some apartment with a map probably, you find your way to this apartment and you have a lot of trouble getting in because the key is acting funny, and finally you get into the apartment and it's 11:00 at night and you have no idea where a store is and you have nothing. Nothing. It wears you out. We just need to be taken care of, sometimes in very small ways. And the first four years when I was traveling around, I was probably gone at least two weeks of every month traveling to different regional theaters and I got really depressed. And I know a lot of young designers who, at about a four-year mark, come to me and say, "I just don't know if I can do this." And I encourage them and say, "You know what, it's very natural. The adjustment from school to the lifestyle of theater can be very different. Hang in there. You'll find your home. You'll find your collaborative homes with your directors and your other designers and you'll find your theatrical homes. You'll find the places that do treat you well and it'll be okay." But those first few years can be very, very difficult. So I think what we keep saying here is the value of the human resource.

VOGEL: Also safety. Safety for young women artists.

The Fundamental Value of Artists and Trustees Getting to Know Each Other

HOUGHTON: When I was at the O'Neill, I created a program called the Trustee Residency. At the O'Neill, playwrights, directors, designers and actors gather in July to stage readings of new plays. Since each play develops over a week, I thought there was the opportunity, in this very condensed period of time, to walk trustees through the highlights of the entire creative process of a play. The O'Neill has a very open-door policy, so we could immerse trustees in the process and open their eyes to what it takes to make theater happen from the artist's perspective, from the inside. But, conversely, it was my hope to start opening up the artists' idea of what a board member is. I think there are many notions out there that are pretty extreme, such as board members are people who just write big checks. There's no merging of ideas, which I think we were able to do in this very intense environment up at the O'Neill. We were able to get rid of many preconceived notions and witness a board member as an advocate for a theater. We heard their stories, they heard ours, we shared meals, we began to open up those lines of communication.

VOGEL: When I had the opportunity to hear the board members talk at the O'Neill, I was very moved. I suspect that those board members are, in essence, the ones who want to engage in the common ground of being uncomfortable. It was incredible listening to them.

HOUGHTON: One thing that kept coming up that really surprised me at the Trustee Residency at the O'Neill was that trustees were often intimidated by the artists coming into their theaters. They didn't know how to talk to them. But, by the end of our week, the trustees had overcome that and felt a renewed spirit and energy. They had a real desire to take back to their communities this idea of embracing and getting to know the artists, or at least creating an environment that feels more sympathetic and welcoming to them.

BUNDY: If boards of trustees don't know the people who work in the theater, it's a huge disadvantage. Virtually every institution I know that's really maturing is realizing that boards of trustees need to have face time with every employee in the theater in order for both sides to understand their shared interests and why they're *all* working within the constraints they're in. Institutions can only move forward when everybody is sacrificing, which means sacrificial giving on the part of the board as well as sacrificial investment of time on the part of the artists and the staff. I do think that the face-to-face contact we've been talking about and the breaking of bread is wonderful. In my experience, there's no single act that has been more successful at theaters than dinner with the company. It's the most important thing that's ever happened on a consistent basis that has improved the working relationship for me.

HUGHES: That's true in my experience, too.

Vogel: Again, I think Perseverance and Molly Smith, when she was artistic director there, have spoiled me for life. But my notion is we should celebrate when we start working on a play, rather than when we finish—that we should all be coming together when we start the process, when we're all there. We're always having opening-night celebrations, but the designers have left and we're not all together. And opening nights are really another performance. With so many people in the room, there's no chance for intimacy. Molly opened her house at the beginning of *The Mineola Twins* in Alaska and everyone brought a potluck dish. It was one of the most fun, funny evenings. Everyone in the room could talk to each other at a different level. It's a little thing, but I like the notion of a celebratory process starting at the beginning, so it's not a product, not a reward. Rather, it's just the fact that we're all in the same room.

Houghton: That's a great place to finish. Yes, we're all in the room together, and that's what counts.

THE SPIRIT OF GOVERNANCE:

Six Interviews

The six distinctive voices in this chapter focus on their belief in the power of collaboration and partnership. Each speaker begins with the centrality of the artistic vision, then turns the prism to reveal a unique perspective. Collectively, they support the idea that the selfless interaction among trustees, artists and staff collaborating on the inner workings of an arts organization and taking the time to know one another can be perpetually productive.

Judith O. Rubin

We begin from the perspective of a trustee. Judy Rubin is the long-time president of the board of Playwrights Horizons, a theater in New York City whose mission is developing new work. She has broad community experience, including serving as the president of the board of the 92nd Street Y. Perhaps uniquely among trustees, Judy is still a member of Actors Equity, dating back to an earlier career as an actor and singer.

Why do I do this work? Without meaning to sound too rhapsodic about it, it's the theater and the mission. Our mission is to present the new work of today's playwrights, and I love that. New work, to me, is the most interesting. And I like the identification with an institution I care about. I really believe in the place.

Playwrights Horizons has a very strong culture. There is great internal loyalty, and the staff really cares about what we do. It's Tim [Sanford], the artistic director; it's Leslie [Marcus], the managing director; it's that we do new work. Every writer is beautifully served. We have a strong sense of identification with our mission, which provides us with a sense of security, a foundation. It's like a kid knowing where he lives. It gives you a sense of groundedness. And it's a wonderful mission, because it's narrow—you can state it very quickly—but within it, it's huge. You can do so many things, you can move to the edge. It's very much the glue that holds us all together.

I believe the responsibility for any place has to reside with very few people who are ultimately responsible for its welfare. While the chairman does not, and should not, run the organization on a day-to-day basis, he or she has to answer for the decisions made and the direction in which the organization moves. I've spoken to friends who are artistic directors or managing directors of other theaters, and if they have a chair who isn't willing to take responsibility for the board leg of the structure, they feel they are really in trouble and unsupported. You've got to be willing to be one of the few who lose sleep over the fate of your theater.

The flip side of that is the temptation to think you can do it alone. That can be really harmful. When things get hot and heavy—in a capital campaign or building a building or in other difficult situations—you find you need other people. My philosophy of governance is based very much on openness. If a problem is particularly thorny and the road to a solution doesn't readily present itself, my first step is to reach out to a logical helper—board or staff—and seek advice. I rarely attempt to solve problems alone. If I have a real-estate problem and I have someone on the board who's good at that, it's wonderful. When we started the seeds of an endowment, we quickly put in place an investment committee that could take the lead. We have a board member who is a lobbyist, and he helps with political issues. He works with the development staff when they write proposals to the city and the state, and then he and I go together to see the legislators. So I rely to a great extent on the other people on the board.

But I have also found that, because you really need these people, you have to bring them along, all the way, all the time. You just can't turn to them and say, "Oh, by the way. This is what's happening. I need your help." People need to be kept in the loop. Inclusiveness is terribly important. If you want people to feel invested, you need to give them information, as much information as you can. You need to be solicitous of their points of view and, even if those views are impractical, they must be heard. And you need to find a way to do it that's real, because there may be the nucleus of a good idea in what they have to say.

And when a theater needs loyal and thoughtful people, the relationships have to be already in place. I have found that you can't do relationship-building wholesale. You have to do it retail—one at a time and slowly. I'm on the phone all the time with board members: "This is what's happening." During a particularly difficult time for our theater, I would get up in the morning and start calling board members. This went on for weeks and weeks. Just telling them what was going on, telling them where we were, what was at stake, what we were planning to do, how we were going to handle it—and collecting their suggestions. It was scary, and I was scared, and the only way I knew to handle it was to bring the board into the process. If you don't do that, people will feel corked-up and there will be resentment. For me, a large part of creating an atmosphere of openness is this continual transmittal of information. People need to be kept up to date. Of course, there are some things that you don't want disseminated before their time, but I've found that bringing the board up to speed informally, regularly and as a matter of course pays off.

The other danger of trying to do too much yourself is that you run the risk of getting too involved in the work of the staff. I had an earlier experience chairing a board of an organization where I had to become very active because we were without an executive director for some time. When we finally hired someone, I probably didn't step back as quickly as I should have. I am very aware of that now, and sometimes, when I feel I am getting too involved, I even say, "I'm sorry. My micromanagement gene is really overactive this week." So much of governing is about balance.

When people ask me, "What do you want in a board member?" my response is, "Ideally, the person should have some feeling for theater, and the more the better—or a desire to develop it." You've got to be very careful about who joins the board. It's easy to make a mistake, and you never know until the person is on the board for a while whether it's going to work for the institution and for that person. I want somebody who's thoughtful, with good judgment, who makes himself available. And somebody who's willing to learn about the institution and learn the ins and outs of the issues, who will know the material and can synthesize and give a good, reasonable response.

You have to work to find people like that. When we are interested in someone, we visit, we have lunch, we have breakfast, they meet the managing director, they meet another board member. Usually someone—often another board member—has suggested we consider the person. It becomes a delicate dance. You may not like them, they may not like you. And it is sensitive not only for the candidate but for the person who proposed him. "Don't you like my cousin? Why don't you like my cousin?" The most awkward situation is when someone comes along who has his own agenda, such as a script in his back pocket or an interest in producing our work elsewhere. This is really difficult, because serious conflicts can arise. For every new person who joins our board, I'd say we see maybe eight or nine people with whom we visit but don't ask to join.

Our board meetings are informative and educational as well as being decision-making meetings. There's a good deal of discussion. We provide a lot of information that people can read, but the important focus is really on one or two issues about which we have a full discussion. If you don't do that, I think you leave yourself open to real problems. If you have a critical decision ahead of you and it hasn't been fully aired, you leave the door open for a lot of second-guessing and resentment. I recently re-read the minutes from an earlier board meeting where we were dealing with a particularly thorny issue, and as I read, I felt that we had all been in it together and had tossed a lot of ideas back and forth about what had to happen. The day following the board meeting, we had a conference call with about eight people to discuss steps going forward and to synthesize a reasonable plan to resolve some of the problems. There was no accusing and no second-guessing. It was looking at what was before us and how to deal with it.

We try to create opportunities for socializing as well as connecting our trustees with the art. We have one board-meeting dinner a year, held in the private room of a restaurant. We try to restrict the agenda to a single, current, important item. We've taken apart a production budget, one year the casting department told us what we didn't know about the complicated side of casting, and we do other things involving the artistic side of the theater. Everyone's invited to readings, to "meet and greet" events and to dress rehearsals. We're constantly encouraging board members to read scripts and to invite people to the shows. For every show, we have one dinner in a nearby restaurant before a performance, to which we invite a group of patrons, a few trustees and the creative team from the current production.

Involved people have busy lives, and sometimes it's hard to get people to come to meetings and events. When we were building our new theater, we invited everyone to come to the design meetings, but very few came. I don't think it was because people weren't interested or didn't think it was important. They were just too busy. That is the reality you have to live with, particularly in a city like New York.

We are very lucky to have a smart board that understands that they are there to best serve the institution, and not the other way around. A great board is comprised of people who are able to give up a piece of themselves for the good of the whole, and while they derive satisfaction from what they do, they understand that the theater doesn't exist to give them a place in the world or an identity. And it is important that, in periods of stress or crisis, which we all experience at some time, board members don't lose their patience, balance and containment of ego. If that happens, they only magnify the situation, making everything worse, because now there are unhelpful personalities that must be dealt with.

I think so much of the culture and spirit of a board depends on the chair. And because of that, you need to think about and plan for who is going to replace you down the road. I am afraid I have not done a very good job of cultivating somebody else to fill my seat. I have not brought anybody in with the express view of, "You know, you should think about maybe some day assuming this job." I need to focus on that, because the health of the theater is directly connected to the bench strength of its leadership.

Every place is complicated and every place has quirks and history and ways of operating that make each problem different from a similar problem at another place. There is not "one way" and certainly no "right way," and a problem within an organization can have multiple viable solutions. You always have to be open to new ideas and new possibilities, to keep learning and grafting new pieces of information on what you already know or have experienced. You have to help people learn to trust themselves and encourage them to believe that something—even something difficult—is possible. In theater, this is particularly essential.

Tonen Sara O'Connor

Tonen Sara O'Connor was managing director of Milwaukee Repertory Theater for twenty-one years and is now the resident priest at the Milwaukee Zen Center, where she carries out the administrative affairs of the center, writes for its newsletter and is a pastoral counselor to inmates in seven state prisons.

The life of a theater company is a kind of impossibility. Economically, it doesn't make sense. It's exhilarating, but it's often discouraging and difficult. The kind of spirit that one wants in a board is one in which the people have truly involved themselves in something they enjoy. They really love going to the theater, even if they're very busy and they're running a bank and they don't get there very often. Still, they have some instinct for the theater, so it's a pleasure for them to be standing behind the effort.

Boards need people with a sense of humor. When I say a sense of humor, I mean an ability to accept something that happens that wasn't what you wanted, figure out what to do about it and move forward without pouring a lot of salt on the wound. The toe gets stubbed and everybody says, "Oh, no!" then, "Oh, well," and you go on. Board members particularly need this because they have ultimate fiscal responsibility for the company. Obviously, the more people come into the theater, the better off you are financially as well as emotionally. But there can be a tendency to put too much hope on play X. Well, it turns out audiences didn't like play X. And maybe the play you were really worried about, everybody loved. So, I would also look for flexibility in addition to a sense of humor.

"Trust" and "respect" are wonderful words and qualities needed in the relationship between the trustees and the staff of a theater: I *trust* you to do your job. I *trust* you to care. I *trust* you not to backbite. I *trust* you to leave your egos home. I *respect* you for what you can do and what you are doing.

Trust yourself. It doesn't sound stupid if you ask a question—it means that you are an intelligent person who needs information. Trust that the person whom you're asking the question will not slap you down, but answer seriously. You will not learn the way a theater company operates unless you ask questions. It isn't always apparent who's connected to whom, who is responsible for what.

Trustees who trust themselves learn the skills to read and understand the balance sheet, because the budget and the balance sheet tell where a theater's artistic priorities are. You can tell where the artistic emphasis is by where the money goes or what is not getting funded in the efforts to stay stable. A board member needs to be able to see that—and to see, sometimes, that we're starving those areas that affect the art, and we have to somehow not do that.

Trustees should also be willing to fly the flag in the community (or grow to become comfortable doing that), with little signs on their chests saying, "I am a trustee of this theater company. You can talk to me (and I'm not worried about whether you liked the last play or not). Basically, I'm here as a warrior for this cause and not just as a kind of affiliate because it's slightly glamorous. I'm here to fight the good fight." You cannot have too many people who are able to do that. They must also be informed, so they don't make up answers that aren't correct. And they must never be tempted to gossip—ever. That's a very hard one, because you feel you're more on the inside if you know the so-called inside gossip.

A trustee should be someone who wants to get to know the members of the company, particularly the management staff. They have to know their managing director really well, so they can talk to him openly when they need to. A managing director should be able to call a trustee and say, "I think we have a problem. I want to talk to you," and know that he can do that safely and that he will get a clear and honest hearing. There's that *trust* again—real trust. Nobody is ever covering up. A board member is not covering up how much money he's really raised (turns out they're all pledges and they're all due fifteen years from now!). That happens, but that's something that we should know. Or a managing director who's beginning to see red dripping off the bottom line in mid-season is not covering that up because he doesn't feel secure in his relationship with the board. You really are comrades in arms.

When I was a managing director, what I needed most was a sense that the board *trusted* me—that I didn't always have to make good with them. That was a personal, emotional need. I really got it from the board at Milwaukee Repertory Theater (and I was with them for twenty-one years). I had a sense of being supported, that they were genuinely appreciative of the art, even when there were rocky reviews or the community didn't seem to care for what was going on.

We had some tough times when we were doing a building project at the Rep. Construction came in more than the budgeted amount. So I had to take that to the board, who thought we were going to come in on budget. In the end it turned out that we came in less than ten percent over budget, which was quite brilliant in terms of construction costs. However, that wasn't what they expected, nor was it what I expected. We went through a difficult time trying to solve that problem. We did solve it and it was okay. But I learned at that time to deeply respect the pressures that a theater trustee is under. I realized that if the whole thing somehow went belly-up, I might lose my job, but they would lose their reputations in the city, which can be more damaging. We got together, and they helped me find a way to solve the problem, as opposed to just pushing all the blame off on me. They were more concerned with solving the problem than distributing blame. That's hard to do because it means you have to take a little of the blame yourself. Trust means: "Let's solve this together," not, "My trust is gone the minute the going gets hard."

The nominating committee, above all, has to understand the spirit of the board and the qualities that contribute to that spirit so that they will be looking for the right people. Their job goes beyond looking for someone who is well known or has an interesting job or contacts, or: "We think they go to the theater." At Milwaukee Rep, the nominating committee interviews prospective board members at a lunch with the artistic and managing directors. The committee really has to look for the important qualities and not just make a quick list of the most influential people in town. It's a hard job, but it's very important, finding the spirit while looking for the skills. Because the nominating committee is so important, the board president should choose committee members from among those who most fully exhibit the theater's spirit themselves. Like looks for like. They are creating the organism that in some ways can make or break the theater company. It isn't just the artistic side that can wreck the train; it's also the trustee side. Fundamentally, the culture of the organization is in their hands.

I want a board president who is a working colleague, a friend who is accessible to me and to whom I am always accessible, who will go the extra mile to understand the workings of the company. And I want someone who will really *lead* the board, not manhandle it. The board is a group, and a group will just go around in circles without guidance.

The board president must give the managing director freedom to operate. At Milwaukee Rep, I actually had a contract that spelled out, in broad terms, the areas in which I had authority. It meant, and they assumed, I was going to have both responsibility and authority. But it does mean that the managing director has enormous responsibility for communicating with the board president, because you are partners. And it means that the information flow from the managing director to the board president must be clear and frequent. So while you're being left alone, in a sense, to do your job (which is a huge relief), you need to express what's happening with that job to the person who's going to be sharing some of the fallout, good and bad.

The relationship of the board to the art is also crucial. An artist is someone who takes all of his extraordinary intellectual, emotional, sensory and memory input and makes something out of it or sees something in it. He is an intuitive thinker. The relationship between the board and the artistic director has potential for friction, because the board is composed primarily of linear thinkers and problem-solvers. Fortunately or unfortunately, they hired the artistic director because he doesn't think that way. He chooses plays for complex reasons: "This is it. This is what I want to do." Then he has to translate that into linear terms to the board.

The culture at the Rep was to take all new board members in hand and be very clear about one thing: The board does not choose the plays. And to me, coming from a situation where that was not the case, it was like falling into cream. I thought, it isn't all left to me to do this. They are all creating and perpetuating a culture of artistic support through thick and thin—sometimes it is pretty thick and sometimes pretty thin. It was wonderful. Occasionally, there was the worrier: "Are you sure this will sell tickets?" And that's okay, because that person also raised money and cared about the theater. You have people with personal styles, and you have to get used to this.

What have I got so far? Respect, trust, a sense of humor, flexibility and a willingness to ask questions. And a real love of the theater, a love that says we like being in the room with live actors who are onstage creating characters and performing just for us. The ideal trustee has to have that gut reaction. There should be the overarching response that the event, the fact of it, is wonderful. Throughout my entire career, when things got bad, I would step into the back of the theater, and then it was all right—I knew again why I was doing this. I think for theater trustees and for managing directors who can get so exhausted and are being sucked away from the art by the need to raise money, that's the time to go into the theater. It might be the time to say, "I want to sit in on a rehearsal or go into the scene shop." But at a minimum, just go to the theater and you'll see what's happening. The event is life-giving.

Gwen Cochran Hadden

Gwen Cochran Hadden has served both as a trustee of arts organizations and as a consultant to major performing arts organizations and arts service groups. Her work has focused on arts management and issues of diversity.

Her depth of experience and her thoughtfulness have been of great service to many arts boards.

It is estimated that by the year 2050, one in three Americans will be black, Hispanic or Asian. The spending power of the minority population of this country equals the gross national product of Canada, and minority markets buy more than any U.S. trading partner. A diverse population is here to stay, and that diversity creates new partners in every facet of American life. These partnerships include the performing arts, where opportunities for participation exist throughout the field. Theaters are beginning to reflect the diversity of their communities among their actors, managers, staff, volunteers and boards of trustees. Arts organizations in particular have led the way in pushing our country forward, giving us opportunities to know each other. When people come together around an art form, they build relationships that enliven the organization and contribute to the notion of "spirit."

What are we talking about when we talk about diversity? Are we talking about skin color? Are we talking about physical features? Are we talking about ethnic background? Socioeconomic status? Are we talking about sexual orientation? What do we mean? I think the mixture that we are looking for is people who are different ethnically, different racially, somewhat different socioeconomically, but not so different that you can't put them in a room and have them come to some understanding of each other and be comfortable. People have to have more in common than they have different. I have been pushing organizations to pay attention not just to differences but also to similarities, especially around the issue of liking theater or being open to liking theater.

Whenever I go into an organization, I ask these questions: Why diversify your board? Why are you interested in broadening your organization? What diversity are you talking about? How does diversity fit into your mission? Who are your stakeholders and what is their position on diversity? What is your plan and what is your timeline for it?

I think you start with asking: "Why diversity?" Each organization has to answer that question for itself. First of all, arts organizations are community based, so doesn't it make sense to open the doors and bring people into the organization's fabric from the community? Another reason is that our world is diverse. That means learning about each other's cultures. Kids who have never seen certain environments see in the theater a world that they didn't even know was out there. It can be a way of helping them understand how they can be more successful in the larger world. Best of all, I would love to see that we not only learn about each other's art but that we also learn what each other's art means. When August Wilson did *Jitney*, how many white people really understood what jitneys were?

One thing I have learned over the years is that diversity needs to be grounded in the mission. The mission shouldn't change just for reasons of diversity. I always feel very strongly that diversity should mesh with the mission of the organization, and you shouldn't have to change the mission in order to have diversity. Diversity might not even be good for an organization. It really has to reflect the organization's phase of development and a deep understanding of why it wants diversity. I have seen theaters in organizational turmoil that needed to reorganize, who started a diversity initiative when they really needed to concentrate on survival. Sometimes, rather than one theater trying to reach everybody, it might be smart to partner. Suppose a smaller Latino theater and a larger white theater are in the same community. Instead of the white theater trying to do Hispanic plays, why not create a partnership between the two groups? But let's say a theater is going through a neighborhood change. Then diversity might be the answer.

When an organization decides on a diversity initiative, there are some important steps it needs to take. The first step is to ensure the support of every board member. Facilitating a full board discussion on diversity will ensure that each board member knows of the effort, understands the preliminary extent of the endeavor and the reasons for it and is aware of his role in supporting it. The discussion will indicate to the leadership how prepared the board is to participate in such an effort, what needs to be done to make board members receptive to new members and how the new members should be prepared for participation on the board.

The second step is to analyze and identify the culture of the organization and the board. Identifying the cultural orientation of an organization is the most important piece of diversity to me. This will indicate what the profile of new board members must be in order for them to be successful in the organization. One of the biggest problems is that most of us don't know what our organization's culture is because we are too close to it. So look at it: Who talks to whom? Who eats with whom? Look at the range of behaviors of trustees and staff. The cultures of organizations vary from formal and prescribed to informal and relaxed. Sometimes, organizations promote a freedom between staff and trustees that is obviously welcoming and friendly. But in other organizations, if a trustee walks through the door of the theater, he must be announced to the managing director and go directly to his office. If he is going anywhere else, the managing director escorts him, like a chaperone. If a new trustee doesn't understand this culture, he might think he is being treated this way because of his difference.

If you want diversity strongly enough, you might need to change some things. Trustees who have worked together for several years have natural groups. Certain people will sit near each other and talk with each other at a board meeting. Maybe they do things together outside of the theater. Maybe they know each other professionally. Perhaps you notice that a new trustee of difference is not feeling comfortable and you say, "Aha, this person isn't talking to anybody at the board meeting." Or, when you have coffee at the meeting, this person is standing around. Imagine if you were that new trustee. You come to the first meeting and see these pockets of people. Then it happens again at the second meeting, and you start to think to yourself, "If I'm not going to meet anybody, why am I here?" One thing I often suggest is to create a buddy system so that new trustees can be introduced to their fellow board members as well as to the culture of the organization. It is incumbent on the organization to create a welcoming environment.

Of course, efforts toward achieving diversity don't always go smoothly. Sometimes the old guard can get too comfortable. When a trustee of difference is so well accepted—his education, his speech, his background make him part of the group—sometimes a white person forgets to monitor his words and says something insensitive or thoughtless. The flip side occurs when a person of difference has a great relationship with fellow trustees and raises an issue around culture or ethnicity or color that makes the majority feel uncomfortable. For example, once I said, "Let me just say as a black woman . . ." You could hear the room get quiet and later people said to me, "Why did you have to say that?" It's much easier to pretend that we are all just exactly alike, so nobody really wants to be reminded that there are differences.

When these things happen, the best thing to do is to address them. If I were in an organization that I know really wants to work on diversity, I might say to the board chair or the managing director, "Something happened that I am not comfortable with. Could you please facilitate a discussion about ethnic differences and the appropriate words to use around them?" Or we might have a discussion about why I think of myself as a black woman and not just as a woman. Those are pivotal times for organizations. Unless they step up to the bat and address the issues, people of difference will feel pushed away.

I can't stress to you enough how much people want to be made to feel comfortable. One of the reasons that performing arts organizations have had so much difficulty attracting minorities is that minorities want to be with people with whom they are similar and comfortable. I urge organizations not to focus on huge disparities of difference, because it is not going to work. Don't look to bring people into your theater by giving tickets to people in the projects. Don't target the broadest ranges of diversity. Target the ranges of diversity where there is likely to be some common ground.

It is also important to be aware that there are many not-so-great reasons for diversity. One is just to get money. That is the worst reason, in my book. Another is: "Butts in the seats." When organizations reach out by saying, "We don't have enough people coming to performances and therefore we want you to become involved," who wants to go under those circumstances? People of difference have a negative reaction to feeling used. And a third not-great reason to attempt diversity is because the organization has a grant that requires it. What typically happens then is that the organization has diversity for only as long as it has the grant, but it doesn't work to maintain the diversity after that. There is no real commitment.

Have you ever seen *Three Mo' Tenors*? I went to see the show with my daughter at a theater in downtown Boston. Now, Boston is still very segregated, but I have never seen an audience like that in Boston. People were talking to each other, turning around in their seats saying, "Did you see that? Did you hear that?" and they didn't even know each other. We were all standing on our feet and singing along, and the guy next to me gave me a big hug and said, "Oh, my God, this is such fun," and I had never met him before in my life. For me, that was diversity at its best.

I really believe that we have an opportunity to get beyond whatever barriers we have and to realize that we are not that different. Once we get past the differences, we can start figuring out what the things are that we have in common and how can we work better together. I am especially optimistic about one thing: When diverse people come together around an art form—and I mean white and black and gay and straight and young and old, you name it—they can build wonderful relationships, and I think those relationships can actually change the world.

Liz Lerman

Founding artistic director of the Liz Lerman Dance Exchange in 1976, Lerman has had a twenty-seven-year career as a dancer and choreographer. With colleague John Borstel, she has authored Critical Response Process, *an approach that helps laypeople talk to artists in a thoughtful and informative way about their work. The Process has been embraced by people in a range of disciplines for such varied purposes as curatorial decision-making in gallery settings and audience talkback for staged readings of scripts-in-progress.*

How can trustees talk about the art with their artistic director, with artists or even among themselves? This is always such a touchy question. Most organizations believe that trustees shouldn't interfere in the artistic work of their organization. But, at the same time, trustees are asked to carry much of the financial responsibility for the organization. Sometimes the board's need for fiscal stability and the artists' need to push the field may feel like conflicting agendas. How can a constructive conversation be created? What is the role of the trustee and the artist in the conversation?

I first became aware of these questions not in relation to trustees, but in relation to my own role as an artist, teacher and colleague. As an artist, I had a complex relationship with critique and opinion. At its worst, I often felt misunderstood and somewhat brutalized by criticism. As a teacher, I gradually realized that I needed to engage my students so they could truly find their individual voices, rather than produce work that reflected my own aesthetics. And, as a colleague, I needed something to say besides, "That was really great," or abject silence when I couldn't think of anything positive to say. As a field, we needed a way to talk about work so that people could in fact have a dialogue and strengthen their own ability to solve the problems inherent in creative endeavors.

As I started to think about these questions, I asked myself what positive experiences of feedback felt like—feedback that pushed me into the studio and made me want to go back to work, not the kind that puts you in bed for three days. As I talked to others about this question, I realized that most people can name the qualities that make an experience of feedback a positive one. Some will name hard-to-define but easily recognized qualities like trust and respect. Others will cite very concrete approaches like pointing out details or suggesting things to think about. Based on the kinds of values and approaches that had made critique effective for me and others, I wanted to develop a series of practical steps to facilitate a genuine dialogue with artists, and that became what I call the Critical Response Process. This formal Process, which usually includes four steps led by a facilitator, is described in the book my colleague John Borstel and I wrote. But the spirit of the Process has broad applications, and that's what I'd like to emphasize in our conversation, because it is a method for getting useful feedback on anything you make, whether it's artwork, a job performance or even dinner. The Process helps me constantly in my conversations with peer artists, with people I am mentoring, in the development of my own artistic work and even in my personal and family life.

Central to the spirit of the Process is that when we respond to an artist's work, we always begin by stating what was meaningful to us as hearers or viewers. To start with "meaning" is to begin with the essence of the artistic act. So a great way to start a conversation with an artist about his work is to imagine that you have been asked, "What was exciting, stimulating, evocative, memorable or meaningful about the work you just saw?" The answer does not have to be, "That was the best thing I ever saw in my life," but, if you have been paying attention, answers can invariably be both honest and positive. This can be done by naming details, because nothing is too small to notice (to an actor: "The sidelong glance you gave as you opened the letter was very telling."). It can be pointing out a particular aspect of the work (to a director: "The pacing of the dialogue made the scene really suspenseful."). It can be telling of a personal connection (to a lighting designer: "The atmosphere you created reminded me of my great aunt's house. I remember how the breeze used to blow through the lace curtains in her bay window."). Meaning has broad possibilities.

Meaning and the ability to talk about it is important for trustees in a couple of ways. Often, boards talk about money, personnel, fundraising, but they don't take the time to talk about why it matters that they're even in the room. They don't tell their stories. We might say to the board, "What's the one story you tell everybody about why you're on this board?" or "When was the time in your early life when you were touched by something artistic?" Those kinds of stories. I hope lots of boards are practicing that. You can open a meeting with that and it changes everyone. That's one notion of spirit.

Our arts trustees also need a way to talk with artists and to talk about our art. Sometimes trustees don't even feel that they know how to talk about the art. The artistic director reports to the board: How can the trustee probe his thinking? Or, imagine the trustee on opening night, knowing he's going to the cast party later, anticipating conversations with cast members: What can the trustee say to genuinely connect with the artists? The trustee is going to be watching and perceiving the work in a whole new way if he begins simply by looking for what is meaningful.

So, begin with a statement of what the work means to you. Remember the trustee at opening night. Maybe he says, "I really understood the intentions of the characters in this classic better than I ever have before." Or, he might say, "I was struck by the use you make of props." The point is to learn to make a habit of noticing things and to discipline yourself to open a conversation by expressing the meaning you find in the content. If you do that—or if the trustee does that when speaking with an artist it may allow him to go deeper in the relationship.

For example, I frequently go backstage after performances. When I see a performance now, I am always looking for what is striking, memorable or meaningful for me. It is a wonderful way to see a performance. Even in the worst production, you can find something of meaning. And I make sure I do it in every single experience I have with art. When I go backstage, I first tell the artist what I found meaningful in the work and then I say, "I can't wait until when we have some more time. I have some questions for you and I am sure you have some questions for me. I am available later tonight if you want to talk."

This doesn't mean that you don't have strong opinions as well. Perhaps you go to opening night and you think the costumes are a real liability to the production. In fact, you almost want to suggest that the artistic director get rid of the costume designer. You can get at what's bothering you, but not by starting with the opinion. My advice is: Wait! Start by stating what *was* meaningful for you and let that stand on its own. Then, ask a question—and not just any kind of question. A large part of the Critical Response Process is how you pose questions. The goal is to ask a neutral question whose purpose is informational, or that explores the artist's thinking or process or the practicalities of the situation. For example, instead of saying, "The costumes are gaudy and unflattering" (an opinion) or, "Why are the costumes so out of sync with the spirit of the play?" (a question that couches an opinion), you might ask, "How do you think about costumes as a way of communicating ideas to an audience?" or, "Tell me about your process for collaborating with designers on this production." This approach allows the artist to share information which might influence how (or whether) you choose to express your opinion. It lets you be curious before you're opinionated.

One of the most powerful aspects of Critical Response is to understand that your opinion matters. You are not being Machiavellian by transforming it into a neutral question. You are coming to grips with what piece of your opinion is truly important to the particular artist. To choose a different example, let's say you are talking to me, a choreographer, and are troubled because my dancers close the piece in a circle. You have to decide what it is you want me to think about. Is the problem the movement rather than the circle? Is the problem that the dancers are too slow when they are in the circle? You have to give it a little thought. What is the question? What you want me to do is *think*. You might ask: "Liz, can you talk about the timing of the different sections of the dance?" Or you might say, "Talk about where you think the emotional impact of the dance is," because you feel that when the circle closes with the backs of the dancers to the audience, the audience feels emotionally shut out.

Although forming a neutral question can be difficult, the actual process of forming opinions into neutral questions enables the questioner to recognize and acknowledge his personal values and biases. For some people, the neutral question may sound like a cover-up for their real opinion, and it can indeed function that way. But even the most hard-edged, "I-can-take-anything-you-dish-out," artists seem to become more receptive and involved in the critical session as a direct result of the neutral question. When defensiveness starts, learning stops.

Finally, a useful idea we employ in the Process is something we call the "permissioned opinion." It works like this. After beginning with a statement of meaning followed by questions that clarify information, the questioner can express his opinions more directly. However, he must first ask the artist if that is all right. Questioners first name the topic of the opinion and then ask the artist for permission to state it. For instance, "I have an opinion about the costumes. Do you want to hear it?" In response, the artist has the option to say, "Yes," or "No."

Sometimes my colleague John demonstrates one of the functions of the permission step by doing this: He'll wad up a piece of paper in his hand while he's talking, then throw it at somebody who is focused somewhere else, who'll usually flinch and fumble in response. Then he'll pick up the paper, make eye contact with the same person and say, "Here, catch," to a now deft receiver. Opinions can feel very much like objects thrown at us. If we have no preparation, we can often feel affronted rather than engaged. But with a little notice and a moment to adjust to what's coming at us, we can be in a much better position to "catch" the opinion.

For example, when someone on our administrative staff has written a grant proposal, they will ask me to look at it. Now, they gave it to me to read for a response, but even so, I don't think it means I have global ability to go back to them and say *anything*. First, I'll say something positive: "Look at the way you worded this. We've been struggling so hard to say this. It's really great. I have an opinion about this paragraph. Can we go there?" And then we talk about it. Another example: My daughter asks me to come into her room to help with a homework question. I can come in and help her with her homework, but she hasn't given me permission to ask: "When are you going to clean up your room?" The difference is huge.

Critical Response is good for anything you do. It's a way of teaching people how to live with their judgments. Some people are used to stating their opinion as often as they want, like an overdeveloped muscle. Many board members come out of hierarchal organizations where they're at the top. For example, after one Critical Response session we led, a woman approached us and said, "I am a really opinionated person, and I am always getting in trouble because of that. You have given me a structure through which I can still be who I am but be sure that I am heard." The Process offers a different way of expressing opinions.

Artists and trustees are committed to their organization's mission, and each gives passionately (and frequently sacrificially) toward that end. Yet, we stumble, we skirt around, we avoid, we put our foot in our mouths about essential issues. A trustee's ability to respond to artistic content thoughtfully, articulately and from the heart can be a great asset to our organizations. The *spirit* of the Critical Response Process offers an authentic way of communicating. It is honest without being confrontational. It is questioning without implying the answer. The Process cuts both ways, both in terms of structuring the encounter to serve the artist and giving people, who otherwise might not know how to broach things or who are being silent because they don't have the tools with which to communicate, the opportunity to speak.

I'm not sure that I agree with the common wisdom that boards shouldn't get involved in discussions of artistic content or quality. I believe that with good tools in place, conversations between trustees, artists and staff members can be effective, valuable and a great way to increase everyone's involvement.

Peter Culman

Peter Culman was managing director of CENTERSTAGE in Baltimore for thirty-four years. Manager and fundraiser par excellence for his theater, he worked from the simple principle of creating relationships among people. Currently a consultant for not-for-profit organizations, he conducts board retreats around the country.

At CENTERSTAGE's first rehearsal, we invite all of the staff (artistic, production and administrative), trustees and any people we are introducing to the theater. The goal is to gather the community of CENTERSTAGE at a key juncture—the first time the play is read. It's a collective start. It recognizes the collaborative nature of theater. Subject to how much you wish to be a part of the rehearsal/production/audience-gathering processes, it takes you all the way through previews, opening night and to the end of the run. I start with this point, because for me, ahead of everything else, theater is about collaboration—the give-and-take among artists, artisans, administrators, trustees, other volunteers and, when performance occurs, our audience. The culture that emerges from this is generous: As we get to know each other, a mutual understanding of theater evolves. Through that we begin to have relationships, the start of compassion for each other and, in time (this does not happen overnight) we have trust. That journey to compassion and trust, coming to a state of mind—soul, spirit, I'd say—when I can be a dumb turkey with you and you can be a dumb turkey with me, is important because it fosters maximum interaction in our dealings with each other.

Next, I would like to bring up the question of how boards of trustees best interact with each other and/or with the staff. In this country, when the resident professional theater movement first started, we understandably turned to the corporate model, which for the most part is strongly vertical with almost everything funneled through a CEO. In a theater environment, it might be through a producing director or an artistic director and a managing director. And, while there is some kind of interaction between the trustees and staff through certain committees, funneling has been the dominant image describing the interaction. More often than not, the trustees called themselves *directors*, not trustees.

But the second model of interaction is I think radically different. It is horizontal. It is a partnership. And it is driven by certain recognitions. The first is the potential for what I call "enlightened studentry."

When doing a play, you have text available, which, if you're interested, can introduce you to the entire process of theater. For example, if your theater were going to produce *Hamlet,* you could send copies of *Hamlet* to trustees who wanted to read the play. You could offer one or two discussions, reviewing the cut script to understand what went out and why, and what stayed in and why. Having studied the script, the trustees could go to the first reading, attend a dress rehearsal or a preview, see the performance and possibly return a second time. By the end of the whole experience, these trustees would have not only a much greater knowledge of Shakespeare and *Hamlet* but also a much greater knowledge of the theater-wide cast-of-characters, starting, obviously, with the actors and extending throughout the organization. So, when it came to the deliberations of the board, the trustees would have a much greater, global, firsthand view of what goes on. They would know theater in their tummies.

If we were to do this for trustees for two or three productions a season, when budgeting for the following season all the numbers would make experiential sense to the trustee. When they met someone at a gathering who asks, "I understand you're a trustee of ______ theater. What do you think of their recent production of *Hamlet*?" they could talk knowledgably about it. They would know what the viewpoints were of the director, the designers and the actors. They would be glorious—not only knowledgeable, but glorious—spokespeople for the theater. If collaboration and enlightened studentry (becoming a willing student voraciously trying to absorb theater) are present in the interaction, I believe passionately that great things happen for the trustee and for the theater.

There was a time in my life when I thought that I could keep the professional and the personal separate. In fact, you don't really need to have them both present. If you're serving on the board of a bank, they want you because of your knowledge of numbers, of getting more depositors, etc. It's not important for people to get to know you. That's bupkes.

I first came to realize the importance of what we're calling the "spirit of governance" through the counsel of a wise trustee. CENTERSTAGE was founded in 1963. I arrived in November of 1966. I was twenty-eight years old and the managing director. A wise trustee said to me, "Without really understanding what you're doing, I see that you are trying to create a partnership between the trustees and the staff. You're reaching for this partnership intuitively, but don't know what it takes to make it work. You have to learn key things about your staff and their interaction with the trustees, and you also have to learn about the trustees and what kind of people they are." He continued, "CENTERSTAGE is in a precarious state. You're understandably clinging to little branches of good news while at the same time wondering if the tree will continue standing. You must tell the trustees all the news, good and bad, all the time—don't color it. It's not that you're not telling them the truth now. It's just that you have to tell them *all* the truth, and they must trust that and you. If you're concerned about cash flow, you must convey that concern, because you're the only person in a position to tell that story." Then, of course, it becomes an issue of how the trustees respond to this direct approach. It's not an issue of, "Culman, you screwed up. The next time you screw up, good-bye." (Because Culman can't function if he's living with an ax hanging over his head.) "What's worse, you're not drawing anything out of the trustees, taking advantage of their experience, their minds and their wisdom."

He went on, "People who are one-man-band successes—self-styled entrepreneurs—don't easily become collaborators or partners. It's a different way of interacting. So, as you recruit people for the board, try to see if there's something about them that suggests they want to be partners. And as you work with current board members, realize you're trying to head this group into a partnership, a horizontal relationship with everyone interacting with each other. As the partnership begins to emerge, the trustees and staff will feed each other. Mutual compassion surfaces. Not far behind comes trust. When compassion and trust are present, when you can be a dumb turkey with a trustee and vice versa, there is nothing you can't accomplish together."

Invariably I'm asked about the relationships among the president of the board of trustees, the artistic director and the managing director. Let me tell you a story. When Stan Wojewodski was the artistic director, he enjoyed great success, and as artistic director he stretched us all the time. I remember he gave me a play called *The Increased Difficulty of Concentration* by Vaclav Havel to read. I read it three times. I went to him and said, "Stan, I just don't understand this play." He responded, "I understand that. Peter, trust me. I think I know how to do this." So, when we announced the play, Joe Langmead, then president of the board, said to me, "What do you think of the play?" And I said, "I know that Stan has a strong view about it. I've read it three times and I don't get it. We must get behind it because Stan has an energy attached to this play that I've rarely seen before. That feeling convinces me that it's worth doing." We did the production. I thought it extraordinary. Joe thought it extraordinary. And Stan's choice was fully vindicated. I mention this example because I think in these relationships there's a time when you just have to believe in one another, almost fly blind, particularly when supporting the artistic director. I might add parenthetically that I had a culture with Stan in which I would never say, "No," until I had examined every conceivable way to realize his ideas. Sometimes I would say, "I don't think we can realize all your ideas, but if we do this and that, let's see if we can make it happen." We kept each other out of corners. Joe sensed that and helped to keep us out of the corners.

I think a person behaves totally differently with another person when an effort is made to get to know him. I watched Joe Langmead and his successors, Katherine Gust, Nancy Roche and Jim Brady, all consciously sit down and not only get to know the trustees, but also get to know the staff—get to know them as people. They knew about our private lives—if we were married, if we had significant others. You name it, they knew it about us. So when we interacted with these people, we felt welcomed, we felt embraced, we felt known. That's important because then you feel, "I'm glad to be in your company and I want to work with you. Yes, we're going to have bumpy times ahead, but we're going to get through them." Now, someone might say, "That's touchy-feely." But I'll say, "Well, maybe it is, but I don't care." It's also rewarding. It's about the richness that can happen. You can have fun doing this.

When someone comes on the board as a trustee, you're asking for their time—you're asking, in some measure, for their family's time. You're asking them to offer up some, if not all, of their friends. You're asking them for their business activity, to the extent it's possible, to become involved in your theater. What are they getting in return? What they're getting back is, ahead of everything, participating in the art form of theater, which can deliver knockout punches in the way it affects you. Sometimes it fails. It doesn't matter. Once you're knocked out, you want more of it. If you're knocked out because you've gotten it through this gathering of what I call "backstage information," the experience is that much richer.

Another thing that happens when you have horizontal relationships is that you are building a community. Monica Sagner, a longtime trustee, says, "Some of my best friends, indeed many of my best friends, are trustees of CENTERSTAGE. I've gotten to know them through the theater, we share the common ground of the productions and now we share the cumulative experience of attending these productions together." People want a community. That's important in life. If you can create a community, you can do anything.

Diane Morrison

Our chapter on "spirit" ends as it began—from the perspective of a trustee. Diane Morrison joined the board of Signature Theatre in New York City in its early days and served as its second president during a period of tremendous growth. Currently executive director of the Laura Pels Foundation, she remains passionate about theater.

I like the word "spirit" because it acknowledges the emotional impact that a board has on a theater company. Oftentimes, that's overlooked as you go down the list of board responsibilities. The spirit (and it is a wonderful word) needs to be recognized—the fact that a board should exist to really lift the theater, to add some confidence to what they're doing.

My experience with Signature (and this is something that I think many boards go through, or need to be cognizant of) is that things change. Signature's mission is to produce the work of one major American playwright each season. When I joined Signature, we were in our third year in a tiny ninety-seat house down on Bond Street. The board was composed of people who brought specific skills like accounting or insurance. It was very typical of the kind of people who would come on the board of a small theater. Our financial responsibility to Signature was quite small. We were just trying to get through every day. Edward Albee, our third playwright, was with the theater the season I joined. Edward had not been produced in New York for ten years at that point. There was a wonderful sense on the board that we were doing something important and something that, in a large sense, was going to mean something to the American theater.

Jim Houghton, Signature's founder and artistic director, was always interested in the theater's larger context. It was around that time that I became aware of Theatre Communications Group (TCG). I started going to their conferences and encouraged other board members to do so. At TCG, I learned what other people were doing, so I had a marvelous time just stealing ideas. I remember a theater company in Philadelphia that began each season by reading the plays they were going to do with board members taking the roles. We did that a couple of times in my living room, and we had a wonderful time. As I recall, one was a John Guare play, and it was great fun, and we had a delightful time over tea, laughing and just enjoying ourselves. People choose to be with a theater company because it touches them in some personal, wonderful way.

Another thing that I thought was important was to go see other theaters' productions. You assume that people who join your board are doing that, but it's surprising to find out it's often not the case. Going to the theater with trustees was a way for Jim and me to get to know people on the board in a more informal way, but it was also tremendous fun to see and then talk about other people's work. You get so wrapped up in your season or your budget, it's nice to get out and see other perspectives. One of the things that we did that I am most proud of in those early days was to organize an evening for the boards of four theater companies to get together at Signature—Playwrights Horizons, the Atlantic Theater Company, Classic Stage and Signature. I know it was important because people are still talking about it. Again, it's a matter of stepping outside of yourself and embracing other people who are "doing it."

We also worked very hard to connect the board with the art. This really starts at the top. It starts with an artistic director who appreciates and values a board and why they are there. As a board president, it's important to be in sync with that and therefore be mindful of it. Jim was very good at inviting artists and playwrights to board meetings. It was sometimes intimidating because, as much as board members might think they'll feel comfortable with artists and playwrights, they are often shy and overwhelmed by them. And, in reverse, it's wonderful for the artists to see what a board looks like. Everyone already understands the fiduciary responsibilities of a board, and that is taken seriously. However, everyone should be there because of the mission and because of the art. Jim would always bring things back to the mission: who we are, what we are about and what people had to understand.

Small things—dinners with new members, dinners after a meeting, getting together during rehearsals, sitting in on readings—all these things help. Meeting with designers and seeing their plans are always marvelous. The president may not do all the work to make the connection with the art but, unless the president sets that tone and establishes that value, it's not going to happen. It becomes just a finance committee meeting or a special events committee meeting. It's not going to speak to the spirit. Why someone stays with your board or leaves your board—it's about that connection. Unless it really becomes a part of their soul, you're going to lose them.

The biggest thing that new board members have to learn is how understaffed and how undercapitalized our theaters are. That's why I always started with determining if there was a willingness to just sit and listen and learn for a period of time. That's hard because you have people coming from important backgrounds with significant skills, and there's the assumption of, "In my company, we do it this way. Can't we do it this way here?" Our wonderful theaters are very different organisms, and it takes time to listen for what they need and what they want. Board members need to be sensitive to the staff. I remember a time when the Signature board became quite cohesive and strong, but we were taking up too much time from the theater. Finally the people on the staff had to say, "We are a staff of four people and you are overwhelming us with your ideas and your desires."

When I think about staff, I also think that it is important to orient new staff members to who is on the board, what their role is and how they operate. Not enough time is spent doing this. We can't assume that they will simply know everyone by osmosis.

As a board chair, I always tried to use people's time well. Another idea I brought back from a TCG conference is that you were better off assigning people tasks, as opposed to just having committees. We tried that and it helped tremendously. When you are really able to identify what a person wants to do and then let them do that, it makes for much better board meetings.

Signature grew very quickly, doubling its budget every year for a few years. When I first came on board, the budget was about $300,000. Now it is $1,700,000. As the numbers changed, so did the board. When we were a smaller theater, everyone had to pitch in and everyone showed up. As we became more successful, that changed, with a lot of folks joining our board for many different reasons. We started adding board members who could contribute financially. After a meeting, many were not interested in getting together, but simply in getting home. And that's okay too. The same way the theater company changed, the complexion of the board changed.

We also had to take on greater risk as we grew. Theater companies, particularly their artists, are really quite wonderful at risk management. They live their lives unemployed for periods of time, often do not know if rehearsal is going to go well today, and in many ways are better able to live in this world of uncertainty. Most people who sit on boards have a bank account and own their apartments and are used to things being in a nice little pile. That's not the way theater companies work. We do all this planning, but ultimately, we're just going to jump in the pool and hope it's okay. It was fine at Signature when we were a smaller theater company. But once we took on our own theater building, I think people's risk tolerance was severely tested. We'd never had a theater before. We didn't know how it would work out. Jim didn't know how it would work out. But he's someone who inspires people to "come along for the train ride," so to speak.

As the numbers and the risk became higher, some people said, "I'm tired and I just don't want to do this anymore," or, "What this theater company has become is too hard for me." There were other people on the board whose abilities to function effectively no longer existed or who were no longer financially able to help. I knew that the only way the board would move forward was if we shared a sense of respect for one another. Sometimes people need to be asked to leave a board. The thing that I love, whether it be the gala or an opening night, is that there's lots of folks there who, for whatever personal or professional reasons, are no longer on the board, but they're always welcomed. They support what we do, and that's quite wonderful.

In the end, though, it is the mission of the theater that gives people goose bumps. I sound like a high school kid when I talk about it. I have said many times to my friends that the Signature Theatre board experience changed my life. At Signature, I experienced a group of people getting together and working on something that was bigger than themselves in an unselfish, caring way. It was absolutely remarkable to me to experience artists working the way they worked on their words and their lines and their lighting, and wanting to express different feelings and thoughts, and doing it in such a focused, loving sort of way. I know there is often a lot of turmoil connected to theatrical productions, but I never saw it when I was at Signature. Everyone was working at the top of their game, and I knew they weren't doing it for the money because they weren't being paid that much. And the board members were really lovely people who, with every phone call, asked what they could do and how could they help. I certainly hadn't experienced that in my professional life. That's the level of caring that you experience, oftentimes, only with your family.

For me personally, books and words are what I've always valued. As a little kid, going to the library was always the best for me; to have stories all around me was very exciting. So being in the theater environment and knowing that there was something I could do to help make our theater strong and secure has been a tremendous honor. And, in that environment, when people say, "Thanks. I'm glad you're here," you'll gladly show up the next day and do a few more cartwheels for them.

Part II

THE PRACTICE OF GOVERNANCE

BOARD DEVELOPMENT

Nancy Roche

GEORGE BALANCHINE, the legendary founder of the New York City Ballet, is quoted as saying: "Après moi, le board." In other words, after the founding genius's vision is no longer steering the institution, a continuum of trustees replaces the founder. In collaboration with the artistic and administrative leadership, it is the board that articulates the mission and sets priorities. It is the board that hires the artistic leader and the managing director. It is the board that assumes fiduciary responsibility for a sound institution. Board members of arts institutions are aptly called "trustees." They, in partnership with the professional leadership, hold the mission of our institutions in trust for our artists and for our communities.

If trustees are so important, how can you ensure that your organization has the caliber of trustee it needs to fill these crucial roles? You begin at the beginning: You form a committee. Because the board development committee is the most important committee of the board, the makeup of this committee needs to be considered carefully. The committee should be liberally sprinkled with community connectors plugged into their professional and social arenas and experienced on other boards. Committee members need to be trustworthy, wise and discreet because their work will involve frank discussions. Their responsibilities are the framework of this chapter.

This chapter is largely based on my almost twenty years of experience at CENTERSTAGE in Baltimore, partly because it is the theater I know best, but, even more, because the CENTERSTAGE approach is one of the most thoughtful and comprehensive I have seen. It was natural for me, in developing this chapter, to turn to my fellow trustees and ask: "What do you need to know? When do you need to know it? What makes a board experience fulfilling?" Their candid, insightful opinions highlight this chapter.

Board Culture

Understanding your board culture is the framework for beginning the process of recruiting, educating and evaluating board members. My fellow CENTERSTAGE trustees told me:

> "The art of theater is the acknowledged heart of discussion and action at CENTERSTAGE."
>
> "The lack of a 'we/they' culture is critical."
>
> "A spirit of collaboration is profound and pervasive. That spirit underlies CENTERSTAGE's culture. The staff's enthusiasm is contagious. The staff supports and responds to every board member and welcomes suggestions from any quarter."
>
> "The board chair and the managing director make a conscious effort to nurture involvement and interaction between board and staff. The key to this is frequent personal contact. Regular reaching out fosters a sense of responsibility within the board for the health, growth and sustainability of the theater and its art."

All boards have a culture. When recruiting new trustees, you need to begin with an understanding of what your board culture is and be mindful of "fit." "Culture" is the animating energy that enlivens the interactions among trustees and between board and staff. It is the subtextual environment that underpins the work of the board. Effective board culture begins with respect and collegiality and includes fun, frequent communication and gratitude for accomplishments.

Board culture is *created*. The best board culture is created by the conscious effort of everyone involved and is modeled by board leaders and key staff, especially the artistic director and the managing director. The board chair sets the tone. She has high personal standards and interacts with colleagues with respect and professionalism. Trustees with long service on the board implicitly teach board values to newer colleagues as they work with staff, discuss issues of consequence on which they may differ and enthusiastically support the theater's programs.

Relationship building is the key to creating an effective board culture. Social activities are a relaxed way for trustees and staff to get to know each other. Encourage digressions, anecdotes and personal stories—and have fun. Remember that we're talking about people. The essence of creating an effective board culture is grounded in people skills.

Some formal and informal social opportunities you can create are:

- Build in social time at board meetings. CENTERSTAGE's board meetings start at 5 P.M., and we offer drinks (including wine!) and light hors d'oeuvres for about fifteen minutes before the business of the meeting begins.
- Arrange lunch with one or two trustees, hosted by the chair or the managing director. (Sandwiches in the managing director's office works fine.) It offers an opportunity for greater give-and-take, perhaps more in-depth than a formal meeting permits, and the valuable chance to get to know each other better.
- Celebrate opening nights. It can be as simple as cake in the lobby.
- Consider an end-of-the-year party for board members and staff that includes partners and children. It's a time of thank-yous and kudos. Also, there's no better way to know someone than by getting to know her partner and kids.

A strong partnership between board and staff underpins the best board cultures. The board is inspired by the staff's enthusiasm and expertise and is welcomed to participate. The board does not micromanage the staff. The board respects the time limitations of an overworked (and frequently stressed) not-for-profit staff and particularly honors the staff's personal time, not calling them at home unless it's an emergency.

Recruiting

Why do people join boards?

> "I joined the board primarily because of Joe Langmead [former board president]. I had a strong personal interest in theater going back to high school, and knew and liked CENTERSTAGE from having attended productions. Joe was positive about his experiences at CENTERSTAGE, particularly about the people

> he worked with. He strongly encouraged me to become involved in a meaningful way."
>
> "When I moved here, I was looking for a fun and exciting way to connect with Baltimore. I associate with bankers every day, so I wanted to connect through the cultural arts, because that appeals to my heart."
>
> "I joined because of my fondness for Peter Culman [former managing director], as well as for several individuals on the board. I was also eager to be involved with and support an institution that reflects so positively on Baltimore. I was looking for an opportunity to be involved with and support theater beyond mere financial support (our financial resources being quite finite), to learn more about what goes into the production of the art of theater and to enhance my enjoyment of CENTERSTAGE."

Recruiting is a year-round job. Well, maybe not year-round, but the board as a whole and the board development committee in particular are always on the lookout for potential trustees. When we meet a subscriber who loves our productions, when we meet someone new to our community looking for important volunteer work, when we meet someone well connected in a corporation, church or synagogue, for example, we consider that person as a potential trustee. That does not mean, however, that a board member, or even a committee member, issues an ad hoc invitation. Names and recommendations are simply passed on to the committee and the committee's recruiting process. The work of the committee is an ongoing process of identifying the theater's needs and cultivating and recruiting potential trustees who meet those needs.

ATTRIBUTES OF AN EFFECTIVE TRUSTEE

The 3 Ts

Time, Talent and Treasure

The 3 Ws

Work, Wealth and Wisdom

The 3 Bs

Brains, Bucks and Balls

A good way to begin is by creating a picture of the current board. It could look something like this:

BOARD COMPOSITION						
	Age by decade	*Gender*	*Race/ Ethnicity*	*Professional Expertise/ Skills*	*Geography*	*Other*
NAME						
NAME						
NAME						
NAME						
NAME						

Add the numbers up and see where you are. Is there a reasonable balance by gender? Have you attracted any trustees in their thirties and forties, or are you too dependent on an old guard? How many lawyers and accountants do you have? Do you have community volunteers, the mainstays of running galas? If your organization has a broad geographical reach, does your board reflect that in its membership? How does your board respond to the diversity of your community?

The picture of your current board may suggest some obvious holes. In the next step, the committee talks about what the board needs and what the theater needs. Different kinds of theaters look for different kinds of trustees. A theater whose work evolves jointly with community participation may look for different trustees than the theater whose work is defined by ethnicity or by gender. Do you need a specific area of influence or expertise? Do you need access to people well positioned in corporations? Do you anticipate a campaign? Do you need individual wealth? Are there gaps in future leadership? For example, do you know who will be the next head of the finance committee? Do you have several potential board leaders in the wings?

Check your strategic plan. How might that change your focus when recruiting your next generation of trustees?

At the same time that the committee is developing a list of needs, the committee also needs to create a set of expectations or responsibilities for trustees of your organization. For CENTERSTAGE these responsibilities include:

RESPONSIBILITIES OF A CENTERSTAGE TRUSTEE

1. Understands and advocates the mission of CENTERSTAGE.
2. Attends theater activities and participates in the work of the theater

   a. Subscribes to the season (Trustees are encouraged to bring guests to performances as often as possible. The staff arranges complimentary tickets.)
   b. Attends regularly scheduled quarterly board meetings and theater-related activities, such as fundraising events, board discussions and phonathons
   c. Serves on at least one committee
   d. Serves on the finance committee as a first-year trustee and may have other committee assignments.

3. Supports and participates in fundraising programs to meet the theater's annual and long-range goals

   a. Commits to make a contribution that reflects CENTERSTAGE as a priority in his or her charitable giving
   b. Contributes to the annual fund and any other CENTERSTAGE fundraising campaigns or events (e.g., the Annual Radio Auction, the "CENTERSTAGE Presents" gala)
   c. Is responsible for soliciting new or increased contributions to CENTERSTAGE campaigns and events.

4. Promotes the sale of single, group and subscription tickets.

And so the list-making of candidates begins. Over time, the list is refined into "hot prospects," "long-term cultivation," "maybe next year," and an archival list containing rejections and the reasons why. Names are suggested, abilities weighed, attributes tested against what the board and the theater need. The question is not only: "Do we need a lawyer?" but more fully, "What lawyer has the ability/interest to understand our mission, our culture, our style of governing?" The point is not to fill empty seats. Apart from your artistry, your board members are the public and personal face of your theater. Their quality mirrors your institution's quality.

So, what makes a good trustee? How do you know whom to ask and whom to reject? I like Harvard Business School professor Regina Herzlinger's word choice: She says that board members should have "footprints." What mark has a prospective trustee already made on her community? Has she reached out to make a difference in other organizations? Has she demonstrated a level of thinking, energy and commitment that would contribute to your board? Has she expressed an interest in your theater? Most important, does this person display personal qualities that would make her effective in the culture and style of your organization? In other words, does she tend to be a one-person show, or does she play well with others? Try not to get carried away with an impressive-sounding candidate if she's not what the board really needs.

Let's say the committee has identified several candidates. Now what? Get to know them better. The indirect way is to offer opportunities to participate in committee work without offering a board seat. Would she serve on the gala committee? Would she sell tickets to an event? Would she contribute expertise to a committee? Perhaps you have a junior board. These situations give you a better opportunity to size someone up (and to allow them to do likewise) and connect each candidate with the mission of the theater.

More often, you take the direct route. You meet with the candidate. Who meets with the candidate? The best combination is the managing director and one or two members of your committee. Sometimes you include the board president. But don't make the conversation so lopsided that your candidate feels uncomfortable. Frequently, the committee member is the chair, but it's important that all committee members have a stake in the decisions and participate in the screening process. Besides, each committee member has her own unique testimony to offer.

This meeting is not a telephone call. It's a face-to-face meeting, frequently over breakfast, lunch or tea. The time you spend with the candidate communicates the importance of your conversation. The meeting is not an automatic invitation. But this can be tricky. It's best to establish the ground rules when asking the person to meet with you: "I chair the board development committee of CENTERSTAGE. I'd like you to meet Michael Ross, our managing director. We want to tell you more about us and explore your interest in CENTERSTAGE."

You may treat the candidate to a lovely lunch at a good restaurant, but consider, instead, lunch at your theater—a simple salad in your managing director's office. When you bring a potential trustee into your space, she gets a palpable sense of who you are and what you value. One first-time visitor to CENTERSTAGE, upon seeing our administrative offices, said, "You certainly don't put your money into your office space." Later on, when we asked him for a gift, I was glad he knew that about us.

What do you talk about at lunch? What do you want your potential trustee to understand right from the start?

> "I tell candidates that the place is very well run. I give them expectations about time commitments, committee assignments and financial expectations."

> "I tell them if they cannot develop a passion for the organization and don't believe in our form of theater, they shouldn't join the board. Service on this board should not be just a line on their résumé. Passion can be cultivated, but is essential to some degree from the start."

> "New trustees should know the importance of the artistic vision. If you don't attend the productions, you miss the reward."

This introductory meeting with a potential candidate tells a story about your theater and the people who lead it. Do you have high expectations? Are you prepared? Are you friendly? Now is the time to communicate your own commitment and love of your theater. What are some of your favorite productions?

Let your conversation evolve. Although you have specific points to make, you also want to get to know the person and to test the issue of chemistry. *Listen.* What does the candidate want to talk about? What are her memorable theater experiences? Do you sense a depth of interest from her in your theater? Does she have a curiosity or want to know more? Does she communicate a respect for the art and for artists? You can meet with someone who doesn't necessarily know or love theater, but you need someone who is doing it for the right reasons and has a willingness to embrace the culture.

Be clear. What is the mission of the theater? What is a trustee expected to do? How many committees are there? What are the financial expectations? What are the fundraising requirements? How much time do you expect them to give? Clearly communicated expectations are best coming from a trustee rather than the managing director. Review the current season and provide an overview of the theater's financial condition (last season's annual financial statement and the latest financial status report are good to share).

The question most frequently asked by prospective trustees is: "How much do you expect me to give?" Some boards believe in a "give or get" philosophy that explicitly states the amount of money each trustee is required to produce. If your board values racial, social and economic diversity, establishing a specific dollar amount may get in the way of achieving the desired balance. Another approach is to ask that a trustee's contribution reflect that your theater is among his top two or three philanthropic priorities. And an even more specific way is to provide a new trustee with the range of trustee giving, including a mean and an average, when you request a specific amount. That sets a tangible benchmark. Create your trustee giving pyramid. It could look something like this:

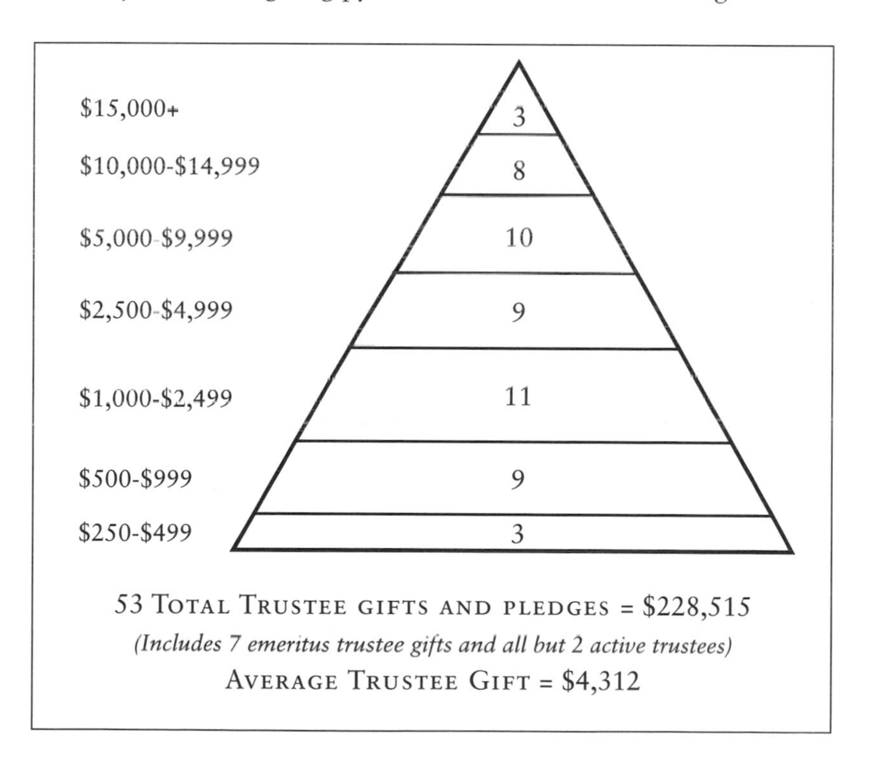

Successful invitations focus specifically on why your theater wants this person: "We need a depth of experience working with not-for-profit boards." "We are embarking on a real-estate project and could use your help." What does she bring to the table that your theater needs? How will you use her talents, expertise and connections? Set designer Doug Stein puts it this way: "What is this person's special gift?" If a potential trustee asks, "Why me? What do I bring to your board?" you'd better have an answer ready.

The first meeting with a prospective trustee is also a great time for a tour of the facilities. Introduce her to artists and artisans as you visit the shops, briefly engaging them in conversation about their current projects. You want your prospective trustee to taste and smell the passion of your theater. I love to actually take people onstage, ask them to point out where they usually sit and show them how visible they are to an actor onstage. The intimacy between actor and audience becomes palpable.

If you have a good sense of the candidate's interest, the meeting can conclude with a description of the committee's process. Tell her you are delighted to know of her interest and that the committee will conclude its work by nominating and electing candidates at the June (or whenever) board meeting. Set a time when you will get back to your candidate, and write her a letter thanking her for her time and interest. If and when a person is elected, be sure to welcome her by phone and letter and give her a general idea of when to expect an orientation.

What if the committee has identified several people who would be great additions to the board but who haven't shown much interest in your theater? These potential trustees are notable for their personal qualities and have the capacity to give of their time and their money. How do you develop that interest? How do you sow the seeds of future involvement? No wonder we call it "cultivation."

Cultivation is all about making friends for your theater through relationship building. Look for ways to connect people with your art. Buy four subscriptions rather than two, for example, using the extra seats for cultivation opportunities. Invite a group of friends from church or the office for dinner at the theater, and ask someone from the theater to speak during dessert about the current production. A backstage dinner is always engaging. One of my favorite locations at CENTERSTAGE is the costume shop, lit by votive candles, but still surrounded by the paraphernalia and detritus of the work, including mannequins dressed in costumes. We also entertain on the paint deck or in the scene shop. The most seductive setting is dinner on the stage itself. These encounters may result in a financial contribution or, ultimately, a board seat, but on a certain level, it doesn't matter. You're developing a network of friends.

Orientation

What can you do to prepare new board members for their board service?

> "Expectations need to be clear. Financial statistics and details on how the organization operates are critical. The history of the organization and its mission, goals and culture must be talked about."

> "Spend a lot of time on the strategic plan—not just what the plan is but how you got to it. By understanding a theater's plan and how you are implementing it, new trustees will know a great deal about the theater."

> "I would appreciate a Q&A of fifteen questions prepared by people in the community."

> "A better understanding of how CENTERSTAGE supports a trustee in fundraising is needed. For example, who puts together a dinner at CENTERSTAGE? Who picks up what costs? What is the availability of complimentary tickets?"

Who's invited?

All new trustees, the chair of the board development committee, the board president, the managing director and the artistic director. At CENTERSTAGE, we also include our resident dramaturg and department heads at scheduled times. Consider inviting resident artists for part of the meeting. Starting from day one, you are building a team.

When should you hold orientation?

New trustees are usually oriented sometime before the first board meeting of the season or before the board begins its work for the year. At CENTERSTAGE, we schedule our orientation session in August. If necessary, you can provide more than one orientation date. Part of the work of the meeting, however, is developing camaraderie among new trustees, mentors, staff and current trustees. Collegiality works better when it's created from the beginning.

How long should the orientation be?

If you're lucky, you can schedule a two-hour morning meeting followed by a working lunch. That gives you about three hours for information and conversation.

What is the agenda?

1. This is the time to tell stories about defining moments in the theater's history. How was the theater founded? Why? By whom? How has it changed as the organization has grown?
2. Let the artists speak about the mission. You want the new trustees to catch their passion. What do the artists value? What are their interests?
3. What is the board's relation to the art? If the board has a hands-off policy toward play selection, be clear about what the artistic vision is.
4. Not-for-profit, resident, professional, regional theater: What do these terms mean?
5. What are your big concerns and challenges? Give an overview of the kind of work the board will be doing over the next few years.
6. What is the big financial picture of the theater? What are the significant numbers trustees should pay attention to—subscriptions, single-ticket sales, contributed revenue, ratio of contributed versus earned income? Where do you get your income and how do you spend it?
7. What are your trustees' responsibilities? (Though you covered this topic in a preelection visit with each prospective trustee, it's important to repeat it.)
8. Maybe you'd like the chair of the finance committee to present the operating budget, or the chair of the development committee to talk about annual fund goals. This is another way for trustees to meet each other—it's always more effective when trustees interact directly with their peers.

9. ALTHOUGH YOU MAY DECIDE TO HAVE DEPARTMENT HEADS speak briefly, your priority is new trustees learning *their* job, not the staffs'.
10. IF YOUR THEATER HAS A HANDBOOK, PROVIDE A CURSORY OVERview of its contents: bylaws, trustee address list, spouse names, contact preferences, staff list, etc. Providing an informational booklet to take home avoids information overload at the orientation.

WHAT'S THE NOT-SO-HIDDEN AGENDA?

1. ORIENTATION IS THE START OF YOUR TRUSTEES' EDUCATION IN board style and culture. Trustees need to know basic issues: Do meetings start on time? What do I do if I disagree with a board decision? Whom do I call? How do trustees handle calls from the press? Can I contact senior staff directly? What if I hate a show? What if my friend tells me she hated the last show? What do I say?
2. MOST IMPORTANT: ORIENTATION FORMALLY STARTS YOUR process of getting to know one another. Allow time to make a personal and emotional connection with each other and with the art. From this very first meeting, establish that the experience with your theater is holistic—not just business. For example, as part of the around-the-table introductions, you could ask each new trustee to respond to the question: "What was my first (or most memorable) experience of theater?"
3. CONSIDER THE IDEA OF SETTING UP A MENTORING PROGRAM FOR new trustees. Pair each new trustee with a veteran trustee. The members of the board development committee make good mentors. Sometimes an obvious fit suggests itself; sometimes an unexpected pairing works better. A mentor is a first-year buddy, so he does what a buddy would do: He calls to welcome the new trustee; he comes to orientation; he calls his mentee to remind her about an upcoming meeting, sits next to her at the meeting and introduces her to fellow trustees; maybe he invites her to lunch, perhaps with a fellow trustee.
4. THINK OF YOUR NEW TRUSTEES AS "NEW" FOR THEIR ENTIRE FIRST year. Cast your new trustees with sensitivity in their first-year committee assignments. Where will they fit best? CENTER-STAGE requires every new trustee to sit on the finance committee because numbers tell a story—the story of the theater's val-

ues and priorities—while simultaneously making the case for fundraising. Some theaters require a first-year stint on a development committee to underscore that fundamental need.

5. ORIENTATION CONTINUES IN A DIFFERENT WAY AS THE YEAR progresses. You're helping now to immerse new trustees in your theater's culture. Look out for them at board meetings. Call them to see how they are doing. And continue to provide opportunities for them to learn.

Education

The more knowledge a trustee has, the more effective she is on the board. The board development committee invests not only in the education of new trustees but also in the continuing education of all trustees. Educate your trustees about your organization's art and governance. Trustees need knowledge to be effective ambassadors for your theaters. Are they well informed about the current season? Can they field the tough questions: Why did your artistic director choose the last play? Why do you do so much (or not enough) Shakespeare? Why don't you do last year's Broadway hit?

Trustees need to know about your theater and its history. How and why was it founded? What is your mission? What values underpin your institution? What kind of art do you produce and why? What kind of choices do your artists have to make?

Board meetings are an opportunity to deepen your trustees' understanding of the art of making theater. The artistic director's report is an opportunity to share his thinking on current issues: "What play choices am I making? Why am I making these choices? What are my alternatives? Why do I love this play? What difficulties am I experiencing? What roles am I trying to cast? What factors affect play selection? Am I trying for a balance? If so, what is it?"

Here are two examples of programs that provide an interesting way in for trustees:

Arena Stage Board Internship Program

Arena Stage's Internship Program invites one or two trustees to participate in an in-depth look at the creation of a production, starting with the first rehearsal and culminating in the final two weeks before the first preview. All trustees are encouraged to participate, especially within their first year on the board. Trustee David Shiffrin describes his experience this way: "Each internship has been a deeply personal experience. Even if you attend only a few rehearsals, sit backstage one night during the performance, come to a dress rehearsal or attend one night in tech week, you get a perspective that is far richer than just sitting in the audience. It's given me a greater appreciation of the artistic process, and it's also given me a better basis from which to operate as a trustee."

CENTERSTAGE's Board Discussion Program

CENTERSTAGE schedules Board Discussions before the opening of every production. Trustees host these discussions in their homes on Sunday evenings at 7:30, and other trustees and their spouses are invited. Some bring their interested children. Invited artists are drawn from the cast currently in rehearsal, the director, the dramaturg and occasionally a designer (anyone who can be enticed by light refreshments to interact with our board after a long week of rehearsals). A discussion of roughly one hour follows a modest time for socializing. The director and dramaturg open the discussion with information about the play, its history (if relevant) and our production. Why did we choose this play? What are the challenges? A discussion between artists and trustees follows. The event is an informal social occasion that prepares the board to talk about the production to our community. Best of all, it allows trustees and artists to get to know each other better.

Trustees also need to know about the larger theater world. What does it mean to be a not-for-profit, regional, resident theater? What is the history of not-for-profit theaters? How many exist today? What are the similarities and differences between your theater and others in your budget size? What national issues affect these theaters? How do the economics of your theater compare with the industry? Who are your competitors? How do they affect your work and your ticket sales? What are your community's demographics? How do they influence ticket sales and future funding? What is Theatre Communications Group? How can trustees participate in TCG? What does *American Theatre* magazine offer trustees?

Public funding is a complex jigsaw puzzle that trustees need to understand. How is theater funded in the U.S.? What is the NEA? Does your organization receive an NEA grant? If so, how much and why? How has that funding changed over the last decade? Are you funded by a state arts agency? Who runs the agency? Do you have a state advocacy organization? How can you advocate for better funding? Are you funded by a city or local agency? How can a trustee affect that funding?

Board meetings are obvious opportunities to invite outside speakers knowledgeable about the local or the national scene. Invite the executive director of your state arts agency or your city arts agency to your board meeting. Invite the mayor. Invite someone from TCG. The topic doesn't even have to be theater-specific. Ben Cameron, executive director of TCG, believes in infusing meetings with speakers with cutting-edge thinking, which in turn makes us more informed trustees. Lifelong learners make the best trustees.

As you plan agendas, don't forget to look internally. Board meetings are a chance to get to know the staff better, especially the production staff. Get to know the inner workings of the costume department, the sound, lighting and props departments. Choose a department that plays a significant role in the current production. Encourage trustees to attend first readings, designer presentations and dress rehearsals.

Trustees also need education about the governance process itself, knowledge that will help them be better trustees. Trustees come to us with varying board experience. It's easy to presume knowledge that doesn't exist. How do you create opportunities to level the playing field?

Governance has become a hot topic in the not-for-profit (and for-profit) arenas. Circulate articles about governance. In addition to books that you can make available to new trustees, speakers on effective trusteeship are available to talk to your theater. Once a year, consider inviting a speaker to your board meeting to discuss the roles of trustees in the development process, financial oversight, the nominating process, the roles of board and staff, etc.

Meetings offer opportune moments to educate. After a spirited discussion, maybe it's a good time to remind trustees of the confidential nature of their work. Or if a decision isn't unanimous, maybe it's a good time to remind trustees about the collective nature of board decisions and what to do if a trustee continues to disagree about a particular issue.

Once a year, ask each committee chair to report not only on the business of the committee, but also on the role her committee plays in the larger work of the board and how the committee and the board work together. This "need to know" is especially true for the finance committee and the board development committee. An annual retreat is another opportunity for education on topics ranging from artistic policy to training in fundraising skills.

Encourage trustee attendance at TCG's Fall Forum, designed specifically for trustees, or TCG's National Conference. When a trustee or a staff member attends, ask her to network, bring back ideas and report at a board meeting.

Evaluation

Now for the hard part: The board development committee has the responsibility to evaluate board members annually. It can do this implicitly or explicitly, informally or formally.

Let's say you're more comfortable with an informal assessment. Once a year, the committee discusses who is rotating off the board and who is invited to stay on for another term. You consider:

- Does the trustee know your theater? Is she a passionate advocate?
- Does her presence on the board make a difference?
- Does she attend meetings faithfully?
- Does her annual gift indicate that your theater is a philanthropic priority?
- Does she contribute time and talent?

The committee also reviews the entire current board. Is anyone's "disconnect" egregious enough to focus on? Is anyone's board presence making little or no difference—a wasted opportunity that could be better used by someone else? With such a trustee, you have choices. The first is to talk with her (make it a two-way conversation). The president of the board or perhaps the chair of the board development committee visits with the trustee. What is going on in her life? What are the demands on her time? How has her board experience been? What is or isn't working from her perspective? The idea is that in a mutual conversation, you help the trustee evaluate herself. Lives have many chapters. For some, the current chapter, with its responsibilities of family and work, doesn't allow for volunteer time. That's fine. The president or chair simply says: "Thank you. We are grateful for all you have done. We wish you well. We hope you will always be a friend of our theater." The second choice is a more hard-nosed version of the first. It's unilateral and precludes a conversation: "We recognize that this is not the right time in your life to participate as a board member in the work of our theater. Thank you, etc." The challenge is to find the line between counseling and confronting and to know when to employ each.

The participation of each and every trustee should make a difference to your theater, but it is also not inconsistent to define broadly the standards for what makes a trustee effective. Using her unique talents, each trustee strengthens your theater, makes it a little better. One brings in church members, developing bridges to a new audience. Another negotiates better insurance rates. Another, a young dot-com-er who can't come to meetings, raises dollars using email. It's not that you shouldn't set high standards, but your standards should allow for diversity of talent as well as wealth.

Some boards use more formal means, even actual contracts that formalize the board's expectations and the trustee's responsibilities. But contracts come with a caveat: The style with which you choose to communicate says something about your board culture, so carefully consider the *how*, not just the what and why. Some contracts are so legalistic and detailed that the fact you are a creative institution gets lost. Other contracts are so standardized that they automatically suggest you aren't interested in a diversity of talents, much less anything else.

One effective but time-consuming method is for the president of the board to meet personally with each trustee once a year. A personal meeting is the single best way to build a relationship. It can also underscore the implicit contract between a trustee and your theater. Ideally, the president of the board chooses to do this. However, the meetings could be shared among members of the board development committee. These one-on-one conversations may include an exploration of how the trustee would like to contribute. What committees would she prefer to serve on? Where does the theater need her help? Will she consider buying a table for the gala? The visit may also include a personal request for her annual gift.

Another way to think about your trustees' experience is to understand what makes a satisfied trustee. A satisfied trustee feels that she is growing as a person. She has a sense of achievement. She is recognized for her good work. Occasionally, it's worthwhile to turn the tables. Is your theater offering your trustees a satisfying experience? Do they have a chance to learn? Do you say "thank you" enough? Do you laugh a lot? Do you create a sense of community and inclusiveness? Do you make a sincere effort to get to know your trustees? Do you communicate your respect for them? Finally, do you have a true partnership between trustees and staff?

Conclusion

If you have done your work well, you should have the basis for an effective, energetic and creative board, capable and ready to support your theater and your art.

> "The board president sets the tone. Leadership, leadership, leadership."

> "One of the things that is special about CENTERSTAGE is that it is not managed as a 'one-size-fits-all' organization. Our leaders have done a terrific job of engaging trustees on an individual basis and figuring out how they can best contribute to the theater."

> "Understanding the mission makes an effective board: seeing the results of your work on an ongoing basis; evaluating what worked and what didn't; being honest about how you're doing; being unafraid to face hard times and hard questions; building relationships with the people you work with."

> "First, give the board meaningful work. Then, say, 'Thank you.'"

> "Cheerlead for the contributions and achievements of the board and staff. Cheerlead again."

Effective board development:

- Ensures that experienced, savvy trustees serve on the board development committee
- Recognizes that every board has a culture and takes an active role in creating it
- Makes recruiting new trustees a twelve-month responsibility of identifying and cultivating prospects
- Recruits candidates because of an identified board need
- Clearly explains the responsibilities of a trustee, including financial contributions, to prospective candidates
- Carefully orients new trustees
- Values ongoing education about your theater and its governance
- Evaluates all trustees annually, and is not afraid to say, "Goodbye," when necessary.

THE NEW WORK OF THE NONPROFIT BOARD

Barbara E. Taylor, Richard P. Chait and Thomas P. Holland

EFFECTIVE GOVERNANCE BY THE BOARD of a nonprofit organization is a rare and unnatural act. Only the most uncommon of nonprofit boards function as they should by harnessing the collective efforts of accomplished individuals to advance their institution's mission and long-term welfare. A board's contribution is meant to be strategic, the joint product of talented people brought together to apply their knowledge and experience to the major challenges facing the institution.

What happens instead? Nonprofit boards are often little more than a collection of high-powered people engaged in low-level activities. Why? The reasons are myriad. Sometimes the board is stymied by a chief executive who fears a strong board and hoards information, seeking the board's approval at the last moment. Sometimes board members lack sufficient understanding of the work of the institution and avoid dealing with issues requiring specialized knowledge. Individual board members may not bring themselves fully to the task of governance, because board membership generally carries little personal accountability. And often the powerful individuals who make up the board are unpracticed in working as members of a team. No matter which cause predominates, nonprofit board members are often left feeling discouraged and underused and the organization gains no benefit from their talents. The stakes remain low, the meetings process-driven, the outcomes ambiguous and the deliberations insular. Many members doubt whether a board can have any real power or influence.

The key to improved performance is discovering and doing what we call the *new work* of the board. Trustees are interested in results. High-powered people lose energy when fed a steady diet of trivia. They may oblige management by discussing climate control for art exhibitions, the condition of old steam lines or the design of a new logo, but they get charged up when searching for a new CEO, successfully completing a capital campaign or developing and implementing a strategic plan. *New work* is another term for work that matters.

New work has four basic characteristics. First, it concerns itself with crucial, do-or-die issues central to the institution's success. Second, it is driven by results that are linked to defined timetables. Third, it has clear measures of success. Finally, it requires the engagement of the organization's internal and external constituencies. New work generates high levels of interest and demands broad participation and widespread support.

New Work Requires New Practices

New work defies the conventions that have regulated board behavior in the past. Whereas the customary work of a nonprofit board is limited to scrutinizing management, new work requires new rules of engagement and unorthodox ways of fulfilling a board's responsibilities. The pressures on most nonprofits today are too great for the old model to suffice. Nonprofit leaders can take the following steps to improve board practices:

1. Find out what matters. Traditionally, nonprofit boards and CEOs have agreed that management defines problems and recommends solutions. A board might refine management's proposals but rarely rejects any. Why? Few trustees know the industry or the institution well enough to do more, and those who do dread being labeled as meddlers or micromanagers. Board mem-

bers sometimes are made to feel that asking a thorny question or advancing an alternative opinion is disloyal to the administration. A vote on an issue is a vote on the CEO. But how can a reactive, uninformed board know what opportunities the organization is missing? And how much damage must the organization sustain before the board realizes something is amiss?

To do new work, trustees and management together must determine the important issues and the agenda of the organization. Trustees need to understand what the CEO sees as the critical issues. They also need to know what other stakeholders and industry experts think, because no chief executive knows enough to be a board's sole supplier of information and counsel. Knowledgeable trustees can help inform the CEO's judgment. They can also perform a useful function for the CEO by focusing the organization's attention on issues that are unpopular within it or that fall outside the staff's capabilities. In addition, the board can find out what matters by engaging in the following sets of activities:

- Make the CEO paint the big picture. The litmus test of the CEO's leadership is not the ability to solve problems alone but the capacity to articulate key questions and guide a collaborative effort to formulate answers. As one member of a museum's board observes, "What I want most from the president are the big ideas." The CEO must be willing to share responsibility and the board must be willing to follow the CEO's lead—and ask questions. "If you don't do that," says one college trustee, "the board doesn't really have a clue about what is going on. When a problem arises and the CEO needs the trustees, they won't own the problem or be willing to help solve it."

  The CEO should review the organization's foremost strategic challenges annually with the board. The board, for its part, must consider whether the CEO accurately targeted and defined the issues. This is a moment, maybe *the* moment, in which the board adds value. Together, the CEO and the board must agree on the institution's priorities and strategic direction. Those considerations, in turn, will shape the work of the board and its evaluation of the CEO.

  The board of a college in the South has formalized this process successfully. At a retreat each January, the CEO and the trustees rank the most important challenges facing the institution. Then the board structures its committees to reflect those priorities. Last year, for example, the board concluded that marketing and technological infrastructure were its top concerns. The board formed task forces of trustees and constituents to study those issues, to specify the decisions the board would have to make during the coming year and to clarify the board's needs for information and education. At the May board meeting, the task forces provided initial reports and the board decided how to organize in order to pursue the issues. Trustees also developed measurable expectations for the president that were linked to the board's top concerns.

- Get to know key stakeholders. Boards and CEOs have to know what matters to the constituents they serve. The interactions of the old work—which were mostly social events and show-and-tell sessions—will not do. New work requires two-way communication. As a college president remarks, part of the reason for such communication is "to make the board vulnerable to constituents"—to make it accessible and accountable rather than insulated from the ordinary life of the institution. In that spirit, the boards of several colleges now meet routinely with leaders of student, faculty and alumni bodies to explore matters of common concern.

  Consider the example of a residential treatment center for children with emotional disabilities. When a major benefactor died, the center needed to find new sources of income. While interviewing leaders of social service organizations (a major source of referrals), several board members were shocked to discover that the center was seen as elitist and interested only in easy cases. In fact, many professionals referred the easy cases to less expensive care and assumed that the center would reject the difficult ones. Alarmed by these misperceptions, the trustees formed a task force to guide a public relations effort. The board expanded to include trustees with ties to sources of referrals and strengthened its relationships with other constituents through educational events and joint programming. "I want to make sure this board is never again so out of touch with its community," said the board's chair at the end of the process.

  Close ties between the board and constituents unnerve CEOs who are determined to be the board's sole source of information and who fear that direct communication between trustees and stakeholders will weaken time-honored lines of authority. That reaction puzzles board members; as one college trustee asks, "Why not have students talk to trustees? What's there to hide? These are our clients. I'm old enough and smart enough to know that some people just want to complain. Trustees are as qualified as the president to interpret the views they express. The closer I get to reality, the better I can sympathize with and help the CEO."

- Consult experts. Many nonprofits are susceptible to competitive forces and to changes in public policy. Consider, for example, the impact of cuts in funding by the NEA on museums, or the effect of efforts to reform federally funded health care on hospitals. Unless trustees understand the basic economics, demographics and politics of the industry, boards will be hard pressed to separate the trivial from the significant and the good news from the bad. New work requires learning about the industry from many sources.

  One of those sources should be experts on the board itself. Although boards regularly recruit trustees with expertise in functional areas like finance, law and marketing, new work requires a board to have more than a few trustees with relevant professional expertise: physicians on a hospital's board, social workers on a clinic's board. Expert trustees can guide fellow board members through a foreign culture. For example, one Ivy League institution counted a former university president among its board members. At one point, he criticized his colleagues for second-guessing the administration's disciplining of a fraternity, saying, "I'd be furious if my board did this." The board backed off. And at a liberal arts college, a trustee who was a professor at another school helped educate the board about the complexities of measuring teaching quality and reallocating academic positions from departments with declining enrollments to those with growing demand. At the same time, he helped establish the board's credibility with the faculty.

  Another source of knowledge is outside experts. They can help boards understand competition, client demographics, trends in government support and public policy debates. For example, the board of a Protestant theological seminary faced with declining enrollment conferred with experts on professional education and the demographics of its own denomination. The trustees learned that their denomination's population would continue to decline, further eroding financial support for the seminary and job opportunities for new ministers. On its current course, the institution would be bankrupt in a few years. The seminary decided to leverage the strength of its high-quality faculty by becoming a resource to the broader Protestant community, offering theological education to laypeople and continuing education for church workers and ministers, both on campus and in local churches.

- Decide what needs to be measured. Corporate boards typically monitor a limited number of performance indicators. Those vital signs convey the company's overall condition and signal potential problems. Nonprofit boards often lack comparable data, largely because the trustees and the staff have never determined what matters most.

  Together, the board and management should identify ten to twelve critical indicators of success. For a college, that may mean scrutinizing its tuition discount (the average remission the institution gives to students as financial aid). For a museum, it may mean measuring its total return on endowment investments. For a hospital, the board may monitor occupancy rates. Distinctive strategies can suggest novel measures. A boarding school focusing on computer literacy monitored the ratio between students' dial-ups to the campus network and their phone calls from their dorm rooms for pizza delivery. A rising percentage of network calls meant that students were becoming more comfortable with new technology. Using comparable creativity, an orchestra with an aging subscriber base monitored ticket sales to single people in their twenties and thirties who had attended chamber music programs with wine and cheese receptions.

  Graphic comparisons against fiscal projections, past performance or industry norms focus a board's attention on crucial issues and remind trustees that the ultimate goal of the board is to influence those indicators in a positive way. As the CEO of a college in the Midwest says, "We have a set of key performance indicators, explicitly linked to the strategic plan, that are reviewed at every meeting. We even put them on a pocket-size card that trustees can carry around."

2. ACT ON WHAT MATTERS. In the world of *old work*, the lines were clearly drawn: The board remained on the policy-setting side of the net, management on the implementation side—and so the game of governance was played. In new work, the board and management are on the same side of the net as partners in both roles. The question is not, "Is this an issue of policy or implementation?" Rather, the question is, "Is the issue at hand important or unimportant, central or peripheral?"

   Today few nonprofits can risk barring the CEO from policy development or divorcing the board from policy implementation. In a capital campaign, establishing priorities and goals is "setting policy," identifying prospects and making calls is "implementation." In the search for a new CEO, determining selection criteria is "making policy," designing the procedure and conducting the interviews is "implementation." In brief, most important matters cannot be subdivided neatly into policy or administration.

   In many instances, implementation is far more consequential than formulation. For example, in face-to face meetings, trustees of a Catholic women's college persuaded affluent older alumnae to support a new institutional focus on serving poor minority women from the inner city. The board of another college, troubled by the decline in students able to pay full tuition, selected three trustees to assist the administration with the design of a marketing strategy aimed at attracting more students better able to pay.

   In another case, a university owned a commercial radio station. The board questioned how the station fit in with the school's mission. After deciding with the president that the university could turn profits from the sale of the station to better educational use, the trustees negotiated the transaction. Afterward, the president exulted, "This was the board at its best." The board members knew more than the staff about the radio business and about selling a major asset and they put that knowledge to use.

   Involving trustees in policy implementation can be critically important during a crisis. In the aftermath of the scandal at the United Way of America (the CEO used more than a million dollars of United Way money for personal expenses), the board and CEO of one local chapter agreed that each of the trustees would interview five business leaders to learn what the chapter might do to improve community support for an upcoming campaign. The advice was consistent: Admit that the national organization had blundered badly, stop all payments to the national headquarters until the charges were resolved, promise that all funds would remain in the community, allow donor-designated contributions, and promise that the board would issue a public report of allocations. The CEO and the trustees accepted those recommendations and inaugurated an intense public-relations effort that engaged every board member. In the end, the campaign was almost as successful as the previous year's and was substantially more successful than those of other chapters in the region. That would not have been the case had the board only set policy.

3. Organize around what matters. The board's new work must be organized to deal with the institution's priorities. That may seem self-evident, but boards often organize their work in functionally oriented committees (physical plant, finance, public relations) that channel trustees toward low-stakes operational decisions. For new work to happen, substance must dictate structure. Committees, work groups and task forces must mirror the institution's strategic priorities.

   For instance, a theological seminary replaced most of its operationally oriented committees with ones that reflected the major goals of the strategic plan: globalizing the curriculum, improving relations with local churches and providing continuing education for the ministry. The committees included trustees and constituents. One result: On the recommendation of the committee on church relations, the seminary established a clearinghouse to provide local churches with technical assistance in such areas as financial management, adult education and church governance.

   In another example, the board of a preeminent women's college created four "councils" (business affairs, campus affairs, external affairs and governance-board affairs) as umbrellas for clusters of standing committees. The council on campus affairs, for example, would oversee the activities and orchestrate the annual agendas of the student-life, admissions and trustee-faculty relations committees, which would meet only as needed. The council chairs would coordinate the annual agendas of the four councils and suggest strategic issues for in-depth discussion at board meetings.

   Task forces that include both constituents and nontrustee experts can tackle critical yet discreet matters, such as outsourcing certain functions or installing a total quality-management program. For example, the board of an independent day school appointed two task forces to explore accreditation issues with the appropriate state and federal agencies. The task forces gathered information about demographic trends, accreditation requirements and possible legislation that would affect independent schools. At a special Saturday session, the task forces presented their findings, the board discussed whether to become more selective and the task forces disbanded. The work had been done.

Such "tissue paper" task forces (use and discard) drive the board toward real-time results, multiply leadership opportunities and prevent longtime members from dominating standing committees. As one college trustee confesses, "Many of our standing committees don't really shape policy or identify needs. They're an empty ritual, a burden, not an asset. In contrast, task forces are very effective. For example, we're looking at the cost and shape of a marketing plan. A task force helped the board understand the problem and recommended directions. There was a material difference in the sense of ownership."

4. FOCUS MEETINGS ON WHAT MATTERS. Boards are boards only in meetings and yet meetings are where boards underperform most visibly. Many trustees think that lack of time is the most significant barrier to a board's ability to perform new work. In fact, the greater problem is the failure to determine what matters and to let that imperative drive the frequency, format and duration of board and committee meetings. And if a board can meet only infrequently or for short periods, trustees should consider realistically what they can deliver. The chair, the CEO and perhaps the executive committee should design each meeting by asking the questions: What is the purpose of this meeting? How can we organize it to fulfill that purpose? Four common responses will help illustrate the point:

- We need more background to make a decision. This answer calls for a discussion led by a moderator. Discussion sessions can engage and educate the entire board about issues facing the institution. The goal is to air views, invite questions and consider alternatives—not to win an argument. No specific decision is on the table and no votes are taken.

  Consider the case of the college board that was generally concerned—but not sufficiently informed—about the interrelated issues of student quality, tuition charges and financial aid. Each year, the finance committee, usually under pressure to balance next year's budget, presented a tuition recommendation to the board. The process afforded no practical opportunity for the board to study the causes and effects of tuition increases. Last year, the board convened explicitly to learn more about the effect of tuition and financial aid decisions on enrollment and student quality, as well as on the bottom line. Subsequently, the board devised principles to govern the finance committee's recommendation for the following year. Those principles included the decision to hold institutionally funded financial aid to below twenty-five percent of overall tuition, but to use grants to attract better students. The board also decided to increase average class size in order to free up resources to enhance learning partnerships, including student-faculty projects.

At another university, each of the board's key committees appears once a year before the whole board for a half-day session to present information on a substantive issue or special area. For example, the finance committee led a board session to explain capital budgeting, deferred maintenance and depreciation of assets. A task force on instructional technology, which included faculty and students, held a panel discussion to describe how technology was being used on their campus to transform the learning process. As a result of such sessions, reports the chair, "The whole board becomes more knowledgeable about the issues. The old bean-counters on the finance committee now see other aspects of the institution."

- We don't know what to do about a current problem. New work, by definition, grapples with complicated issues that defy easy solutions. Trustees and management must be able to present multiple perspectives and develop solutions that reflect the group's best thinking. A meeting's design is critical to making that happen. Discussion must center on the explicit question at hand, such as: What should be our top three priorities for the capital campaign? Or what specific steps can the board take to improve ties to the corporate community?

Small groups create a more comfortable environment for trustees to speak freely. Says one college board member, "I may have a comment worthy of sixteen pairs of ears, but not one worthy of sixty." Small groups provide venues for brainstorming, arenas where there are no dumb questions or insane ideas. A board member of a midwestern university explains, "Before we added small group discussions, all fifty trustees sat passively and listened to a few people impart information. The process was superficial, and substantive participation was limited to the executive committee. Small groups allow everyone to participate genuinely."

- We face a crisis. In times of crisis, business-as-usual must be pushed aside to allow the board to concentrate on the matter at hand. Crises might include the loss of a major source of funding, the sudden departure or death of the CEO, the rise of a competitor, or even a split within the board itself.

  For example, a local Alzheimer's Association chapter lost a major grant in 1993 and had no immediate prospects for significant new funding. The chair called a special meeting of the board to discuss restructuring the chapter's services. A review of the mission statement reminded trustees of the organization's purpose; an examination of what it would mean to reengineer the organization helped open up discussion of key issues. By the end of the meeting, board members accepted responsibility for specific tasks to help manage the crisis, explaining the chapter's mission to potential sponsors in the community, exploring the restructuring experiences of other chapters and examining with staff the best ways to smooth the transition to a smaller, more tightly focused organization.
- We need to deal with sensitive governance issues. Executive sessions without the CEO present open lines of communication among trustees. "We have an executive session after each board meeting," says one college trustee. "We feel free to bring up anything at all. This is a time for us to really ask questions and probe." Among the questions a board might entertain in an executive session are: Did we deal with the important issues? How did the meeting go? Can we better serve the CEO? Differences of opinion among trustees or between the board and the CEO can be treated more candidly in an executive session. Says one board member of a women's college in the South, "If there are sensitive issues, the executive session gives us a chance to counsel one another."

These examples of new work and new structures are far from exhaustive. Boards should experiment with different formats for different purposes. Use what works.

Leading the Way

Trustees protest regularly that artists, academics, physicians and other professionals stubbornly resist change. Yet, governing boards are among the least innovative, least flexible elements of nonprofits. Boards are as reluctant to forsake committees as faculty members and physicians are to eliminate departments. Trustees resist varied formats for board meetings more than musicians resist novel formats for concerts. And board members oppose new membership criteria as strongly as teachers oppose nontraditional certification.

This hypocrisy was plain to the chair of a midwestern university's board: "It's tough for a group like this to be self-conscious. They're classic CEOs. They can tell stories about empowerment and team building, but that's not how they got where they are. They are uncomfortable with questions like, 'How are we doing? And how should we improve?' Most of our members are heavy into productivity. The board isn't hesitant to ask faculty and administration to answer these questions. The board wants everyone else's time to be more efficient and effective, but the board should look for ways to improve, too."

Too often, trustees assume that organizational success proves that the board has performed well, even when there is little evidence that the board played a significant role and even when staff members say privately that the success was achieved despite the board. "Most boards have the attitude," a trustee of a women's college notes, "that if it ain't broke, don't fix it. But I think it's better to fix it before it breaks." A sympathetic explanation for the reluctance of most boards to experiment with substantial governance reforms would be the trustees' desire to do no harm. A less charitable explanation would be the trustees' desire to do no work.

Moving to new work *takes work*. As the CEO of a midwestern university recounted after the institution's board had changed, "It required getting people out of their little corners, the areas that they had learned and owned. They wanted to work on what they knew best and leave the rest to others. Now they had to rotate around and learn *everything* in order to govern the organization. They moved from being just guardians of the physical plant, overseers of the administration and suits with deep pockets."

Boards across the nonprofit sector are calling on institutions to change. As trustees demand evidence of productivity gains, efficient processes and enhanced outcomes, they should model the behavior they seek in others. If boards demonstrate the capacity to discard shibboleths, dismantle old structures and desert deeply ingrained modes of operation, the professional staff may follow suit. If the board does not do new work, the trustees' hypocrisy will be blatant and the value added by the board will be too meager to inspire organizational reform.

Originally published in the Harvard Business Review, September/October 1996. Permission to reproduce granted by Harvard Business School Publishing.

A GUIDE TO STRATEGIC PLANNING: Taking Aim Before You Fire

Ronnie Brooks

"READY! FIRE! AIM!" That's the planning sequence that many theaters follow. Pressed by deadlines (curtain times, foundation schedules, loan payments), organizations and the people who lead them are usually challenged just to keep functioning. They often cannot find either the time or the energy to launch a planning process to determine if where they are headed is where they really want to go, much less if the current path is the best way to get there. Who has the time to plan? Action is what's needed!

The answer is that you really cannot afford *not* to take the time. Action *is* needed, but a thoughtful planning process will increase the likelihood that the action you take will be wise and effective.

This essay seeks to make the case for developing some kind of *thinking* process that is collective, disciplined and forward-looking—in other words, a strategic planning process. The form of the process is not critical, nor is its duration or cost. What is important is that the process address a few key questions with a fair degree of rigor.

This article is organized around a set of key questions that form a guide to designing and implementing a strategic planning process. It is intended to be accessible and useful to people in very different kinds of organizations with varying resources and experience.

What Is Strategic Planning?

Strategic planning is a way of thinking. It connects an organization's purpose, its resources and the environment in which it functions. A theater cannot operate in a vacuum. In order to be effective, it must consider not only its own reason for being, but also the pool of money and talent it has to work with and the things going on in the social environment that will affect its ability to achieve its mission.

Good strategic planning is preparation for action. Intense thought, analysis and communication are necessary (but not sufficient) characteristics. The goal is action, and strategic planning is the rational process of organizing for action.

There are lots of different kinds of planning, and the consultant-rich field is full of jargon. It would be an impossible and probably useless task to try to get through the language here. However it is important to make a distinction between strategic planning and comprehensive (or long-range) planning. The latter is more like dreaming: Comprehensive planning tries to address *everything* an organization wants to accomplish. It is necessarily long-range and draws heavily on an articulation of the vision of the future the organization wants to create. It is idealistic in that it is based upon the most desirable situation the organization can envision, and it addresses everything the organization wants to achieve over a long period of time. In that sense, it is a useful exercise when time and resources allow, and can provide part of the context for strategic planning.

Strategic planning, unlike long-range planning, is not about *everything* an organization wants to accomplish. Rather, it is about the *most important* things for that organization to accomplish in the near future. Depending on the nature of the situation (Is the organization new or experienced? Does it have a high level of certainty about its resources? Are the times stable or turbulent?), the time frame for planning can be longer or shorter. Greater stability lengthens the planning horizon. These days, most organizations look at a period of one to three years, except when major capital projects are involved.

Beyond that time, the exercise is more like wishful thinking than a disciplined attempt to allocate real resources to real priorities.

Why Do It?

There are really only two reasons to do strategic planning. The first is change. Change is constant: a new artistic director, a different community demographic, a closed factory in town, a budget deficit or perhaps even a surplus. Strategic planning assumes change, and it also assumes the ability to act. If an organization does not think the world is changing or is not prepared to change the way it acts, there is no point bothering with strategic planning.

The second reason to do strategic planning is that choices need to be made. There is simply not enough time and resources to do everything that is desired. And a strategic planning process lets you set priorities and make those choices wisely—that is, in a way that reflects the purpose of the organization, makes the best use of available resources and takes into account the forces at work in the external environment.

Think of yourself in a canoe on a river. If you do not know the direction and the speed of the flow of water, you could find yourself swept away by the current or paddling upstream just to stay even. Strategic planning helps you determine where to put your canoe, which way to point it and how to use the force of the river to help carry you to the desired destination.

What Can It Accomplish?

Planning allows an organization to manage change and make wise choices, but the process can yield additional benefits to an organization as well. Keeping these benefits in mind will help an organization design a process that maximizes them.

Strategic planning can help an organization respond quickly to change. The planning process tries to anticipate change, and because of the thinking required in that analysis and the process of making choices, needed actions can occur quickly. A second benefit is that it focuses attention on a few important issues. Again, if the process is well managed, consensus will build within the group, bringing people together and preparing them for concerted action.

Strategic planning also gives people a framework for solving problems and building real teamwork. All of the people in the organization get to see what it is they have to contribute and how their work fits into the organization's overall success. Not only can this be a big motivator, but it can also be a way of maximizing both efficiency and effectiveness.

In many ways, the best strategic planning processes are educational. The people feeling only their little part of the proverbial elephant get a chance to see the whole beast and where it's headed. That information helps each and every person in the organization align his/her work with that of his/her colleagues. The result is better coordination, more clarity and increased energy.

What Makes for a Good Plan?

Above all, the plan that emerges from the planning process should be *useful*. It should guide action, keep people focused on the important things, make the best use of available resources and take maximum advantage of forces at work in the environment.

To achieve these things, a good plan is *clear*. It should not require a great deal of interpretation. In fact, the clearer and simpler a plan is, the more likely it is to stay alive as a guide to action. If it is turgid and voluminous, if people need to look up its major provisions, it will have very little real life within an organization.

A good plan builds on an organization's strengths and uses its resources fully and wisely. Resources that are thought to be strengths ("Our staff is so friendly!") but are inaccurately assessed ("Their staff is so grumpy!") can doom a plan in its implementation. And resources that are real assets but are ignored will needlessly reduce the performance of the organization. For example, skilled and enthusiastic board members can be real assets to the organization if they are recognized as such and prepared to use their skills. Consider a board member who is a respected community leader, willing to contact public officials regarding funding for the arts in general or for a specific zoning change to help the theater address its parking problem. If that board member is not contacted by staff, or not properly armed with relevant facts, or not told whom to contact, that resource may be wasted. Accurate assessment of all the organization's strengths—from staff capacity to community reputation—and effective allocation of those resources to key challenges are essential to a good plan.

A good plan takes advantage of opportunities that the external environment presents; at the same time, it tries to mitigate or avoid threats. Think again of the canoe and the current in the river. That current presents a force moving in the world. If the paddler is able to find a way to use that current, he can expand the resources available to him in his journey. Without that perspective, he may find himself wasting energy paddling upstream or trying to change the direction of the river's flow.

As you think about getting started, it is important to realize that the process of strategic planning need not be complicated. Many steps can be followed in a reasonably logical manner. In each step, it is important to focus on what needs to be accomplished. In some organizations, important steps may already have been taken, while in others extra time and resources may be required. So what are these steps, and what critical questions must each address?

The Steps in a Strategic Planning Process: A Simple Model

1. Planning to Plan: Designing the Planning Process

Although the process of strategic planning is logical and rational, it is neither automatic nor easy. Therefore, it is a good idea to "plan to plan" and be sure you design a process that will be effective for your organization. You want a plan that will energize and focus the organization. Therefore, it is important that you think through what the process should look like and answer the following questions:

- Who should be involved?
- How much time should we spend?
- How much will this cost?
- Do we need outside help or can we do this ourselves?

There are two rules to remember here. First, you should design a process that is appropriate to the culture, experience and resources of your organization. If you are part of a small organization that has never done planning before, it is probably appropriate to have a very simple and informal process that brings people together for a short time, does not require too much analysis and educates people about the process step by step. If the organization is facing a lot of contentious issues or there are clear factions to be reckoned with, it is probably desirable to have an outside facilitator, focus initially on the external context, and relax the schedule of decision-making. At the same time, it is important to design a process sensitive to the time frame in which decisions are required, such as the budget cycle, the production schedule or key personnel changes.

Second, involve key leaders from the very beginning. Leadership is an essential ingredient for success. Before the process begins, make sure that the leadership of the organization understands the nature of strategic planning, endorses the purpose for undertaking the process and the process design and sees that the process has adequate resources (time, money and attention) to be successful. This admonition applies to both staff and board leadership. In the context of a theater, it is important that the strategic planning process involve those with both artistic and administrative responsibilities, since both are essential to the theater's ultimate success. In fact, it is the planning process that can expand understanding of the way in which the two are intertwined.

When designing the process and deciding who really needs to be involved and in what way, think about the people who are in a position to thwart the plan's implementation if they are *not* in agreement with the results of the planning process. They are the ones who must be involved in some way, though not necessarily in every meeting all the time.

Planning to plan is a key step in ensuring implementation. Remember, effective action is what the process is designed to achieve. The all-too-frequent alternative is what some have called "SPOTS" (Strategic Plans On The Shelf).

Two common errors that can give strategic planning a less-than-stellar reputation are designing a process that fails to fit with an organization (it is too long or too boring or too detailed), or one that never engages the key leadership needed for implementation. Avoid these and you have greatly increased your chances for effective planning.

A third frequently made error in the planning process is that participants begin by making decisions about what they need to do and laying plans for doing it before they have defined the shared context for their work. On occasion a person will come into the planning process and declare, "We need to create an endowment fund," or, "We need to do a musical," before they have agreed on why they even continue to operate.

2. Articulating Our Purpose

Thus the second step in the planning process is articulating the purpose for which the organization exists—its mission. At its core, the mission statement must explain who you are and why you exist. It is the beacon that shines into the future and lights the way for the organization.

A mission statement provides a motivating sense of purpose and direction for the organization, and it provides guidance when it comes time to make difficult choices. It is what all people in the organization have in common, and it is the glue that holds them together. Therefore, it should be the expression of what the organization believes the world needs and that it can provide.

A good mission statement is *short*, so that people can remember it. It is *compelling* in a way that makes it worth committing one's energies to. It is *understood* and *shared* within the organization and does not require much interpretation. And it is *useful* in providing real guidance when choices need to be made.

Some organizations place comity above clarity—they burden their mission statement with several conjunctions linking too many verbs because they want to avoid the pain of leaving someone's idea out of the statement. For example, a mission statement might say that the theater produces plays *and* educates kids *and* entertains *and* brings the community together *and* provides a transformative cultural experience. It well may do all those things, but the mission statement must make clear what is the core purpose that the theater exists to serve.

One way to avoid this problem is by having planning participants articulate why each of them is present, what they cherish about the theater and its work and what they believe is fundamental to its purpose. Have the person guiding the process take notes on those core elements and then later—separate from the group—draft up two or three possible statements for the group to consider at a future meeting. (Drafting mission statements within the full group is a surefire way to derail the process. People lose their focus, haggle over language and become bored and intransigent at the same time.)

Defining the mission is an important anchor to the planning process, so do it carefully. Clarity of purpose is critical to both the definition of success and the achievement of it. Take the time to understand why the organization exists—not everything it may do, but the one thing it *must* do. A real discussion among key stakeholders in the mission can really pull the organization together and help it understand whom it exists to serve and what is the difference it seeks to make in the world.

3. Understanding the Context in Which We Are Operating

If strategic planning prepares an organization to make wise choices in pursuit of its purpose, it is important to understand what is going on in the environment that will affect the organization's ability to achieve that purpose. For example, the demographic trend toward a growing number of retired people combined with their relative increase in wealth could suggest such things as greater audience in matinees, a bigger pool of volunteers in the ticket office or gift shop, or—for theaters in northern climes—reduced sales for January shows.

There are several ways to accomplish this task of understanding your environment. At the most elemental level, it is helpful to simply ask people about changes they have noticed in different areas relevant to the organization's mission. This can be done by asking people to reflect on changes they see in the theater field, the community they serve or the economy upon which they and their patrons depend. What is happening to the people you care about, to your colleagues and competitors? These changes or trends can be classified as political, economic, social or technological. ("PEST" is a helpful acronym.)

A slightly more sophisticated approach has participants do some research on trends in each of these areas and then project their possible impact on the organization's key constituencies (e.g., audiences, employees, donors, sponsors and community members) and on its principal business activities (e.g., securing production rights, hiring actors, pricing and selling tickets or educating school groups).

Whatever the approach, encouraging discussion of the trends put forward will enable people to note that most of these changes present both a negative side that can be a threat to the organization and a positive side which might later be construed as an opportunity. The key point is to be able to understand the forces "out there" that affect your ability to move in your chosen direction. You want to ride the wave rather than crash into it.

4. Recognizing Our Assets

The internal analysis identifies what the organization has to work with, including the strengths or assets that can be used to implement the plan. These fall into a variety of categories and can be identified through a simple listing process that covers things, such as people and their talents, facilities and capital equipment, money, subscriber base, etc. It is also helpful in preparation for the planning process to visit with key stakeholders, such as season ticket holders and major funders, and have them respond to these early questions about what they value about the organization and its work, what they see as its strengths, what they think will affect the organization in the future. Checking in with stakeholders provides a reality check for an organization that otherwise may overlook important factors or make up assets that don't really exist.

Some planners also take time to identify organizational weaknesses. For reasons stated earlier, this is not always helpful to the process. It can cause carping or finger-pointing without providing useful information. A good plan is based on strengths that exist and assets that can be applied in the future. Spending time on what is lacking adds little. If the organization needs something in order to progress, then that need will emerge as one of the strategic issues in the next phase.

5. Identifying the Critical Questions the Plan Must Address

Up to this point in the process, the attention of the participants has been on drawing the picture of the world as it exists for the organization. The participants have identified their "true north," clarifying the fundamental purpose of the organization, which will be used to set the overall direction. They have described the forces at work in the external environment that will affect the work they do, and they have taken stock of the assets they can use to move in the desired direction. And in this process, there has been involvement of key leadership and consultation with important stakeholders. It is almost time to plan!

But first there is one more critical step: Articulate and prioritize the key strategic issues the plan must address. One of the values of strategic planning is that it lets you sift through a lot of information and focus the attention and energy of an organization on a few priorities that fundamentally affect the direction and success of the organization. These are the key *strategic issues*: policy questions or choices that relate to something fundamental about the organization, such as the field it is in, whom it serves, what kinds of services it provides or how activities are financed or managed. A strategic issue is one that has a fundamental impact on an organization's purpose, position in the community, programs and operations. In the case of a theater, it might relate to the kind of plays it produces, the audience it seeks to attract or its ticket-pricing structure.

This is a critical stage in the process and the most difficult to do in a truly systematic way. Strategic issues arise out of the interaction between external forces and internal resources, but the catalyst for recognizing those issues can come from anywhere. Thus, it is especially important to provide some freedom and creativity here, particularly if the organization has done strategic planning several times in the past. There is an understandable tendency to narrow in too quickly on issues that were identified in the past.

At this point, it is critical to focus on the issues first—not what to do about them. Too often, people identify issues, frame them in a biased way and settle into the fact that all issues are problems. Such an approach really dampens enthusiasm for the planning process.

One way to keep that from happening is to ask participants to identify strategic issues as questions to which there can be more than one answer. For example, the first instinct might be to say, "We need more money for our education program." But on reflection, addressing the issue as, "How can we get the resources needed to support programs for school children?" will open up more possibilities for resolution.

Once the group has generated a full list of possible strategic issues, it is important to prioritize them so the group can deal with them in an orderly fashion. There are numerous ways to sort them out, and the method selected will depend on the number of issues, the nature of the issues and the level of consensus in the group. It is important, however, not to simply cast a vote. Give people a chance to reflect on the issues and understand their meaning, scope and potential impact. Before actually asking people to indicate their priority, it can be helpful to ask them to consider each issue in terms of several different criteria, such as how central it is to the mission (Will this have a big impact on what we do?), how controllable the issue is (How much of a difference can our organization make?) or how urgent it is (What will be the consequences if no action is taken?). All of the issues identified are important to the organization, and they will arise throughout the process. The key factor here is naming them, thinking together about them and collectively deciding upon a place to begin.

6. Setting Goals

Up to this point, the process has been preparation for creating a plan. We have set the context, and if the process has proceeded smoothly, the participants have a shared view of what issues the organization must address and in what order. It is now time to set some goals for the organization.

Starting with the highest priority issue, the group needs to articulate what it will consider success and how that success will be recognized. For example, if the top-priority strategic issue is, "How can our theater increase our audience?" the group might work to envision what success would look like by saying, "Success is having eighty percent of available seats filled with paying customers." Alternatively, success might be a ten percent increase in ticket sales each year for three years. Or it might be defined as doubling the subscriber rate.

The way success is envisioned and measured greatly affects how it is achieved. If a goal is simply defined as "increase audiences," it is so general that it does not give much guidance as to the type or degree of improvement needed. Would the organization be satisfied if the audience was increased by one person or by one percent over the previous year? Clarity in goal-setting gives strength.

For each of the priority issues, goals should be set and agreed upon by the planning group. It is also helpful to specify how the group will know when the goal is achieved. Is it by counting ticket sales at the end of the season, counting revenue from tickets sold or counting attendees? Again, the clearer and more consensual the goals, the stronger they are as guides and motivators to action.

7. Developing and Selecting a Strategy

Thanks to our mission statement and priority goals, we know where we are headed. Now we are ready to develop a strategy for getting there. A strategy is a road map designed to move the organization from where it is to where it wants to be. It explains where you are going, the path you are taking and how you are getting there. At this initial stage of consideration, a strategy can also be thought of as a general approach to answering the strategic questions identified earlier in the planning process. For example, if one of the priority questions identified is, "How can we increase our audience?" and that question has become focused by the goal-setting process so that it is now, "How can we increase the number of tickets sold?" we can begin to outline possible strategies for consideration. One strategy might be to launch a two-for-one campaign giving buyers the chance to bring a friend at no extra cost. Another approach might be to find a sponsor who would underwrite the cost of tickets for special, new audience populations. Yet a third could be to have more big-name stars in the cast. There are, no doubt, many other (and better) approaches as well.

The important thing at this point is to generate as many strategies as you can for each of the priority goals. Creativity is important; brainstorming is effective. So is working backward from the vision of success that has been developed and imagining how you might have arrived at the desired place. Suspend judgment as you generate options.

Once the options have been generated for each priority goal, they must be evaluated. A good strategy is one that gets the organization to the desired place and uses its resources most efficiently. It builds on strengths, takes advantage of opportunities and mitigates threats in the environment. Thus for each option, it is important to determine first whether the group believes the strategy will work to accomplish the stated goal and, second, whether the organization has the resources to carry it out.

There are several methods for doing these ratings, all involving ways of measuring group preferences. It is not science, really, but, rather, good judgment. No matter what technique is used to evaluate and prioritize strategies, at the end of this step there should be two or three clearly defined goals, each with a few possible strategies for accomplishing them.

8. MAKING A PLAN

With all this as background, we are now ready to draft a plan and to structure these deliberations into actions.

This is the most mechanical part of the process because, by now, a fairly clear map of the future has been described and the process has generated a high degree of consensus around a few major points. Now the task is to allocate resources to get the job done in the most effective and efficient way possible. Sometimes, the board drops out of the process at this point, and the staff constructs the implementation plan.

It is important to start with the highest-priority goal and the highest-ranking strategy to achieve that goal. You want to give the organization the best possible chance to succeed in addressing its most critical issue. Therefore, it is important to give the highest-priority strategy for the highest-priority goal all the resources it needs to succeed. It is no good to skimp or you may not achieve anything important to the organization.

So, in this planning process, it is important to define the component elements of the strategy and determine what resources they require ($14,000, two full-time staff people, a computer, or the contacts of the board chair, for example). Whatever resources needed to implement the strategy must be subtracted from the list of assets and resources constructed in an earlier stage. They can only be used once.

One of the biggest mistakes organizations make is to keep allocating the same human resources over and over again. The artistic director or the managing director gets assigned to every major project, regardless of the number of hours its takes. Conversely, certain resources (board talents perhaps or junior staff) might be underutilized. All resources—not just financial ones—need to be budgeted. Deficits are to be avoided.

After the first strategy has been made into a "plan" that includes resources and a timetable with measurable objectives and assigned leadership, it is time to move on and do the same thing for the second highest priority goal. Brainstorm different possible strategies, evaluate them and select one in which to invest the resources needed for success. Again, once resources are allocated, they must be "subtracted" from the initial list of assets.

It should be apparent that the more resources on the asset list, the more goals you can support and the more strategies to achieve those goals you can have. It should also be apparent that as this process continues, it has to be more creative to succeed. After the initial one or two goals and strategies, it is generally harder to find strategies that utilize the resources remaining on the asset list. Toward the very end of the process, participants may be saying, "We have only this asset left—how can it contribute to achieving one of our goals?"

A lot of strategic planning slips at this point. People write down what they intend to do as if every task is equal. Proper planning at this stage focuses on priorities, starts working with the most important priority and only proceeds as far as resources are available. This is a discipline critical to effective planning, and it is what distinguishes wishing from planning.

When you think you have completed the plan, take time to review it for clarity and internal consistency and for opportunities to accomplish multiple objectives with a single activity. The strategies cannot all draw on a single resource, and they cannot all be done in the same time frame. To make the plan workable, there is often a need for adjusting; sometimes effective implementation requires reordering priorities to make full use of available resources.

When the plan draft is done, it should make clear how the actions relate to the strategic issues: Who is doing what, when and how, and what should happen as a result? Communication is critical here. If people are not clear about who is supposed to be doing what, nothing will happen. Similarly, if people do not have the resources (time, money, know-how) to do what is expected of them, they will fail.

9. MONITORING AND EVALUATION

Even if everyone does what is expected of them, things will never go exactly as planned. The world has too many variables to be completely predictable. That is why it is the planning *process*, even more than the plan itself, that has real value. The planning process clarifies goals and generates alternatives, so if someone is thwarted in carrying out strategy A, he or she can go back and try strategy B. The *goal* need not be abandoned. If the plan is a road map and you are headed to Chicago on the Interstate (your first choice strategy) and there is a bridge closing, you do not need to give up on your goal of reaching Chicago. You can go to your second choice strategy, the county highways.

To create this agility—a requisite skill in turbulent times—monitoring and evaluation are essential. If your plan has a three-year time frame, you cannot wait for three years to see how things worked out. By then it will be too late to adjust things that are not going as well as expected or to capitalize on those things that are going better than anticipated.

Because you constructed strategies in a way that identified the actions that were desired, the resources they required and the results that were anticipated, you have key points along the way to see how things are going. For example, suppose for the audience-boosting goal of selling ten percent more tickets than the previous year, your theater had decided upon a strategy of having a big-name star headline the season's opening show. And the media gave lots of publicity to the star's arrival, advance ticket sales boomed and the show sold out. In this obvious and easy example, early monitoring would enable you to revise your ad spending, schedule additional performances, take the additional revenue and sign another big name for a future show or offer attendees a price break on subscriptions for the remainder of the season.

Conversely, if ticket sales did not increase, you would want to know whether the potential audience did not get word of the star's presence, whether the star had no drawing power or whether the strategy itself was a poor choice—or even whether there was a blizzard that kept people away.

You cannot know how to adjust if there is no regular and systematic monitoring of the plan. Did we carry out the plan? Did it work the way we expected it to? What was different? What can we learn from it? What adjustments are needed now? How can we do better in the future? To do this with discipline and dispassion is to learn from experience and enable the organization to plan and implement more effectively in the future. Keeping good, reliable records of key indicators of progress made on your priority goals and objectives will enable you to take the organization's pulse on a regular basis.

There is really a cycle of planning, implementing and evaluating; and then planning again based on the evaluation of the implementation. Effective organizations develop this practice as part of their culture, and they become strong because of it.

Some Cautionary Notes and Frequently Asked Questions

Why do people growl when asked to be part of a strategic planning process?

There are two principal reasons why people may dislike and/or be disillusioned with strategic planning. First, because the last time they were involved in planning, it took a lot of time and nothing happened. The plan was not *used.* The second reason is that the process ran away with any enthusiasm people might have brought to it. It was either too long or too turgid or it failed to focus on things that really mattered. Therefore, it is advisable to keep the process as simple as you can, focus on a few things and *do* something. If you are successful, you can do a new process the following year when you will know even more and have some planning experience to boot!

How many goals and strategies can an organization pursue?

Not too many. Less is more in planning. Having too many goals dilutes focus, energy and resources. It is a sign that the group is not really making the hard choices that are required. Again, start modestly and make sure effective implementation occurs. Then, with some success under your belt, plan again and do more. A good number of goals is somewhere between one and four, again depending on resources. Whatever the number, everyone in the organization should be able to remember them and understand the strategy being pursued to accomplish the goal.

What about using a planning consultant?

Since consultants cost money, they are most valuable when their skills and expertise are applied to things in which the organization has limited experience. In most cases, a consultant can be very helpful in designing a process that will increase involvement and effective implementation. The consultant pays attention to process so others can concentrate on the substantive choices. The consultant can also ask the direct and difficult questions that others are hesitant to raise and can bring fresh energy and insight to both the process and the issues that emerge from it. If you decide to use a consultant, choose someone who not only has the necessary expertise but whose background, manner and responsiveness resonate with you, someone with whom you would enjoy discussing the future of your theater.

How often should we revise our plan?

Plans should be revisited on a regular basis, perhaps monthly by the people with leadership responsibilities in a given area and quarterly by the whole planning group. Revisions should occur when needed, and the full plan should be reconstructed somewhere between a year (in the case of a small, start-up organization with a lot of change) and three years (for a larger, more stable organization). The real factor in timing is whether or not the plan is still providing useful guidance to the organization.

Could this work for us?

Yes, if you let it. Don't overburden either the process or the plan. Manage it well. Consult with stakeholders. Get to the heart of each question. And use all your resources—but don't overuse them.

UNDERSTANDING FINANCIAL STATEMENTS

Patricia Egan and Nancy Sasser

WELCOME TO THE WORLD of numbers, arguably the least understood aspect of your service as a trustee. In this article we will describe the financial oversight role that a trustee should play. In addition, we will provide the tools you need to understand not-for-profit accounting and show how to use these tools to interpret your theater's finances. While the laws require that a trustee exercise financial responsibility for the theater, the language of accounting is full of unfamiliar terms, and not-for-profit accounting has distinct differences in presentation from for-profit accounting.

With the implementation of the new not-for-profit accounting standards in 1995 and 1996, interpretation of financial statements became significantly more difficult. Individuals familiar with the earlier fund accounting may have difficulty understanding the new format, and all board members and managers may need assistance in analyzing the financial strength and operating health of their organizations under the new rules.

Because the readers of this article will range from those with extensive accounting and financial expertise to those who have never seen financial statements, we have prepared a brief tutorial, "Accounting Basics," which follows. If you understand what constitutes an income statement (statement of activity) and balance sheet (statement of financial position), move ahead to the next section, "The Financial Roles and Responsibilities of the Board Member." If these concepts are new to you or difficult to understand, read "Accounting Basics" first and then move on. At the end of the chapter you will find a Glossary of commonly used terms to help you as you read through this article.

Accounting Basics

Income Statement (or Statement of Activity)

A trustee needs to understand two basic financial statements—the income statement and the balance sheet. The most familiar is the income statement, which states what income you receive during the year, what your expenditures are and how they compare—whether they are in balance or whether you have a surplus or deficit. The income statement is an accounting of where you are at any particular point during a year.

The most frequent use for the income statement is to track progress against the annual budget, which is prepared in the same format as the income statement. The budget is your financial plan for the year. By comparing the income statement to the budget, you can monitor how you are doing as the year progresses. Is income above or below what you expected? What about expenses? Are you staying in balance or are you in danger of running a deficit? Reviewing regular income statements allows you to take action before the end of the year to offset unexpected developments. The budget is your plan, and the income statement is how you monitor the plan.

To help you understand the basic logic of income statements, let's start with a personal income statement like the one shown below. Your personal income statement is the best measure of whether you are living within your means each year. It is made up of your revenue and your expenses. Revenue consists of all monies you received from all sources during the year. Your personal revenue might consist of your salary from your employer, income from your investments and rental income from a property you own. Your personal expenses might include payments on your home and car, insurance, utilities, food, clothing and other similar expenses. Your net income is the money that remains in your bank account after you deposit the income you received during the year and pay all your expenses. If this is positive, you had a surplus for the year, but, if it is negative, you had a deficit or overdraft.

A theater's income statement is quite similar to your personal income statement—it just has different categories of revenue and expenses, as you can see by comparing the examples below:

PERSONAL INCOME STATEMENT *($ in thousands)*		THEATER INCOME STATEMENT *($ in thousands)*	
REVENUE		REVENUE	
Salary at XYZ Corporation	$75	Ticket revenue	$45
Investment revenue	11	Investment revenue	3
Rental property revenue	5	Contributions	35
TOTAL REVENUE	91	TOTAL REVENUE	83
EXPENSES		EXPENSES	
Housing and utilites	40	Production costs	53
Auto expenses	15	Marketing	13
Food	20	Fundraising	5
Clothing and other	15	Administration and facility	10
TOTAL EXPENSES	90	TOTAL EXPENSES	81
NET INCOME (LOSS)	$1	NET SURPLUS (DEFICIT)	$2

The income statement is your way of knowing where your theater's income comes from, how it is spent and whether income and expenses are in balance.

BALANCE SHEET (OR STATEMENT OF FINANCIAL POSITION)

The balance sheet is probably the less familiar of the two financial statements a trustee needs to understand. Although the two statements are closely connected, each shows a different aspect of a theater's financial life. The balance sheet shows the accumulated financial results of all the years you have been in business rather than showing how you are doing in the current year, as the income statement does. The balance sheet is the best measure of the overall financial health of your organization, since it represents the organization's entire history of fiscal activity. It is a snapshot of your assets, liabilities and the difference between the two at a particular point in time.

In your personal balance sheet, the difference between what you own (assets) and what you owe (liabilities) is your net worth. Your net worth increases or decreases each year by the difference between what you earn and what you spend. Examples of your personal assets are cash in the bank, stocks and bonds, your car and your home. Examples of your personal liabilities are credit card balances and loans. We have created a sample balance sheet below based on these items. A theater's balance sheet is quite similar to your personal statement—it just has different categories of assets and liabilities, and uses different terminology.

PERSONAL BALANCE SHEET *($ in thousands)*		THEATER BALANCE SHEET *($ in thousands)*	
ASSETS		ASSETS	
Bank balance	$5	Cash	$25
Stocks and bonds	85	Investments	50
Automobile	25	Equipment	25
Home, rental property	275	Facility/theater	280
TOTAL ASSETS	$390	TOTAL ASSETS	$380
LIABILITIES		LIABILITIES	
Credit card balances	10	Accounts payable	30
Loans	45	Subscriptions received in advance	30
Mortgage	260	Property and equipment	100
TOTAL LIABILITIES	315	TOTAL LIABILITIES	160
NET WORTH	75	NET ASSETS	220
TOTAL LIABILITIES AND NET WORTH	$390	TOTAL LIABILITIES AND NET ASSETS	$380

These illustrations will help you understand the more complex examples used later in this chapter. You are now ready to move on to "The Financial Roles and Responsibilities of the Board Member."

The Financial Roles and Responsibilities of the Board Member

The board of trustees holds the theater in trust for the community. That trust includes responsibility for maintaining or strengthening an organization's financial position. The board is also responsible for maintaining the balance between the desire to invest in the highest quality programs and the responsibility to sustain financial integrity.

One of the key roles of the board is to help determine the theater's priorities, on both an annual and long-term basis. Understanding the financial position and financial trends of the theater allows trustees to more fully consider strategic issues they will confront. For example, given the constraints of limited resources, how should a theater spend its funds: Invest in program quality? Commission new work? Invest in a facility? Upgrade technology on the stage and in the offices? Hire additional staff? Pay current staff a higher wage? Strengthen working capital to reduce day-to-day cash-flow problems? Raise funds for an endowment? Launch a capital campaign to fund desired priorities? The answers to these questions will determine what is included in the annual budgets and the long-term financial plan of the theater. First we will look at two types of budgets, operating and capital, and then we will review the income statement and balance sheet.

OPERATING BUDGET

The board's oversight role as it relates to finances is generally led by a finance committee. The committee works with staff by providing input and feedback on detailed budgets and financial reports that the board later reviews in summary. Each fiscal year, the theater follows a similar financial cycle. Several months prior to the start of the fiscal year, the committee should review the proposed operating budget for the upcoming year to understand the underlying assumptions and ensure that they are realistic and that the budget reflects the operating priorities and long-term goals of the organization. For example, if one of the top priorities of the theater is to commission a new play each season, the committee should verify that the budget accurately reflects all of the costs related to the commissioning of a new play. The board should approve an operating budget prior to the beginning of a new fiscal year (and generally, it should be balanced).

In the annual operating budget, the staff estimates the theater's revenue and expenses as part of the plan for the upcoming year. The operating budget should cover the twelve-month fiscal year of the organization. Each of the line items shown should be supported by a set of detailed budget items and related assumptions. The summary budget should be presented to the board with comparisons to the current year's budget and year-end projections, as well as to the results for one or two previous years. This history provides the context for the proposed budget.

The following are examples of questions that trustees might ask as part of their budget review:

- Is the operating budget balanced? If not, why?
- Does it provide a small contingency to handle unforeseen events?
- Does the budget include only current-year revenue that is unrestricted and available to be spent on operations?
- What are the riskiest parts of the budget? Is there a fallback position to protect the organization from these risks?
- How do the major budget categories compare to this year's budget and year-end projection?
- What new initiatives are included in the budget?
- Are any existing programs terminated?
- If the budget includes significant increases in earned or contributed revenue, does the staff have a realistic plan for activities to generate the growth, and is the development or marketing budget increased to reflect the new activities?
- Does the budget include depreciation as an operating expense? (Depreciation is a non-cash expense, and each theater must decide how much it can afford to fund.)

Capital Budget

The capital budget is a list of all the expected expenditures for the year for additions and improvements to buildings and for purchases of equipment. As these items are not normally included in the operating budget, the theater must have a separate source of funding available for them. Possible funding sources include special grants to purchase equipment, capital campaigns for facilities and equipment or use of a board-designated reserve that could be replenished by funding depreciation. The board should review and approve the capital budget annually.

Questions trustees might ask include:

- Is capital expenditure and revenue budgeted and tracked separately as part of the capital budget?
- Is the capital budget balanced, with revenue sources identified?

MONITORING FINANCES—INCOME STATEMENT (OR STATEMENT OF ACTIVITY)

Once the operating budget has been approved and the theater's fiscal year begins, the board uses an income statement to oversee the operating results—that is, what the theater is actually earning and spending. The actual results, as shown in the income statement, should be regularly compared to the budget, and differences should be explained. It is inevitable that actual revenues and expenses will vary from the budgeted amounts. It is difficult to accurately predict the audience's response to a show and what the exact ticket sales will be. Despite the best expense budgeting, unforeseen circumstances can crop up in all areas of the operation, particularly during the production process. Budgeting a contingency can provide a cushion for such situations. Ultimately, it is essential that the staff monitor revenue and expenses and reforecast actual year-end results regularly for the board's review. If the projection shows a deficit, the board and staff should discuss ways of closing the gap.

The fundamental difference between for-profit and not-for-profit accounting is that not-for-profit organizations have three types of net assets that come to them through their charitable contributions. When donors contribute gifts to a not-for-profit organization, they can designate whether these gifts are temporarily restricted and must be held until a designated time or used for a specific purpose, or whether they are permanently restricted and can never be used for current operations (such as an endowment fund). The theater cannot restrict a contribution; only the donor can. If there is no designation, then the gift is considered unrestricted and can be used for current operations. Some examples of temporarily restricted contributions are gifts for specific programs or productions, gifts for operations for future years, and capital campaign gifts for facilities that are not yet built. When the restriction is fulfilled, then the net assets are released to the unrestricted operating statement. However, prior to restrictions being lifted, temporarily restricted donations should be segregated and not used to pay for operations. Permanently restricted contributions, such as gifts to the endowment, are restricted by the donor in perpetuity.

Prior to the change in accounting standards in the mid-1990s, contributed revenue for future periods or purposes was considered deferred revenue, similar to subscription revenue for the next season. However, now such contributions must be recognized as temporarily restricted revenue in the year that the gift is received, whether it is cash or a pledge. The gift remains temporarily restricted until the gift terms are fulfilled. It is important that trustees not confuse temporarily restricted activity with unrestricted annual operating activity.

The income statement that follows on page 187 is one example of the kind of year-to-date financial information that should be provided to board members on a monthly basis. It includes an unrestricted operating section that shows only the portion of contributed income that can be used for current operations. This is followed by a section that details nonoperating and restricted funds that should be reported and monitored by the board separately from operating activity. Trustees may want to see other relevant columns of information, such as year-to-date budget, percentages of total, variance amounts, etc. The letters in the right-hand column of the sample income statement refer to how that line is used in calculating the operating ratios presented later in the article.

Let's assume that you are a board member of a theater that sent you this statement accompanied by a set of comments explaining both year-to-date and projected variances. What would you look for to monitor how the theater is doing this year? Let's start with a few general questions.

- Comparing the first two columns, are there any areas where the theater is doing much better or worse than in the previous year? If so, why?
- Reviewing the "Budget to Projected Variance" column on the right side of the table, what has caused any major differences between budget line items and projection of year-end totals?
- Is a deficit projected for unrestricted operations?
- If revenue shortfalls or expense overruns are projected for year-end, are steps being taken today to make up for the variances?

Sample Year-to-Date Income Statement

($ in thousands)

	Prior Year Year-to-Date *Actual*	Current Year Year-to-Date *Actual*	Prior Year Total *Actual*	Current Year Annual *Budget*	Current Year Year-End *Projected*	Budget to Projected *Variance*	Operating Ratio References
UNRESTRICTED OPERATING							
REVENUE							
Earned Revenue							
Subscription	$432	438	1,296	1,357	1,316	(41)	A
Single tickets	165	168	554	569	571	2	B
Education programs	8	8	24	24	25	1	
Other earned	2	1	6	6	7	1	
Total earned revenue	607	615	1,880	1,956	1,919	(37)	C
Investment revenue	9	9	21	22	22	0	D
Contributed Revenue							
Individual	133	149	406	408	408	0	
Corporate	88	96	241	262	260	(2)	
Foundation	122	127	257	276	260	(16)	
Government	64	66	240	244	247	3	
Special Events	52	58	52	57	58	1	
In-kind	1	2	3	4	4	0	
Subtotal	460	498	1,199	1,251	1,237	(14)	E
Net assets released	72	80	144	151	151	0	
Total contributed revenue	532	578	1,343	1,402	1,388	(14)	F
Total revenue	1,148	1,202	3,244	3,380	3,329	(51)	
EXPENSES							
Program							
Productions	502	522	1,490	1,612	1,631	(19)	
Education programs	11	15	35	36	37	(1)	
Subtotal	513	537	1,525	1,648	1,668	(20)	G
Marketing	207	220	630	655	643	12	H
Development	116	130	266	271	269	2	I
Facilities	145	149	342	342	347	(5)	
Administration	186	203	440	452	462	(10)	J
Total expenses	1,167	1,239	3,203	3,368	3,389	(21)	K
INCOME (LOSS) FROM OPERATIONS	(19)	(37)	41	12	(60)	(72)	
NONOPERATING							
UNRESTRICTED							
Investment revenue in excess of spending rule	1	(1)	3	0	0	0	
Net assets released for capital purposes	0	0	0	0	0	0	
Capital gifts	0	0	0	0	30	30	L
Change in unrestricted net assets	(18)	(38)	44	12	(30)	(42)	
TEMPORARILY RESTRICTED							
Contributions	90	110	165	150	140	(10)	M
Net assets released	(72)	(80)	(144)	(163)	(163)	0	
Change in temporarily restricted net assets	18	30	21	(13)	(23)	(10)	
PERMANENTLY RESTRICTED							
Contributions	5	0	50	0	10	10	N
Change in permanently restricted net assets	5	0	50	0	10	10	
TOTAL CHANGE IN NET ASSETS	$5	($8)	$115	($1)	($43)	(42)	

Operating Ratios

The first three operating ratios look at how much of the theater's total expenses are covered variously by earned, contributed and investment revenue. Understanding trends in a theater's reliance on different kinds of revenue may clarify changes in the operations and marketplace. Trends should be reviewed to determine whether they are consistent with the organization's strategic goals and future plans. The measures are calculated as follows (each measure references lines on the sample financial statement):

Earned Revenue Ratio = Total unrestricted earned revenue ÷ Total expenses (C ÷ K)

Contributed Revenue Ratio = Total unrestricted contributed revenue (including net assets released from restriction) ÷ Total expenses (F ÷ K)

Investment Revenue Ratio = Investment revenue ÷ Total expenses (D ÷ K)

The next ratios measure how much of the theater's budget is spent on programs, marketing, development and administration:

Program Ratio = Program expenses ÷ Total expenses (G ÷ K)

Marketing Ratio = Marketing expenses ÷ Total expenses (H ÷ K)

Development Ratio = Development expenses ÷ Total expenses (I ÷ K)

Administrative Ratio = Administrative expenses ÷ Total expenses (J ÷ K)

The development efficiency ratio measures what portion of each dollar of contributions is spent to generate all contributed revenue:

Development Revenue Generation Ratio = Development expenses ÷ Total contributions (I ÷ [E + L + M + N])

The marketing efficiency ratio measures what portion of each dollar of ticket sales is spent to generate the sale:

Marketing Revenue Generation Ratio = Marketing expenses ÷ Total ticket sales (H ÷ [A+B])

(Theatre Communications Group (TCG) conducts an annual Fiscal Survey of theaters. It is useful to compare these figures above to those of theaters of similar budget size in the survey. If your theater participates in TCG's online Fiscal Survey, you have access to customized comparisons with other theaters.)

- How does the year-end projection compare to the year-to-date actual? Given the number of months remaining in the fiscal year, is the projection reasonable?

To give you even more insight into your theater's financial situation, you can look at operating ratios to track financial trends over several years. The most important operating ratios are detailed in the preceding table.

In addition to reviewing financial trends, trustees and staff should identify a small number of indicators that measure critical aspects of the theater's operation. These should be tracked over a period of three to five years to reveal trends. Examples include:

- Number of productions, performances and classes
- Attendance: total, average per production, percentage of capacity, etc.
- Number of subscribers and renewal rate
- Number of single ticket buyers
- Average ticket price for subscriptions and single tickets
- Number of members and donors
- Total employment of actors, artists and staff.

Looking at the income statement, operating ratios and other indicators will give trustees the information they need to assess their theater's current position.

Monitoring Finances—Balance Sheet (or Statement of Financial Position)

The balance sheet (or statement of financial position) provides the best assessment of the financial health of an organization as it reflects the theater's financial history, i.e., the accumulation of all surpluses and deficits plus all the capital the theater has acquired. It provides information on the financial strength and well-being of the organization that cannot be learned from looking at the theater's annual income statement. It reflects the theater's position at one point in time—the day the balance sheet is prepared. In addition to the income statement, the board should receive monthly balance sheets and have the opportunity to question changes in assets and liabilities. The balance sheet may be single-column, or may include a comparative column if desired. The format should mirror the format of your audit.

SAMPLE THEATER
BALANCE SHEET

ASSETS	Fiscal Year-End	Balance Sheet References
Cash and cash equivalents	$329,000	
Accounts and contributions receivable	202,000	
Prepaid expenses	62,000	
Inventory	14,000	
Investments—restricted	400,000	P
Property and equipment, net	2,208,000	Q
Other assets	17,000	
TOTAL ASSETS	$3,232,000	R
LIABILITIES AND NET ASSETS		
LIABILITIES		
Accounts payable and accrued expenses	$169,000	
Subscriptions received in advance	700,000	
Lines of credit	25,000	S
Notes payable	100,000	T
Other liabilities	18,000	
TOTAL LIABILITIES	$1,012,000	U
NET ASSETS		
Unrestricted		
Operating	1,450,000	
Board designated	250,000	
Total unrestricted	1,700,000	V
Temporarily restricted	120,000	
Permanently restricted	400,000	
TOTAL NET ASSETS	2,220,000	W
TOTAL LIABILITIES AND NET ASSETS	$3,232,000	

As you can see from the "Sample Theater Balance Sheet" on page 190, there are three sections: your assets (what you own), your liabilities (what you owe) and your net assets (the difference between what you own and what you owe). The for-profit equivalent to net assets is owners' equity.

Assets

Assets may include bank account balances, accounts and contributions receivable, prepaid expenses, investments, and property and equipment. Some of the assets are worth highlighting:

- Contributions receivable are pledges and grants that have been promised but not paid; trustees should review this number to make sure that the theater is recording pledges and collecting them on a timely basis.
- Prepaid expenses are expenditures that have been made for future seasons, such as for a subscription campaign or production expenses; trustees should be aware of the magnitude of prepaid expenses, especially if cash flow is tight.
- Endowments, reserves and excess cash your theater has are invested in stocks, bonds and other financial instruments. These investments provide a revenue stream that increases the strength and sustainability of an organization. Each theater should target an appropriate level of invested capital after developing sufficient resources for operations or working capital. Investments can be unrestricted, temporarily restricted or permanently restricted.
- Property and equipment is all the land, buildings, equipment and other fixed assets owned by the theater. It is usually shown as the net result of accumulated depreciation. The amount that a theater invests in its building and equipment will vary and should be tailored to the needs of the organization and the larger community. However, every theater should maintain the fixed assets that it owns, providing for upgrade and replacement.

Trustees should understand the nature of the theater's assets. Questions about assets might include:

- How much of the cash is restricted, for example, as grants for future years?
- Are restricted funds held until they are utilized for the intended purpose?

- Are cash balances invested automatically by the bank on a nightly basis (a sweep account)?
- How old are the accounts receivable?
- Has the theater had difficulty collecting any accounts or contributions receivable?
- Are balances of contributions receivable regularly reconciled to development reports?
- What is the inventory and how old is it?
- What kinds of investments does the theater have?
- Is invested capital growing or declining?
- Is invested capital growing in proportion to growth in operating size?
- Is investment in property and equipment growing or declining?
- Is the theater investing in its property and equipment on an ongoing basis to avoid deferred maintenance?
- Has the theater projected the increased operating costs of proposed facility additions prior to adding facilities?

Liabilities

Liabilities may include accounts payable, unpaid payroll taxes, next year's ticket sales and loans. Several of these liabilities deserve attention:

- Subscriptions received in advance (or deferred ticket sales) represent ticket sales for future productions and for future seasons. A review of this line can help a trustee track progress in selling next year's season.
- Notes payable, lines of credit, mortgages and capital leases are contractual obligations of the theater. Together, they represent the total debt incurred by the theater. The ability to repay debt is key to financial health.

Sample questions trustees may want to ask about liabilities include:

- Have all payroll taxes been paid on a timely basis?
- What is the age of the accounts payable? Are vendors paid on a timely basis?
- Are next year's ticket sales held in cash and spent only on next year's season?
- Is debt increasing or decreasing?

- Does the theater have a dedicated source of funds for debt repayment, for example, capital campaign pledges that will pay off a building mortgage?
- Has the theater had difficulty making debt payments on a timely basis?
- Is the line of credit used for the stated purpose, and is it repaid according to the terms of the loan?

NET ASSETS

As previously noted, the fundamental difference between for-profit and not-for-profit accounting is the existence of three net asset classes in not-for-profit accounting: unrestricted, temporarily restricted and permanently restricted.

- Unrestricted assets, liabilities and net assets include your accumulated operating surpluses and deficits, your property and equipment and any board-designated funds, such as a cash reserve, artistic reserve, capital projects or endowment.
- Temporarily restricted assets, liabilities and net assets are restricted by the donor for a specific purpose or time period.
- Permanently restricted assets and net assets are restricted by the donor in perpetuity. Most often, these are permanent endowment funds.

The single-column balance sheet frequently does not distinguish unrestricted assets and liabilities from those that are temporarily or permanently restricted. Sample questions about "net assets" include:

- Are all contributions for specific projects and future years shown as temporarily restricted?
- Are board-designated funds shown as unrestricted? Are the assets intact and ready to be used for the designated purpose? Does the theater have policies regarding the use of board-designated funds?
- Are permanently restricted net assets intact? Is the income being used according to the wishes of the donor?
- Do total net assets grow at least as fast as operating expenses each year?

WORKING CAPITAL

One key element of the balance sheet does not appear as a single line item—working capital. Working capital consists of the unrestricted resources available for operations. It is a fundamental financial building block of an organization and should be a primary focus for trustees. Working capital may be determined by using the traditional calculation of total unrestricted current assets less unrestricted current liabilities. If your balance sheet doesn't include sufficient detail to do the traditional calculation, you may approximate working capital with the calculation shown in the "Balance Sheet Measures and Ratios" table, which follows. Adequate working capital provides an organization with the financial strength and flexibility to meet obligations as they come due and with the ability to take more risks, knowing there is a cushion to fall back on. An organization with negative working capital is likely to suffer periods of cash-flow stress or financial crisis, and will need to borrow to meet current needs (for example, borrowing from a bank through a term loan or a line of credit, borrowing from next year's revenues, borrowing from restricted net assets, or "borrowing" from vendors by delaying payments on outstanding bills).

Questions about working capital might include:

- Is working capital positive or negative?
- Does the theater have periods of cash-flow stress?
- If cash flow is tight, does the organization prepare detailed cash-flow projections that show expected receipts and disbursements?
- Has working capital grown or declined during the past several years?
- Is working capital growing in proportion to the growth in operating size?

BALANCE SHEET MEASURES AND RATIOS

The mix of your assets, liabilities and net assets and the nature of restrictions on each determine your theater's capital structure. A healthy capital structure allows the theater to fulfill its artistic mission and take artistic risk without significant financial stress. Each theater should determine its own ideal capital structure based on the theater's individual operation and future needs. Balance sheet measures and ratios may be used to track the overall health of the theater and to develop targets for capital structure.

Balance Sheet Measures and Ratios

Total Net Assets = Total assets - Total liabilities (W = R – U)

Working Capital = Total unrestricted net assets - Property and Equipment (net of accumulated depreciation)[1] - Unrestricted investments[2] (V – Q)

(The most prevalent format for the balance sheet does not delineate between current and long-term assets, nor does it segregate unrestricted assets and liabilities from temporarily and permanently restricted assets and liabilities, which makes a traditional calculation of working capital difficult. However, if your balance sheet includes this detail, it may be preferable to calculate working capital using the traditional calculation below:)

Working Capital = Total unrestricted current assets - Unrestricted current liabilities

Invested Capital = Total investments (P)

Fixed Assets = Total property and equipment - Accumulated depreciation (Q)

Debt = Short-term + long-term contractual obligations (S + T)

The measures may be analyzed further by calculating the ratios that follow and tracking the trends over several years:

Working Capital Ratio = Working capital ÷ Total expenses ([V - Q] ÷ K)

This ratio relates working capital to the size of an organization's operation. An increase in the ratio over time, which indicates growth in financial strength at least in proportion to growth in operating size, is a healthy trend. Each theater should determine its own working capital needs based on its yearly cycle of cash flow and any extraordinary expenditures that are anticipated.

Investment Ratio = Total investments ÷ Total expenses (P ÷ K)

This ratio relates investments to the size of an organization's operation. An increase in the ratio over time, which indicates investment growth at least in proportion to growth in operating size, is a healthy trend.

The final ratio requires information found in the audit footnotes and statement of cash flows.

Deferred Maintenance Indicator = Accumulated depreciation ÷ Annual depreciation expense

This ratio is used to assess the relative likelihood of deferred maintenance and the need for investment in buildings and equipment. This ratio relates total accumulated depreciation to annual depreciation. An organization that invests in fixed assets at a pace that exceeds annual depreciation will show a declining trend in this ratio, which is a healthy trend. For organizations that own their facilities, a deferred maintenance indicator greater than fifteen years may indicate the need to invest in plant. For organizations that own equipment but no facility, a deferred maintenance indicator in excess of six years may indicate a need to invest in equipment.

1. Property and equipment is generally unrestricted, though in some situations it may be restricted. If fixed assets are restricted, do not subtract them from the working capital calculation.
2. Unrestricted investments may not be broken out separately on an audit, but internal business office records should identify this figure.

We suggest that board members track five measures annually for several years using the audit as the source of the data to calculate:

- Total net assets
- Working capital
- Invested capital
- Fixed assets
- Debt.

Key ratios include:

- Working capital
- Investment ratio
- Deferred maintenance indicator.

The calculation of these measures and related ratios are explained in the table on the previous page (each measure references lines on the sample financial statements given earlier). You should look at these indicators along with the operating measures for your theater over a three-to-five-year time span to identify trends. You are probably already aware of what some of these indicators show, for example, that you have times during the year when cash flow is tight, or you have outdated equipment that needs replacement. But tracking the measures can put this information on a quantitative rather than an anecdotal level. It allows for a dispassionate analysis that makes it possible to articulate trends and financial needs.

OTHER FINANCIAL RESPONSIBILITIES

In addition to understanding and monitoring financial statements, trustees have other financial responsibilities. The board oversees the selection of auditors and the audit process and should approve the audit, management letter and tax return. Trustees should annually approve the selection of an audit firm to prepare an audit report that consists of the auditor's opinion, a balance sheet, income statement, statement of cash flow and footnotes. The auditor, after examining the theater's internal financial records, may issue a clean opinion (no significant objections to the statements) or a qualified opinion (the auditor disagrees with one or more aspects of the financial statements). If the auditor questions the viability of the theater, there will be a "going concern" paragraph in the opinion. The finance (or audit) committee should review and approve the audit engagement letter and discuss any issues of concern with the auditors. When the audit is complete, the committee should meet again with the auditors to review the draft documents and understand any difficulties encountered during the process. In performing an audit, it is key that the auditors complete their work with an objective state of mind, free from any influence or relationship that could impact interpretation or statement of the numbers. This independence should result in accurate financial statements upon which the theater's stakeholders can rely. The board should be aware that the theater's financial results are more accessible to the public since the IRS form 990 became available on the internet.

If your theater has an endowment, working capital reserves or other board-designated reserves, the board should establish policies on their investment and use. The board should ensure that any endowment maintains its value for the future while providing current income to support operations. To accomplish this, the board should establish an endowment investment policy that balances risk and return, establish a spending rule that does not deplete the endowment, select investment managers to manage the investments (if needed) and regularly monitor investment management performance.

Finally, the board should act as a resource to management in evaluating the financial impact of operating and capital investment decisions.

Board Education and Training

Your orientation of new board members should include training on financial literacy. In addition, you may want to suggest that the treasurer or finance committee chair do an annual educational presentation of the theater's finances to the board. Finally, there are numerous external opportunities and sources for both trustees and staff to receive financial training.

Conclusion

You now have a basic understanding of your financial oversight role as a theater trustee. In addition, you have some tools to use to understand and analyze your theater's financial reports. If you have difficulty understanding the financial statements, the most important thing you can do is ask questions, ask more questions and then ask more questions. If you are confused by a presentation or explanation of information, you probably are not alone.

Financial analysis should be considered in light of an individual theater's mission, current environment and strategy. Ultimately, financial analysis and reporting is not an end in itself but a means to inform decision-making that supports the artistic mission of the theater. When you and the other leaders of your theater understand the theater's financial information and trends, you can make better financial decisions that support and enhance your artistic work and build an appropriate capital structure that supports the artistic goals and programs of the theater.

Glossary

Assets are all the resources owned by the theater, such as cash, accounts receivable, investments, prepaid expenses, inventory and fixed assets.

Audit report consists of the auditor's opinion, a balance sheet, income statement, statement of cash flows and footnotes. The auditor, after examining the theater's internal financial records, may issue a clean opinion (no significant objections to the statements) or a qualified opinion (the auditor disagrees with one or more aspects of the financial statements). If the auditor questions the viability of the theater, there will be a "going concern" paragraph in the opinion.

Balance sheet (or statement of financial position) is one of three primary financial statements. It summarizes assets, liabilities and net assets at a given point in time. It provides information on the financial strength and well-being of the organization. It is usually prepared on a monthly basis.

Capital budget is a budget of all capital expenditures or purchases of long-lived assets for a given year, and the resources that will be used to purchase them.

Cash-flow projection contains details of all expected cash inflows and outflows for a given future period (not to be confused with the "statement of cash flows" in the audited financial statement).

Debt includes all short- and long-term borrowings (including capital leases) of the organization.

DEPRECIATION is the method used to spread the cost of fixed assets over the estimated life of the asset rather than assuming the entire expense of the asset in the year it is purchased. Each year the asset is in use bears a portion of the cost. Assets such as software may be depreciated over a short life (three to five years) and assets such as buildings are depreciated over a longer life (perhaps forty years). Accumulated depreciation is the sum of all depreciation expense since the assets were purchased.

ENDOWMENT is an established fund that is invested to produce present and future income for a theater. Endowment may be unrestricted, temporarily restricted or permanently restricted.

EXPENSES include the total monies expended by the theater during a given period. All expenses are unrestricted.

FIXED ASSETS include all land, buildings, equipment and other fixed assets that are owned. Fixed assets (also called property and equipment or plant) have long lives and are generally used by the theater for several years or more. See "depreciation."

INCOME STATEMENT (or statement of activity) is one of three primary financial statements. It reports revenue and expenses and the related surplus or deficit for a given period.

INVESTED CAPITAL includes monies usually invested long-term. It approximates reserves and endowment. Revenue from investments is available for operations or to support specific purposes.

INVESTMENT POLICY is a written policy that specifies how a theater may invest funds long-term. The policy usually includes ranges for the portion of the portfolio that is invested in equities, fixed income and cash. It also includes a "spending rule" (see below).

LIABILITIES include all the obligations incurred by the theater that are unpaid.

MANAGEMENT LETTER is a document issued by the auditors at the same time as the audit that details any weaknesses in the financial systems and internal controls of the theater.

NET ASSETS are what an organization owns after paying off all that it owes.

OPERATING BUDGET is an estimate of revenues and expenses for activities that are recurring from year to year. Operating budgets do not include revenues and expenses related to capital campaigns and additions to fixed assets.

OPERATING RATIOS provide information on the trends in sources and uses of annual financial resources.

PERMANENTLY RESTRICTED ASSETS and NET ASSETS are restricted by the donor in perpetuity. Most often, these are permanent endowment funds.

REVENUE includes all sources of income earned from programs and investments from public and private sources. Contributions can be unrestricted, temporarily restricted or permanently restricted. Most earned revenue is unrestricted, although revenue from some investments may be restricted.

SPENDING RULE is a formula that determines what portion of the endowment market value may be spent each year.

STATEMENT OF ACTIVITY (see "income statement").

STATEMENT OF CASH FLOWS, one of three primary audited financial statements, summarizes the sources and uses of the organization's cash during the period of the income statement. It contains valuable information not available elsewhere in the audit, such as investment activity, purchase of fixed assets and issuance and repayment of long-term debt.

STATEMENT OF FINANCIAL POSITION (see "balance sheet").

STATEMENTS OF FINANCIAL ACCOUNTING STANDARDS (FAS) 116, 117 and 124 were issued by the Financial Accounting Standards Board in 1993 and 1995, changing the way not-for-profit organizations (including theaters) track and present their financial statements.

TEMPORARILY RESTRICTED assets, liabilities and net assets are restricted by the donor for a specific purpose or time period. These can include funds that will be used for operating activity in the future. When the restriction is fulfilled, then the net assets are released to the unrestricted operating statement.

UNRESTRICTED ASSETS, liabilities and net assets include your accumulated operating surpluses and deficits, your property and equipment and any board-designated funds, such as a cash reserve or endowment.

WORKING CAPITAL consists of the unrestricted resources available for operations.

THE ANNUAL FUND

Dawn Rains

I SERVE AS A PROFESSIONAL FUNDRAISER for a major not-for-profit theater. I recently joined the board of another not-for-profit organization and had the experience of being handed a "portfolio" of ten donors that I am responsible for cultivating and soliciting for the annual fund during this calendar year. As I am relatively new to the board, I am still learning about the organization. I have never met the people assigned to me. What if they ask me a question I can't answer? What if they don't even want to talk to me? While some of my concerns may be somewhat irrational, even as a development professional, I find that I have nagging reservations about picking up the phone and introducing myself. Isn't this work better left to the staff with whom the donors may already have a relationship?

Wait a minute! What am I saying? This is what I ask the trustees of the theater to do almost every day of my working life. While I have spent countless hours training and preparing trustees for their roles in fundraising, it has been both wonderful and overwhelming to be put in the shoes that I regularly ask board members to fill. I now have a better understanding of how trustees must feel when asked to participate in fundraising, especially when they aren't even sure where to begin.

This chapter is designed to give you an overview of the fundraising process and your role in it as a trustee. While a trustee's job description includes many functions—such as fiduciary responsibilities, hiring and evaluating artistic and managing directors, and strategic planning—playing a leadership role in both giving and raising money for the organization is one of the most significant and rewarding trustee responsibilities.

What Is the Annual Fund?

The annual fund is a theater's yearly campaign to raise the necessary resources to pay for general operating expenses, including everything from artist and staff salaries to arts education programs, from lumber and paint for scenery to the electric bill. The annual fund usually includes contributions from a variety of sources, such as individual patrons, corporations, foundations and government agencies. Common solicitation methods include face-to-face personal visits, direct mail, phone solicitation, email or web-based campaigns, special events and grant applications.

In addition to providing critical resources, the annual fund is an important tool in building and deepening a theater's relationship with its constituents, including board members, subscribers, single-ticket buyers, volunteers and staff members. The process of cultivating, soliciting, acknowledging and stewarding donors on an annual basis builds and cements the relationship between donors and your organization.

As you may have heard in your board interview, not-for-profit theaters generate a sizable portion of their revenue through earned income, such as ticket sales, commonly in the range of fifty to sixty-five percent of the total operating budget. For example, fifty-five percent, or $4 million, of Seattle Repertory Theatre's current budget of $7.2 million derives from tickets and other sources of earned revenue, such as concessions, building rentals, coproduction revenue, etc. The board of trustees, in partnership with the managing director and development staff, is responsible for raising the remaining forty-five percent, or $3.2 million. Many theater managers think it is desirable for earned revenue to make up a higher percentage of the annual budget in order to reduce reliance on contributed income. In recent years, this has been difficult to accomplish because theaters have experienced a trend away from subscriptions to single tickets as a buying pattern, while single-ticket sales have been affected by weak economic conditions. Due to these trends, many theaters have become increasingly dependent on donations. Theatre Communications Group's Theatre Facts 2003 reported that, on average, earned income grew 11.5 percent, but sustained 8.1 percent less of total expenses in 2003 than in 1999; conversely, contributed income grew 35.2 percent and financed 2.4 percent more expenses in that same five-year period.

Why Do People Give?

There are many varied motivations for making a charitable gift to a not-for-profit organization. Some people give because they believe in the organization's mission and value what the organization brings to their community or to themselves personally. Some contribute because they want to "give back" to the community or to an organization that has supported them in some way. Many give because they have become involved in a theater, perhaps as a subscriber or volunteer, and they want to deepen their investment in the organization. Some want to be viewed by others as generous or as an important member of the organization. Others are interested in the social or business connections they are able to make with others involved in the theater, such as board members, donors, artists or staff. Some give because they are interested in the tax or estate implications of charitable gifts.

However, topping all of these reasons is the one motivation so obvious that it may be easy to miss: *The number one reason people give is because they are asked.* They are even more likely to give generously if they are made aware of the organization's mission, programs and needs, and then are asked to make a gift by someone, usually a peer, whom they respect and like. Do not assume that the people who attend your theater's wonderful productions understand the need for their support or that their ticket price covers only part of the actual cost of that ticket. In a recent audience survey, only sixty-five percent of one theater's subscribers (who, by the way, receive many magazines, theater programs and direct solicitations annually) knew that the theater is a not-for-profit organization in need of community support beyond the dollars generated by ticket sales.

Sometimes, in the process of asking for support, the following question will arise: "Why don't you just charge the full cost for tickets to the theater, then you wouldn't have to keep asking me for money?" The answer to this question is simple. If a theater were to charge the full cost, ticket prices would certainly be seventy-five dollars to a hundred dollars or more, which would greatly reduce the number of people who can afford to attend. I would assert it would also greatly reduce the number of people who are even interested in seeing the theater's work. An important part of the mission of most not-for-profit theaters is to provide the community the broadest possible access to the theater's programming. In fact, many theaters have discount ticket programs for young people and seniors and make low-cost or free tickets available to schools as part of valuable arts education programs, all subsidized by contributed income.

What Is the Case for Support?

Having reviewed the websites and materials for dozens of theaters and other arts organizations around the country, I would argue that very few theaters make a strong case for support from their community. Because "ticket sales only cover fifty-five percent of our budget," while absolutely true, is not necessarily a compelling argument for support—although it is one that almost every major theater uses as a key statement about its need for charitable gifts.

When we talk about ourselves, we find it difficult to express the impact our theaters have on our communities—the intellectual and emotional impact of the communal experience of watching a play that reflects our human triumphs and frailties. We fail to talk about the importance of the arts to our local economy. We don't explore how art both reflects and advances our society. And we talk about our financial need in a way that leaves gaping holes for people to say, "Why does it cost so much?" or, "How is all of that money being used?"

Fundraising is the ultimate test of an organization's mission and how the organization is perceived in the community. The case for support articulates the problem your organization is trying to solve or the impact of its programs in improving the quality of life in your community. It provides a clear, compelling statement of the reasons your theater is worthy of support. As a trustee, you have the right to ask for the tools you need to go out into your community and ask for money and other resources, and none of these tools is more important than the case for support.

Veteran fundraising consultant and practitioner Dan Conway has articulated the key questions involved in developing a strong case statement as follows: Who are you? Why do you exist? What is distinctive about you? What is it you want to accomplish? How do you intend to accomplish it? How will you hold yourself accountable? I would go one step further: How would your community be different if your organization ceased to exist, or better yet, accomplished its mission?

It is generally the job of the development director to write the case for support, with input from the artistic and managing directors and members of the board's development committee. If the organization doesn't have a development staff, this task is usually undertaken by the chief executive, with assistance and feedback from members of the board. Generally, a more extensive internal case statement of some sort is prepared, giving more detailed information about the theater's mission, vision, programs, goals, governance, budget, finances and various statistics that might be helpful to trustees and staff members who are participating in the theater's fundraising efforts. A more concise, persuasive statement is developed for use in brochures, newsletters and other print pieces. It is a good idea to revisit the case for support annually, as there can be substantive changes in programs, goals and needs. Often, key points of the case for support will come directly out of an organization's strategic planning process; indeed, institutional and programmatic direction and goals should be a critical part of the case for support.

Who Does Fundraising?

The simple answer to this question is everyone. The development director and staff generally lead and coordinate the effort, especially in larger organizations, but executing a comprehensive fundraising plan requires involvement from the full board, the artistic director, the managing director, visiting artists and staff members across the organization—not just in development. Fundraising, done well, is labor-intensive because it involves building relationships. The more people who are involved in a comprehensive and coordinated way, the more people you can reach—and the more likely you are to be successful.

Many organizations now require that every trustee serve on a fundraising committee of one sort or another. Others draw up fundraising participation contracts with each trustee at the beginning of a given cycle in which the board members pledge to participate in the fundraising process in specific ways; examples include making a personal gift, hosting an event for donors at your home, providing the names of five people you plan to cultivate and solicit, and filling a table at an annual gala.

Where Does the Money Come From?

In 2003, contributed income provided an average of forty-six percent of total revenue for eighty-five Trend Theaters that have participated in the Theatre Communications Group (TCG) Fiscal Survey for each of the past five years. The following section provides a snapshot of the sources of contributed income. Your theater's contributed revenue picture will likely look slightly different than the percentages outlined below, due to local and regional differences as well as the size and longevity of the company. In order to ensure financial stability, one of your central development goals should be to achieve a diversified base of support, with funding from as many sources as possible, including individual donors, corporations, foundations, government agencies, events, guilds and in-kind goods and services.

1. INDIVIDUALS. Theaters receive individual gifts from trustees, subscribers, single-ticket buyers, volunteers, staff members and the general public each year. In 2003, the Trend Theatres received 35.2 percent of contributed revenue from individual donors, up from 29.2 percent in 1999. While the number of donors has stayed flat, the average non-trustee individual gift jumped from $275 in 1999 to $473 in 2003.

   Development directors across the country have identified individual donors as the primary area of opportunity for growth for the next three to five years. Individual donors represent significant untapped potential, both in terms of increasing the number of donors and the average gift. Additionally, individual donors are by far the most reliable source of charitable contributions. Once invested, most donors continue their support year after year, and many increase their giving as their involvement in the organization grows. Many theaters have an individual gifts or major gifts committee to focus on cultivating, soliciting and stewarding the theater's major supporters; depending on the size of the organization and the donor base, the committee might focus on gifts of $250 and above or $2,500 and above.
2. FOUNDATIONS. Foundations exist to give money to organizations or individuals who match their giving priorities and criteria—in fact, the law requires that they do so. While psychologically, this makes them an attractive source to solicit because they are expecting you to apply, competition for these dollars can be

fierce, especially for national foundations that specialize in your art form. When you do receive a foundation's support, however, it can be substantial.

Foundations may support everything from operating dollars to education programs to capacity-building initiatives, depending on their giving priorities. In 2003, foundations provided about 17.8 percent of theaters' overall contributed revenue. Often, it can be helpful to have connections between your board and the board of a foundation; some larger theaters have foundation-relations committees that work specifically on building relationships with foundation trustees and program managers.

You may have heard the conventional fundraising wisdom that an average of one in ten grant proposals is funded. One of the most important things to remember in applying for foundation grants is that the relationship-building process is as important with institutional funders as it is with individual donors. Most professional fundraisers would strongly advise against sending a grant proposal to a foundation without first making contact with the foundation's giving officer to introduce your organization and discuss whether your proposed project would be of interest to the foundation. It will save your organization a lot of precious time and energy preparing proposals that may not be well received. Often, giving officers can provide helpful tips about how to make your proposal more competitive and therefore more likely to get funded. Also, I would not recommend sending the same proposal to a number of foundations; in most cases, local funding communities are fairly small and well connected. Throughout the year, your organization should also make efforts to keep foundation-giving officers apprised of happenings and accomplishments and invite them to events, whether or not they are currently providing funding for your organization.

3. CORPORATIONS. Corporate gifts usually come in the form of operating, production or programmatic support or gifts to match individual contributions made by the employees of the company. Many established theaters have long-term partnerships with the major and midsize companies in their area; these relationships often depend on the involvement of a senior-level executive on either the board or a corporate-giving council or committee. In 2003, the TCG Trend Theatres received 15.2 percent of their contributed revenue from corporations.

Many companies contribute to arts organizations because they value the impact these organizations have on making their communities attractive places for their current and prospective employees to live and do business. Corporations also generally value the public recognition benefits offered by theaters, as well as the opportunity to cultivate executives, clients and employees with tickets to the theater. To help them attract corporate gifts, many theaters have a corporate-gifts committee comprised of board members with corporate connections and nonboard, senior-level executives to cultivate and solicit corporate gifts throughout the year.

A major component of your theater's corporate fundraising campaign may also be a program to solicit gifts of in-kind goods and services. These gifts of good and services, like airline tickets and accommodations for artist travel and housing, printing, software, catering and the like, help to substantially reduce a theater's out-of-pocket costs and direct more cash contributions to the art onstage. On average, the TCG Trend Theatres reported gifts of in-kind goods and services valued at nearly $162,000 in 2003.

In recent years, there has been increased focus on the difference between corporate philanthropic dollars and corporate sponsorship dollars—the latter generally coming from the marketing side of a company. Corporate sponsorship, often called cause-related marketing, refers to a commercial activity in which a corporation and a not-for-profit organization form an alliance to market an image, product or service for mutual benefit. Some theaters are now dedicating staff time to pursuing these kinds of marketing deals in addition to philanthropic support. Some companies also extend their relationship with an organization beyond marketing, integrating it with employee volunteerism or corporate philanthropy. Another entry point or opportunity for additional corporate investment in an organization involves sponsoring or buying a table at a theater's annual gala, dollars which often come from the marketing side of a company.

Please remember that corporate giving can be an unreliable source for long-term support due to shifting giving priorities and issues around profitability. Many theaters have experienced significant corporate-giving cutbacks due to the wave of mergers and acquisitions in the 1990s. Over the last five years, the average number of corporate donors per theater has decreased from sixty-three to forty-one, and fewer corporations are giving large gifts.

4. GOVERNMENT. Many theaters receive a portion of contributed revenue from federal, state, county and city government agencies; this support can be for operating, production, arts education or other programmatic support, depending on the funding programs of the agencies. While the level of this support can vary greatly from community to community, theaters received an average of eleven percent of their contributed revenue from government sources in 2003. In recent years, the National Endowment for the Arts has been a much less reliable source of annual funding, having shifted from operating support to project support (due to the funding controversies of the early 1990s). As with any other source of contributed revenue, it is important to build and sustain relationships with both elected officials and paid staff of government funding entities.
5. SPECIAL EVENTS. Almost all not-for-profit organizations raise a portion of their income through one or more major special events. Special events are often seen by board members as an attractive way to raise money because they can be fun to attend, and there is relatively low personal risk in asking friends and colleagues to support the organization through attending a splashy annual event. However, events are costly to produce, both in terms of dollars and human capital. Events are one of the least efficient ways to raise money, often costing thirty to fifty cents for each dollar raised. In addition, there is no better formula for volunteer burnout than big fundraising events.

   That said, events can raise a lot of money and can be a great way to raise the visibility of your organization and introduce new people to your theater. Most successful events depend on committed, high-profile event chairs and a volunteer committee of ten to forty people, whose main responsibility is to ensure that people attend the event. Many theaters produce annual black-tie gala dinners, auctions, performances or opportunities to meet artists or celebrities in an intimate environment; others hold participation-based events like golf tournaments, fun runs or theater tours to New York or London. It is advisable to somehow incorporate your theater's mission into a special event to remind those in attendance what they are there to support.

   Generally, special-event income comes from either individual donors or corporate sponsors; an event is sometimes an effective way to attract an additional investment from a current corporate donor. Trustees are generally expected to support and attend major special events in addition to their annual fund gift.

6. Other. Many established theaters also have other sources of contributed revenue, which for some can account for a substantial portion of their income. Many theaters have guilds or support organizations whose focus it is to raise money and provide volunteer service to the organization. Some communities boast united fund-drives for the arts, in the model of community-wide campaigns like United Way, which provide significant revenue to the organizations that participate. Some theaters also operate under the auspices of another organization, most often a university, which may provide substantial operating support or facilities at low or no cost. While not the direct responsibility of trustees and staff, these auxiliary sources of revenue usually require a fair amount of attention to keep these relationships running smoothly and the dollars flowing in.

What Fundraising Methods Are the Most Effective and Efficient?

Within annual fundraising efforts, there are many ways to solicit support for your organization. Even before you joined the board, it is likely that you received a mailing or a phone call asking for a contribution to the theater. However, there is substantial history and experience to suggest that letters and phone calls may not be the most effective ways to ask for a potential donor's support. The general rule is that the more personal the solicitation, the greater its chances for success. Most theaters use a combination of solicitation methods in the course of an annual fund campaign. The following list provides an outline of these methods, in order of most effective to least effective in terms of success rate and dollars raised:

1. Face-to-face solicitation by a team. You may have heard the conventional fundraising wisdom that "people give to people." This is why a face-to-face meeting is by far the most effective way to raise money. If the theater is requesting a substantial new or significantly increased gift, a personal meeting is highly recommended. The team is usually made up of two to

three people, including a peer of the person being solicited and a staff member from the theater, perhaps the artistic director, managing director, development director or program manager. The peer serves as the passionate advocate for and investor in the organization, and the staff person serves as the expert witness. In my personal experience, the chances of receiving a gift following a personal visit are greater than sixty to seventy-five percent, and the costs associated with securing these gifts are minimal.

2. Face-to-face solicitation by one person. While not as strong as a team approach, this can be effective if the solicitor is passionate, informed about the theater and comfortable in making the request. However, if you do not feel comfortable about expressing the organization's case or asking for the gift, it is a good idea to bring another trustee or a staff member on the visit.
3. Solicitation by letter followed by a personal phone call. As your donor base grows, it will not be possible to meet personally with every prospective supporter. An alternative is to have a peer sign a letter requesting support at a specific dollar level. Generally, a pledge form and return envelope is enclosed with the letter. Within a few days, the person who signed the letter follows up by phone (not email!) to answer any questions and to ask for the support personally. Many theaters use this method in their major-gift fundraising efforts. However, if the prospective donor does not respond to the letter on his own and the solicitor does not follow-up by phone, it is unlikely that a gift will be made.
4. Telephone solicitations. Known as "telefunding," these solicitations can either be done by paid solicitors or volunteers, but paid solicitors generally have a higher success rate. Telefunding campaigns reach out to a theater's current donors, lapsed donors, subscribers, single-ticket buyers and other constituent groups. While recent changes to communications law and technological advances such as caller-ID have made reaching prospective donors more difficult and costly, this is still a far better way to reach people than the mail. Telefunding is also a more effective way to achieve increased gifts than direct mail, as it is more personal. Success rates will vary based on the callers and the type of constituents being called, but are generally in the ten to fifteen percent range; costs associated with paid callers generally range from twenty to thirty-five percent of dollars raised.

5. DIRECT MAIL TO IN-HOUSE LISTS. One of the ways to reach out to and renew the support of existing lower-level contributors is through mail solicitations. Many organizations mail to their constituencies several times a year via direct mail. Generally, the mailing will include a letter signed by a notable artist or a board or staff leader, a pledge form or other response device and a return envelope. Some theaters use direct mail as a pre-approach method to their telefunding efforts, mailing to current donors, lapsed donors, subscribers, single-ticket buyers and other constituent groups. Success rates with in-house lists tend to range between five to ten percent; costs for a substantial mailing printed and prepared by a mailing house generally range from ten to fifteen percent of dollars raised.
6. GIFTS WITH SUBSCRIPTION. Many not-for-profit theaters include a passive contribution solicitation in their subscription renewal packages. This solicitation is based on the idea of encouraging subscribers to become "one-hundred-percent subscribers," paying the full cost of their tickets. Usually, a specific dollar amount is calculated based on the value of the subscription and is printed on the subscription renewal form with language like, "Yes! I'd like to make a tax-deductible contribution and be a one-hundred-percent subscriber." At Seattle Rep, three to five percent of all subscribers include a gift with their subscription, while the costs have been less than one percent.
7. EMAIL OR WEB-BASED SOLICITATIONS. Most theaters are just beginning to experiment with this method of solicitation. Many have websites that can receive contributions via a secure server. However, just because a theater has that capability does not mean that the money will come rolling in. I know of no theater in the country that is currently receiving more than one percent of its total individual contributions via the web. Proactive email solicitations are also a relatively new phenomenon and are now being used to great effect by political candidates and advocacy organizations. Although the method of solicitation is relatively new, the traditional fundraising truths hold true: Relationships are still of the utmost importance (online gifts won't be from new people dropping from the sky); you still have to ask for the gift; it is important to integrate online and offline strategies; and, finally, finding a way to illustrate some urgency is critical. As time goes on and people become more accustomed to shopping and banking online, email and web-based solicitations

may become a more important and effective means of raising individual contributions. The attractive thing about email solicitations is they can be done at little or no cost.

8. DIRECT MAIL TO "COLD" LISTS. Direct mail to cold leads, better know as the general public, has not typically been part of fundraising efforts for most theaters, as we have many prospective donors to contact through people who have already expressed some degree of interest in our organization—subscribers and single-ticket buyers. However, many theater marketing departments trade or purchase lists from appropriate not-for-profit organizations and businesses in order to acquire new subscribers and single-ticket buyers. Direct mail, in the most traditional sense, is generally reserved for securing new donors. As the response rate to cold lists is generally 0.5 to 2 percent, it is unlikely that this mailing will do more than simply break even. The purpose is to acquire donors that the theater can then renew through less costly methods.

The Role of Staff in Fundraising

Especially in larger theaters, you can count on development staff to do much of the behind-the-scenes work related to cultivating, soliciting and thanking donors. In fact, it would be fair to say that about ninety percent of the work will be done by staff. However, the remaining ten percent of the work involves very specific tasks that staff members simply cannot do as effectively as a trustee. These include any task that would be enhanced by a peer relationship: making a connection to someone with whom you have a relationship, asking someone to attend an event, soliciting a new or increased gift or saying thank you via a personal note or phone call. For small theaters, trustees carry more of the responsibility for fundraising.

The bottom-line responsibility of development staff members is to partner with the board in order to maximize each trustee's time and influence. The role of the development staff usually includes the following:

- Develop the fundraising plan, goals and strategies for the review and approval of the development committees and then the full board
- Assist in developing solicitation strategies
- Attend solicitation meetings, serving as the "expert witness"

- Provide information about the prospect as needed and appropriate
- Provide all needed information and materials about the organization, programs and campaigns
- Draft solicitation and thank-you letters for trustees and staff leadership
- Train board members for their role in fundraising, if appropriate
- Prepare meeting announcements, agendas, minutes and other materials in support of the work of development committees
- Update board members on campaign progress
- Coordinate events.

The Role of Trustees in Fundraising

Although it may seem overwhelming at first, fundraising is a simple extension of a trustee's role as ambassador for the organization. Every gift, no matter the source, is the result of a relationship, even foundation and government grants. An important role of the board is to extend the theater's reach into the community—introduce the organization to new people and steward and strengthen the theater's relationships with its various constituencies. The good news is that you are endorsing a great product that has tremendous impact on the people who experience it every night.

When you participate in raising charitable dollars for your theater, you are asking people to join you in investing in a community treasure. You are giving people a unique, totally voluntary opportunity to be involved in something bigger than themselves that makes a real difference in their community. There is no need to be apologetic or feel that you are imposing on people by asking for their support. Look at it this way: The worst someone can say is, "No," and people rarely say no when asked personally for a cause in which they have some interest. Once you can make a shift in your perspective, participating in raising money for your theater can actually become a fulfilling and exciting process.

Trustee Role #1: Give Generously

Trustees demonstrate their leadership and commitment in many ways, but none is more important than their willingness to be involved in the theater's fundraising programs and to give a generous personal gift. As noted fundraiser Worth George says, "It is particularly important that the board act unanimously in its display of commitment, for this lends invaluable strength to its solicitations to outside parties." The board sets the standard for giving for the rest of the community, and the participation of every trustee in the annual fund is crucial. In fact, trustees generally give twenty to forty percent of a theater's total individual gifts. In 2003, the average trustee gift to the 214 theaters that participated in the TCG Fiscal Survey was $6,189 (Trend Theatres averaged $9,184) and represented 30.3 percent of total individual contributions. Even for small and emerging theaters, trustee gifts accounted for between a quarter and a third of all individual gifts received, while the average trustee gift ranged from $1,314 to $2,717 for theaters with budgets less than one million dollars. As you are working with the development staff to build the theater's annual fundraising plan, it is important to set an appropriate and specific goal for annual fund gifts from trustees.

Based on your board recruitment interview, you should have some idea of what level of personal giving and fundraising involvement is expected of you. If you don't, you should ask the board president, managing director or development director, hopefully before you accept trusteeship. Many, if not most, organizations have a stated minimum trustee gift, as well as guidelines in terms of additional financial participation, including purchasing a subscription and supporting fundraising events. You may also want to be clear about expectations regarding current or upcoming special campaigns, such as capital or endowment efforts, before joining a board.

Although every theater will handle soliciting annual gifts from board members in its own way, you can expect a meeting, phone call or letter from a member of the board leadership asking for your pledge at the beginning of each season. The earlier in the season you make the pledge, the better—it saves board leadership and staff valuable time, which they can now spend contacting people who are not as close to the organization. In terms of your personal giving, the general rule is that the organization on whose board you serve should be one of your top three philanthropic priorities in terms of both your financial support and your volunteer time. If you are on several other boards, you may want to consider whether you can be an effective board member for yet another organization. I would strongly encourage you to consider making a personally significant "stretch" gift to the annual fund—whether that amount is $500 or $50,000. The process of deciding your level of support can be a transformative experience; a generous gift will inspire others and give you additional confidence in asking others to join you in supporting the organization.

Some organizations, including many theaters, have adopted what is known as a board "give or get" policy, or what may more appropriately be called a "give *and* get" policy. This policy states that each trustee is expected to make a personally significant gift, as well as go out into the community and raise a specified additional amount. For some theaters, that amount may be $5,000, and for others it may be $25,000 or more. For example, one major theater's board recently adopted a policy that each trustee is expected to give $10,000 personally and raise an additional $15,000 for a total impact of $25,000. Some trustees do this by soliciting their company or a handful of friends or by assembling tables for the organization's gala. While exceptions to the policy are made on a case-by-case basis in order to attract a trustee with specific skills or connections, most trustees on that board far exceed the expectation. A smaller theater could have a similar policy more in line with its budget size and trustee resources—perhaps a $2,500 give-and-get policy, where each board member is expected to give $500 and assist the organization in raising an additional $2,000.

TRUSTEE ROLE #2: KNOW YOUR STUFF

Take the time early in your tenure to learn as much about the vision, mission, programming, management, financials, history, goals, challenges, needs, and facts and figures as possible—but know that the staff is there to back you up. I would strongly recommend that you take advantage of any orientation or training opportunities your theater offers, even if you have participated in similar training programs at other organizations.

Take the lead in developing the tools and training that you and other trustees need in order to be effective ambassadors and fundraisers on behalf of the organization. Be able to articulate your own personal story about why you have chosen to support the theater with your money and, more importantly, your time—and why you believe in what this organization is trying to do. This will help you tremendously as you begin to reach out to others asking for their support.

Trustee Role #3: Participate Where You Can Have the Most Impact

Fundraising involves much more than soliciting gifts—in fact, about ninety percent of fund development involves cultivating and stewarding relationships that will later provide the opportunity to ask for an investment in the work of the theater. Trustees are particularly well suited for these tasks, because board members come from a place of passion and personal commitment; if you are enthusiastic about the organization, that positive energy will speak volumes to potential donors.

Ways Trustees Can Participate

There are many ways that theaters need trustees to participate in fundraising, but the most important include serving on a fundraising committee, introducing new people to the organization, cultivating current and prospective donors, and soliciting gifts.

Join a Committee

Most theaters will request that you join a fundraising committee early in your board tenure. Since expanding the reach of the organization into the community is a primary role of the board, newer board members often have the most to offer. Your willing participation will make you the hero of the board leadership and the staff, and you'll begin to understand and maybe even enjoy the process. This is hard work, but once you are involved, I believe you will feel that it is worth the investment of time and energy.

As was mentioned earlier, many major theaters with large boards will have several development committees organized around the overall development plan and policies: individual or major gifts, corporate gifts, foundation relations, planned giving, government advocacy and special events. Smaller organizations may have just one fundraising committee, which can be a good way to engage and expand the number of nonboard volunteers participating in the fundraising process and thus the reach into the community. Some organizations have chosen to disband standing development committees altogether to send the message that fundraising must be the work of the full board, rather than delegated to the handful of brave people on the development committee. Instead, these boards focus a major portion of every board meeting on fundraising.

The responsibilities of trustees who serve on development committees usually include the following:

- Be enthusiastic about the organization and the fundraising process
- Involve and motivate the full board to participate in identifying, involving, soliciting, thanking and stewarding current and prospective donors
- Ensure the case for support is strong and current and that you have the materials and training you need to be successful in your efforts
- Help develop policies for board and staff related to gift solicitation and recognition
- Help evaluate or rate prospective donors for appropriate ask amounts
- Assist in developing strategies for involvement and cultivation of major gift, corporate or foundation prospects
- Attend donor events to forge personal ties between the theater and its donors
- Solicit prospective donors in collaboration with trustee colleagues and/or staff
- Supplement the theater's official acknowledgment letter and donor's tax receipt with a personal note or phone call to thank the donor.

It is important that you and the theater use your precious time to focus on high-impact efforts and major gifts; most lower-level fundraising efforts, such as telefunding and direct mail, can be handled by the staff. Once you have been on the board a while and feel more comfortable with the fundraising process, offer to share your experience by mentoring a newer board member or serve as a leader of one of the development committees.

Introduce the Theater to Friends and Colleagues

One of the key roles trustees can and should play is introducing their friends and colleagues to the theater. It is not unusual for an organization's major gifts or corporate gifts committee to ask that each board member identify three to five people or companies that they think may have the interest and capacity to become donors at a specific level. This can be an overwhelming request for some, depending on the circles they travel in.

Before you get too anxious about asking people you know for money, take a deep breath. You probably know more people that meet these qualifications than you think. Sit down and go through your Rolodex or email-contact list and make a list of people you think might enjoy an invitation to attend the theater. Think about your business contacts, vendors or clients—are there companies that would benefit from cause-related visibility in front of your theater's particular audience demographic? Think about the other professional, not-for-profit or alumni groups with which you are involved—are there people who attend everything in town or are crazy about theater? If you are racking your brain and are still having a hard time coming up with your list of people, ask the development staff for a list of current subscribers to the theater and then go through it and identify people whom you know already have some relationship with the organization.

CULTIVATE PROSPECTIVE DONORS STRATEGICALLY

Once you have your list, invite your prospects to the theater one night and have an informal reception before or after the show. Invite the artistic director or managing director to join you and speak to your group; the development staff can usually help you coordinate the details of this type of event. Or you can buy four subscriptions and invite people to join you at the theater on different evenings. Alternatively, you can invite them to join you for a development event that the theater is already hosting. This process can be fun—your guests are likely to thank you for including them!

Conventional fundraising wisdom suggests that it takes as many as eight to twelve contacts each year to help a current or prospective donor feel connected to the organization. These contacts might include sending materials or information about the organization, personal contact through a phone call or handwritten note, invitations to fundraising or cultivation events or small gifts related to your organization.

If you are cultivating the people you have identified for the organization, you probably have a strong sense of the right series of contacts with those particular people. On the other hand, you may be asked to take on a "portfolio" of individual or corporate donors with whom you will be the primary trustee contact; in this instance, the staff may be helpful in planning a cultivation strategy. If you are willing to develop relationships on behalf of the theater with theater patrons you don't know, the staff will be very grateful and you will set a great example for other trustees.

It is a good idea to sit down with the appropriate staff member at the beginning of a season and plan a cultivation strategy with each of your prospects. In order to keep the workload manageable, each trustee should have no more than ten to twelve prospects assigned to them at a time. This is why your theater needs the involvement of every trustee, not just those who serve on development committees, to be successful; a board of thirty could reach out personally to a major donor pool of more than three hundred prospects if the systems are in place to support them.

When the cultivation plan (with specific tasks and due dates) has been developed, simply schedule each task for each prospective donor over a period of months leading up to the solicitation. Some tasks will be the responsibility of staff (sending an invitation, newsletter or official acknowledgment letter), and some will be the responsibility of the trustee (handwritten note, a phone call to follow up on an invitation or set up a solicitation meeting). If your organization has a large development staff, the major gifts officer or another support person may be able to set up a system to remind you via email that on January 12, you need to call Mrs. Smith to follow up on that opening night invitation. This collaborative strategy between board and staff has proven highly effective at Seattle Rep (see the Cultivation and Solicitation Plan worksheet at the end of this article for further illustration).

Solicit Gifts from Donors

The process of soliciting a major gift from an individual donor can be a wonderful experience—and it can also cause the participants a lot of unnecessary anxiety. The following section should help to demystify the process and help you feel more at ease.

- Get the meeting: It is most effective if a trustee, rather than a staff member, contacts the prospective donor by phone to ask for thirty to forty-five minutes of his or her time to talk about the theater. Be honest and deal with donors as if they are being perfectly honest: If they say they are busy, believe them and ask for a later date when their schedule lightens up. I would suggest planning a meeting with them at a neutral location such as the theater. If this is not possible, offer to come to their home or office. Avoid meeting over meals or in busy public places, as there will be many interruptions and distractions that may make what could be a short meeting into a two-hour commitment on the part of the prospective donor(s). Let the staff know when the meeting is scheduled and plan who from the board or staff will join you at the meeting, if you have not already done so.

- Prepare for the meeting: Spend some time before the meeting reviewing the solicitation packet that will be given to the donor, and be prepared to present a compelling case for support. Also, learn as much as you can before the visit about the prospects, their capacity, their interest in and relationship with the organization—it will give you more comfort, credibility and leverage. Staff will often prepare a short briefing about prospective donors, their relationship to the organization, their giving to other organizations and evidence of their capacity to make a significant gift. Even if your organization does not have the staff resources to do significant research on prospective donors, a simple search on the internet will often give you some information about where they work, what other organizations they support and what some of their other interests might be. Look for ways that you can connect with each prospect on a more personal level, such as professional background, personal interests, mutual friends or other common threads.

  Especially when you first begin doing solicitations, it is a good idea to get together with your solicitation team for thirty minutes before the visit to plan and rehearse the solicitation. Who will begin the conversation? Who will name the gift amount you are seeking? How will you handle possible objections that might arise? The preparation meeting is a good time to remind everyone that the most important part of a solicitation visit is to *listen* to the prospective donor. The solicitation team should not be doing any more than fifty percent of the talking at the meeting—this is more difficult than it would seem, but keep in mind that the goal of the meeting is to get to know the donor.

- The opening: At the beginning of a solicitation visit, thank the prospective donors for making the time to meet with you and state the purpose of the meeting. You should engage in efforts to build rapport with the prospects, especially if you don't know them well. Thank them for their past support, if appropriate. Within the first few minutes, though, you should try to work the theater and the campaign into the discussion. I have been to painful lunch solicitation meetings in which there was no discussion of the theater for the first forty-five minutes; by that point, everyone around the table, including the prospect, becomes anxiety-ridden about what is coming.

- The involvement: Talk with the prospective donors about their involvement and interest in the theater: how they got involved, if they were ever involved in theater in high school or college (you'd be surprised how many were!), what their favorite shows have been, etc. Ask open-ended questions that encourage the person to share more about themselves. Try to determine if they have special interest in a specific part of what your organization does. For example, some people are passionate about new-play development programs, while others are most interested in outreach programs such as arts education. With this information about their specific interest, you will know where to focus your comments about the theater and the need for their support.
- Make the case: This is your opportunity to talk about the theater's vision, mission and needs. How will their investment in the theater make a difference? Talk about the features and benefits of the organization and the campaign. Mention your own personal involvement with the theater and the campaign and why you have decided to devote both your time and your financial resources to the theater. Listen for the donors to express either praise for the organization or specific questions or concerns that they may have.
- You must ask: In a personal solicitation meeting, someone must request a specific dollar amount, and the whole solicitation team should go into the meeting knowing who is going to ask for the gift. If the trustee designated to make the request fails to do it, someone else has to name the number. The prospective donor can't read your mind—he or she has no idea what you want, need or might suggest—and it will be a relief to all involved to have the number out on the table. When the moment to ask comes, look the person in the eye and ask if they would consider joining you in supporting the campaign at the $X level. Once the number has been named, be quiet and wait for their response.
- The details: Once the donor provides an initial answer, be prepared to offer additional information about the benefits of being a donor, how to make a gift, timing of the gift, payment options, etc. Also, be ready to respond directly to any objections that the

donor may have. Your rehearsal earlier will come in handy at this point, as you should have anticipated possible objections and practiced how you would handle them.

If you find that you are uncomfortable with the idea of asking for money—and almost everyone is in the beginning—start small by calling donors to thank them on behalf of the organization. You can also sign solicitation letters to mid-level donors and phone them to follow up and ask for their renewed commitment to the organization. These experiences will serve to make you more comfortable with the process.

The Annual Fund and Its Role in Long-term Financial Stability

Around the board table, the following question will often arise around the end of the fiscal year: "Do we really have to raise all this money year after year?" Fortunately, the answer to this question is: "Yes!" The annual fund is the process by which a theater reaches out to its constituency to share in fulfilling its mission. As was discussed earlier, the process of inviting constituents to deepen their relationship with your theater through an annual fund gift is an important part of building and cementing each donor's relationship with your organization.

While the fundraising process may seem daunting at first, I encourage you to stick with it. Giving and the process of fundraising encourage people to act on their values. Each act of asking and giving is an honor and a privilege and, if viewed as such, can be transformative for the individuals involved as well as the organizations they care about and, ultimately, the community.

It often takes years to build a solid base of annual fund donors, but their support will underwrite the current needs of the organization and provide the foundation to encourage increased future investment in the theater. That investment might take the shape of helping to establish working-capital reserves, construct or renovate facilities through capital projects, build a permanent endowment or make a planned gift through a donor's estate. It is only through a well-established and solid annual fund and base of supporters that your theater will be able to contemplate larger fundraising efforts that have the capacity to propel your organization and its service to the community to the next level.

Major Gifts Prospect Cultivation and Solicitation Plan

Date created: ____

Prospect: ______________________________ Account #: __________

Contact information: Day __________ Evening __________ Email: ________

Primary solicitor: ______________ Primary development staff: ____________

Who else can help? ____

Targeted solicitation amount: ____________________________________

Prospect profile completed and attached? Yes No

Profile anticipated to be available: ________________________________

SOLICITATION METHOD:

Face-to-face solicitation/Meeting date: ______________________________

Personalized letter with phone follow-up/Date: _________________________

CULTIVATION PLAN (8 to 10 contacts for your prospect throughout the year; can include personal notes, personal contact, event invitations and follow-up, chatting at an event, sending marketing materials, reviews, tangible items, etc.):

ACTION:	ASSIGNED TO:	DEADLINE:	COMPLETED:

NOTES (record results of actions, content of conversations and other information relevant to this donor):

____

____

____

____

____

____

Questions to Help You Develop Your Strategy:

What is the rationale (case) for this specific major gift?

____

____

____

How does this gift support the mission of Seattle Rep?

____

____

What do we know about the prospective donor? Their interests? Concerns? Previous gifts? Relationship with Seattle Rep?

____

____

Who should be involved in the solicitation? Other trustees? From Seattle Rep? From the prospective donor's perspective? Spouse? Financial advisor?

____

____

Who should ask for the gift?

____

____

When is the right time to ask? What cultivation needs to be done first?

____

____

What is the specific request for the annual fund?

____

____

How much time will be involved (from getting the appointment to asking for the gift to negotiating the details)?

____

____

CAPITAL AND ENDOWMENT CAMPAIGNS

Christine Fiedler O'Connor

O THERE YOU ARE: an active member of the board of an arts organization with a well-crafted mission, top quality programs, astute management, strong box-office sales, a growing base of diversified funding and a healthy balance sheet. Then, just when you thought you were safe, a new institutional imperative erupts on the horizon: The Capital Campaign.

While those three words often strike fear in the hearts of the hardiest board members, there's no reason to be afraid. Capital campaigns—be they for a bricks-and-mortar project or to create an endowment—can bring about a board's greatest legacy to a cultural institution and the community it serves. How? By providing the leadership to raise funds to build a new facility, renovate an existing one, or create the permanent financial resources of an endowment, trustees can help theaters meet the changing needs of audiences and artistic programs for future generations. No other initiative may be as valuable to an arts organization's effort to sustain its niche as a cultural treasure for its community.

Ideally, the happy characteristics identified above would describe all organizations about to embark on a capital campaign. Alas, it doesn't always happen that way. This chapter offers an aerial view of how these extraordinary campaigns work and details what to consider—and why—before your theater embarks on a campaign. We'll consider how you as a trustee can provide the leadership and stewardship that will steer a campaign toward success.

What Is a Capital/Endowment Campaign—And How Does It Differ from an Annual Fund Campaign?

Three factors set capital campaigns apart from general operating campaigns:

1. THE NATURE OF THE CORE PROJECT FOR WHICH FUNDS ARE being raised. Typically, capital campaigns involve construction or renovation of facilities or acquisition of major equipment.

   The term "capital campaign" is also used to describe the creation or augmentation of a permanent endowment. Endowment gifts are made with the understanding that the principal will remain intact in perpetuity. All, or more typically a portion, of the income generated by investing endowment funds can be used either to fund general operating expenses or for restricted purposes specified by the donor. National Arts Strategies, the leadership development organization that has guided capacity-building efforts in the arts, recommends that a healthy arts organization have permanent endowment resources equal to two hundred to five hundred percent of the annual operating budget. Only a few theaters have achieved that, but many are taking steps to at least begin creating endowed funds that can help them stabilize their finances and weather fluctuations in earned and contributed income.
2. THE TIME FRAME IN WHICH THE CAMPAIGN IS CONDUCTED. FOR building or equipment projects, extraordinary costs and construction deadlines call for an intensive fundraising campaign that may extend over two to five years but has a clearly defined ending date. Endowment-campaign deadlines are often driven by the need to generate investment income to fund program

expansions. Although endowment deadlines may have more flexibility than construction schedules, clearly defined time limits for endowment campaigns create a sense of urgency that can provide the momentum to stimulate giving.

3. THE MAGNITUDE OF THE TARGETED GIFTS. ALTHOUGH SOME construction projects or equipment acquisitions may have more modest price tags, most capital campaigns will involve multimillion-dollar goals—and may require the organization to seek the largest gifts it has ever solicited.

Why Embark on a Capital Campaign?

For many arts organizations, a capital campaign represents a decisive step toward realizing a long-held dream of greater financial stability, enhanced programs and improved service to audiences and artists. The best reason to embark on a campaign is because it will enable your organization to advance the art form and better serve the community. Put another way, it makes sense to move forward when failing to undertake the initiative will pose a threat to the future success of the organization and its ability to serve its varied constituencies.

For Seattle Repertory Theatre, the decision to begin a capital campaign for a new second space was tied directly to programming and the organization's core mission. "We have a wonderful mainstage in the 856-seat Bagley Wright Theatre," said managing director Benjamin Moore. "But new-play development is an integral part of our artistic mission—and the 99-seat venue we used for new play workshops and productions of more intimate plays just couldn't serve our production needs. We knew that our programming and our audience development efforts would stagnate if we didn't move forward to build a 300-seat second theater that would support our artistic ambitions."

"Our organization is almost twenty years old and we've never had an endowment," explained Elizabeth Kennedy, administrative director of the Los Angeles Opera. "For years, we struggled to keep the wolf away from the door, and we were starting sentences with, 'If we're here next year, then we'd like your support for . . .' We couldn't have convinced anyone that [an endowment gift to our company] would be a wise and safe investment. Even now, cash is king for us, and whenever a donor says, 'You can have it now or later,' we tend to want it now. Still, we realize that we need to take steps to move toward endowment or we'll never have the resources to get out of that endless circle. For us, that means beginning with a focus on planned gifts to build endowment."

When Is a Theater Ready to Embark on a Capital Campaign?

Although unbridled enthusiasm and a clear need are crucial to a capital campaign's success, those factors alone aren't enough to propel an arts organization toward victory. Timing is everything. As this checklist illustrates, you will know that your theater is ready to move forward when:

1. The organization generates sufficient earned and contributed income to cover operating expenses, ending each fiscal year with a balanced budget. Although that wasn't unusual in the 1990s, it has proved increasingly difficult for theaters since the millennium. The 2003 edition of Theatre Facts, Theatre Communications Group's annual survey of the field, noted that fifty-eight percent of the 125 Universe Trend Theatres[1] closed the year with deficits, up from thirty percent two years earlier. In a fluctuating economy, donors may perceive modest shortfalls as harmless. Accumulated deficits equal to more than ten percent of an arts organization's total budget, however, undermine the organization's financial management credibility and may compromise the success of a capital campaign.
2. The theater has working capital reserves equal to at least three months' operating expenses. One of my clients looked at that statement and asked hopefully, "Does it matter which three months it is?" Although it would be easier if the advice pertained to June, July and August—when her organization is not in performance and operating expenses are less than a third of those incurred in any other fiscal quarter—this piece of conventional wisdom refers to a minimum of twenty-five percent of total annual expenses. Reserves provide a safety net enabling the organization to weather short-term cash flow challenges, a cost-efficient, first line of defense to turn to before drawing on an external line of credit and evidence of prudent planning.

1. Universe Trend Theatres are the 125 organizations that have participated in the Theatre Facts survey for the five years 1999 to 2003, as distinct from the 85 Trend Theatres that have been profiled during that period.

3. THE BOARD AND STAFF HAVE TOGETHER CREATED A STRATEGIC plan that maps the organization's goals and the strategies to attain them. Designed to summarize the organization's future direction and articulate goals, strategies and budgets, the plan is a working document that forms the foundation for a successful capital campaign. A three-to-five-year period is "long range" in the performing arts. A plan covering more than five years may require projections of programming, budgets and external market forces that are too vague or speculative to be useful.

    The trustee chair of my organization's strategic planning committee said some years ago, "There are two ways for us to approach this plan—the Santa Barbara model, or the slow, traditional method." The puzzled look on my face prompted her to offer further translation. "Well, you and I can go to Santa Barbara for the weekend, lock ourselves in a hotel room with a laptop and come out with a plan that the board can rubber-stamp. Or, we can spend the next year having monthly meetings with the senior staff and the committee and hammer it out over a conference table."

    While some view the strategic plan merely as a required attachment for grant applications, well-managed arts organizations have found the planning document—and the process of creating it—to be essential navigational tools. Our theater rejected the Santa Barbara model in favor of a process that was more inclusive and instructive for the players. We found that the meetings that were required to build consensus were also opportunities for valuable dialogue and healthy disagreement. For artistic and administrative staff, articulating goals and strategies offered an opportunity to gauge what the board did and didn't understand about the often-mysterious process of producing in the performing arts. For trustees, the planning process presented a forum for balancing the staff's in-the-trenches view of the organization's future with a broader, arm's-length perspective on the theater's profile within the larger community. The planning process also provided an opportunity to develop fresh approaches to articulating the case for support. Trustees assessed financial stability and identified ways they could provide effective advocacy to support ongoing artistic and institutional ambitions.

    For an organization that is contemplating a capital or endowment campaign, the planning process can be a critical tool to build internal momentum and clarity of purpose. Whether prospective donors read every page of the plan is less important than the impact of the planning process on arming trustees and staff with a common view of priorities and a thorough understanding of the organization's needs and potential.

4. THERE ARE STAFF AND SYSTEMS IN PLACE TO SUSTAIN THE PLANNING and execution of a special campaign in addition to normal fundraising operations. Chances are that your organization's development staff is already working overtime to meet the demands of annual fundraising goals. Depending upon the scope of the capital effort, the organization may need to hire additional staff to provide support for the campaign leadership, create grant proposals and campaign materials, conduct prospect research, process gifts and generate reports for billing and stewardship.

   For many arts organizations, capital campaigns may represent the first time the organization has offered donors the opportunity to make multiyear pledges and installment payment plans, utilize a variety of planned giving instruments, create named funds or place specific restrictions on their gifts. Accordingly, the systems required to record, invoice, monitor and report on those gifts may be very different from those previously used in annual fund campaigns. Modifications to computer databases may be necessary and changes must be tested and implemented before the campaign is underway.

5. THE BOARD IS WILLING AND ABLE TO PROVIDE LEADERSHIP for a campaign. Like annual fund campaigns, eighty to ninety percent of the work of a capital or endowment campaign may be done by staff. The crucial ten to twenty percent that remains, however, will require the active, strategic involvement of trustees who share a passionate commitment to the campaign—as well as the project. It's the trustees who provide the influence and evangelism to motivate others in the community to provide their financial support. A board that assumes that the staff will lead the effort will endanger the campaign's profile in the community, raise doubts among prospective donors and handicap the organization's potential for success.

6. THE THEATER HAS ENOUGH PROSPECTIVE DONORS WITH THE capacity and readiness to make major gifts. A capital campaign requires a robust universe of prospective donors with a strong interest in the organization and the financial capacity to con-

tribute leadership gifts. Conventional wisdom holds that a campaign will require three prospects for every gift. Ideally, relationships with those donors have been nurtured by trustees and staff during the course of the annual fundraising programs, and the prospects are ready to hear about your organization's extraordinary initiative. If not, the initial phases of a campaign may incorporate cultivation programs. Regardless of their interest in the theater's work, however, the prospects must have the financial resources to make leadership gifts or the subsequent "quiet stage" of the campaign will stall.

7. THE THEATER HAS DETERMINED HOW IT WILL FINANCE A CAMPAIGN. In addition to the costs of the capital construction project or the proposed permanent endowment, the campaign itself will require funding for staffing, materials, catering, computer upgrades, etc. Will your theater build these expenses into the campaign goal or carry them as separate project costs? Will a portion of each capital gift be allocated to this purpose, or will discrete funds be raised to cover all or part of the costs prior to the campaign's commencement? Whichever approach you take, it will have a different impact on the organization, the campaign timeline and the donors. While the full scope of the campaign costs may not be clear until the campaign preparation process is complete, the theater should consider this issue on a preliminary basis before moving forward.
8. THE THEATER HAS FORMULATED REALISTIC FINANCIAL PROJECTIONS of operating costs in the new or renovated facility. Too often organizations focus their attention on analyzing the campaign costs, but fail to consider the increased operating expenses that will inevitably accompany life in a new or expanded theater. Occupancy costs such as heat, light, power and building maintenance, personnel expenses of additional house management staff, box-office and backstage crews; and increased marketing expenses to attract an expanded audience may conspire to cripple the organization's finances before the glow has faded from a successful capital campaign. Similarly, the costs of financing construction while capital campaign pledges are paid out over subsequent years can also pose a financial hazard to organizations that overlook this cost in campaign and operating budgets.

A wise planning process will analyze these factors before the campaign is underway and account for these expenses in campaign and/or operating budgets. Board and management may be well served, for example, to include a two-to-three-year transition fund for increased operating costs in the capital campaign goal. "Bridge funding" of this nature will give the theater time to bring its marketing and annual fundraising efforts into line in the post-campaign phase, and donors will appreciate the theater's comprehensive approach to long-range planning as a means of protecting their charitable "investments" in your campaign and your organization.

9. THE TRUSTEES ARE EXCITED BY A CASE FOR SUPPORT THAT OFFERS a compelling opportunity to transform the art form and the cultural resources of your community. In the increasingly crowded marketplace for arts and other not-for-profit organizations, the biggest challenge for a capital campaign may be articulating a compelling answer to the: "So what?" question. So you'd like a new building, or an endowment or a major upgrade of your technical equipment. A wide range of similar campaigns are likely to be underway in the community, from the local university to the hospital to the job-training resource center, among others. The reality is that every donor cannot support each at the same level—and many may feel moved to support only one or two campaigns. Why should a donor choose your organization? What difference will your capital or endowment project make to the life of your community, to your cultural economy, to the art form and the citizens who benefit from it? The odds are that you have plenty of compelling answers to those questions, and you and your fellow trustees have enthusiasm for sharing that information with your friends, peers and colleagues. If that's not the case, your campaign is not ready to move forward.

When your theater has addressed these issues, the organization can proceed with confidence to begin a capital campaign. Can you move forward if these factors are not in place? Many organizations do—although the campaign process will be harder, take longer and remain vulnerable to periodic setbacks as the organization stops to address key issues along the way.

How can you determine whether your theater is ready? The first two items on the list will be reflected in the theater's audited statements. The remaining points will benefit from impartial evaluation by outside consultants, as part of the feasibility study discussed in the next section.

What Are the Stages of a Capital Campaign?

As mentioned earlier, capital and endowment campaigns differ from annual fundraising efforts because they focus on a major project that is outside the normal operating budget, require a longer time frame and seek gifts larger than those normally required for annual operations. Capital campaigns also involve a different set of steps, a different rhythm and a different arc in building momentum toward a fundraising goal than annual fundraising programs. The key to a capital or endowment campaign is planning. Generally, the campaign process is divided into four distinct phases.

PHASE 1: CAMPAIGN PREPARATION

Feasibility

The process begins with a fact-finding tour (or, perhaps more accurately, an investigative journey through community perceptions) that is commonly known as the feasibility study. The study is designed to answer a fundamental question: "Is it feasible for this theater to raise the funds necessary to support this capital or endowment project at this time?"

That's not a rhetorical question, although more than a few boards and organizations will ask impatiently, "Why do we have to spend time and money on a feasibility study?" The first reason is that before the campaign begins, you must be certain that your theater has the personnel and systems in place to support this major undertaking. The second reason is that no matter how important you believe your project to be, it is essential to test your community's perceptions of your needs, case materials and leadership capabilities before launching a campaign.

A feasibility study will examine these issues in two phases. The *internal assessment* component will involve interviews of staff and key volunteers and analyses of information provided by the organization—with an eye to determining whether the organization has the infrastructure, expertise, prospective donors and information systems to manage a campaign. The *external phase* will involve one-on-one interviews with key stakeholders and community leaders whose views of the organization, the project and the fundraising goal will inform campaign strategies and timelines. Although effective studies may be based on as few as twenty interviews, your organization may elect to expand that roster to forty or more individuals, depending on the nature of your project and the complexity of your constituency. The interviews will probe perceptions in areas such as:

- The nature of the individual's (or the corporation's or foundation's) involvement with the theater and the factors that promote continued involvement.
- The organization's mission, strengths and weaknesses.
- The theater's reputation and standing in the community, as well as the reputations and standing of its artistic, management and board leadership.
- The strengths and weaknesses of the theater's fundraising programs, as well as its marketing and public relations efforts.
- The fundraising environment in the community with regard to the economic climate, competition for contributed funds in general and competition from other capital or endowment campaigns in particular.
- Reactions to the case statement or similar materials that have been provided in advance as well as to the timing of the proposed campaign.
- Whether it's feasible for the theater to raise the funds required to meet the goal of the capital or endowment project—and, if the goal is perceived to be too ambitious, the interview subject's opinion of a more realistic goal.
- Suggestions by respected and influential volunteers about whom should be recruited to lead the campaign—and feedback on whether the interview subject would be willing to serve in some capacity.
- Specific suggestions of prospective donors who the interview subject believes might be interested in making major gifts at various contribution levels and whose support would be influential to others in the community.
- Feedback on where the theater fits into the interviewee's philanthropic priorities and, if the organization is not at the top of that list, the factors or changes that might raise the theater to a more important level in the interviewee's eyes.
- A sense of whether the interviewee would be inclined to make a significant gift.

The best means of obtaining candid responses in these interviews is to engage an outside expert or consultant. Prospective donors and community leaders who have concerns or criticisms may feel more comfortable sharing these important issues with an objective outsider than with members of the theater's staff or board. Conversely, interviewees may also feel more free to articulate compliments about the strengths and capabilities of the organization, its staff and its governing board—and their responses may carry more weight coming from an outside consultant's report.[2]

"We knew we would learn something valuable from the feasibility study interviews," remarked one theater's development director, "and we were prepared for some degree of criticism from the donors and trustees who were interviewed. As it turned out, we learned that we were much harder on ourselves than anyone thought we should be. Our board and donors had very favorable views about our programs, our staff and our potential for success with the campaign. Their only concern was whether our board was ready to provide the leadership and support that the campaign would require. If we'd done the study ourselves, I'm not sure the people who were interviewed would have been as frank about that. With the consultant's help, we were able to raise those issues with our executive committee and formulate the strategies to address them."

The feasibility study's potential for success will be enhanced by the organization's clear definition of the scope and nature of the issues and the selection of an appropriate consultant to explore those issues with community leaders. The most effective consultant will be one who is willing to tailor the study methodology to meet your needs, rather than applying a formulaic approach that may not be suited to your organization or your constituents. The best consultant is one whose style complements your organization, whose experience includes similar organizations in the arts and/or in your geographic region and whose listening and communications skills will represent your organization well. Your organization will create a narrative request-for-proposals (RFP), seek recommendations from colleagues and others in the community and solicit proposals from a range of

2. Traditional feasibility studies treat each individual interviewed as an anonymous source and feature unattributed quotations to support conclusions in the final report. However, some consultants prefer, unless specifically directed by the interview subject to maintain confidentiality, to share specific opinions and information from each source openly with the client organization. It's up to you—and your stakeholders—to determine which method will succeed in yielding the most useful information for your organization and your campaign.

consultants before winnowing the list to two or three who will make presentations and be interviewed by board and staff.

Consulting fees for a feasibility study may range from $15,000 to $40,000 or more. Fees will depend upon whether you engage a large national firm or a local independent consultant; how many interviews are included and, in turn, how much consulting time must be spent on the study; and whether the consultant's report is to include a detailed plan and timeline or simply a summary of the findings and recommendations for next steps. A feasibility study may take from six to ten weeks to complete from engagement of the firm to submission of the final report.

Formation of a campaign study committee of six to ten members will add value and organization to this phase of the campaign-preparation process. This committee's primary role is to shepherd the feasibility study, select the consultant(s), provide input to the study methodology, evaluate the results and formulate next-step recommendations when the findings are presented to the full board. Although the majority of the committee members may be from the board, it may be useful to include some influential voices from the broader community to participate in this process. Individuals from the corporate, civic or philanthropic arenas who have an interest in your organization's progress will offer fresh perspectives and may be among the first external advocates and advisors for the planned campaign.

The results of the feasibility study will provide your organization with answers to key questions that will form the basis for a critical path for the campaign, such as:

- Does the community have confidence in our organization and our artistic and management leaders, and are they valued and respected?
- Is our need for a capital project or endowment clearly understood and embraced by important members of our community?
- Do we have the right volunteer leadership to spearhead this campaign?
- Do we have a sufficient number of prospects for leadership gifts who are willing to support the campaign at the necessary financial level?
- Do we have the staff and systems in place to support a campaign of this magnitude without disturbing the momentum of our annual fundraising program?

In turn, the answers to these questions will form the basis for the final component of the campaign preparation phase: the creation of a fundraising plan outlining key elements, including:

- The campaign leadership structure, including honorary chairs, working chairs, committees to cultivate and solicit gifts at various levels, campaign policy committees[3] and job descriptions for each.
- The gift table (which appears in "Phase 2: The Quiet Stage"), illustrating the number of gifts that are required at each level in order to meet the goal.
- Rosters of potential campaign volunteers.
- Lists of prospective donors (including trustees) who have been "rated" in terms of capacity to make gifts at various levels, readiness to be solicited and potential to influence other donors in the sequence of solicitations.
- A summary of the types of gifts that will be sought, including cash, securities, gifts of property and, if appropriate, planned gifts and bequests[4].
- A structure of donor recognition opportunities.
- A public relations plan that is coordinated with ongoing institutional promotion.
- A campaign expense budget outlining direct expenses for print and electronic campaign collateral, campaign counsel, cultivation and solicitation events, computer enhancements, donor and volunteer recognition, travel and personnel (total expenses will vary for each organization, but will generally range from four percent to ten percent of the total fundraising goal).

3. Campaign policy committees or subcommittees may include an Investment Policy group to select and supervise the allocation and management of endowed funds; a Gift Acceptance group to determine policies for receipt of gifts of real estate or personal property; and a Planned Giving advisory group to develop guidelines and policies for gifts of bequests, charitable remainder trusts and other planned giving instruments.

4. Bequests and planned-giving instruments, such as charitable remainder or lead trusts, gift annuities, pooled income funds and life insurance, are tools that may enable donors to make significant gifts to not-for-profit organizations while increasing current income and reducing or avoiding certain taxes. Many types of planned gifts may be appropriate for endowment and capital campaigns and require administrative policies and procedures that are different from those for more conventional contributions. Space prohibits us from including specific details on each planned giving opportunity and on regulations and compliance issues that vary by state. Please refer to the resource list at the end of the book for suggestions on where to obtain more information.

- A campaign income budget, outlining projected pledges and gift payments on a quarterly or annual basis through the campaign period and beyond.
- A capital project expense budget indicating, in the case of building projects, how construction expenses will be financed while contributions are being secured.
- A timeline for the campaign outlining deadlines for implementing internal improvements, a cultivation and solicitation calendar and mileposts for reaching key financial goals in order to meet construction schedules or financial projections for investment income.

As with any planning document, these elements will be revisited, refined and updated throughout the campaign with input from staff and volunteers.

Campaign Leadership

With this blueprint in place, the organization is ready to recruit campaign leadership. Beyond passion for the organization and the capital or endowment project, criteria for the top post include influential standing in the community to provide credibility and leverage; capacity to make a significant gift that will set the pace for others; time to devote to the campaign's needs; and a collaborative style to forge strong partnerships with staff and other volunteers and to maintain clear lines of communication between those working on the special campaign and the leadership of the organization's annual fundraising programs.

That's a tall order for a single individual working in a volunteer capacity, and arts organizations may want to consider co-chairs to combine forces in the top leadership position. Pairing a longstanding community leader with a young philanthropist to work together as co-chairs, for example, may enable the organization to reach different segments of the organization's constituency of donors more effectively, prevent "leadership burnout" and avoid any perceptions that the campaign is the pet project of a single individual.

Whether the campaign is headed by one chair or more, the fundamentally intensive nature of fundraising will demand a strong corps of committee members to deploy on various stages of the campaign. A general is only as good as his (or her) army—those captains and lieutenants will enable the organization to divide the prospect pool into groups and provide the human resources to cultivate and solicit these prospective donors thoughtfully and appropriately.

Job descriptions are essential for each category of campaign volunteers, from the chairs to the solicitors of gifts at the lower levels. Avoid the "just say yes—we'll figure out the details later" theory of recruitment. Be specific about roles, responsibilities and time commitments so that the leadership and volunteers begin their involvement with a clear set of expectations—and, if modifications must be made, those can be agreed upon at the outset.

Preparing Campaign Volunteers for Success

Whether your role is that of campaign chair or member of the larger corps of volunteers, every trustee needs to take stock to ensure that he or she is appropriately equipped to contribute to the success of a capital or endowment campaign. Consider whether you:

- Have a passion for the organization. Does this theater represent one of your top three philanthropic priorities? If so, you are philosophically prepared to convince others to share your enthusiasm and support the campaign. If not, consider what it is that keeps you from putting the theater at the top of your contributions list—and discuss that with your spouse, trustee colleagues and theater management as necessary to resolve outstanding issues or concerns.
- Are able to make a case for the organization in your own words. While the formal case statement is a valuable tool, you will find that you need to translate the message into words that are more comfortable for you but convey the same message. Test your understanding of the case and your presentation skills with staff or board colleagues before embarking on a solicitation, and revise the case language as necessary to arrive at a description that you can deliver comfortably and easily.
- Know the facts and have answers to all your questions. You needn't become an expert in theatrical literature or production; you just need to know the key points of your theater's case and organizational challenges. The questions that you may have about the project and the campaign are likely to be ones the donors will have. Clarifying those issues with staff and others before the solicitation process will benefit everyone.

- Are able to ask for help and training. The best leaders often become so by remaining open to new ideas and approaches to the process of building relationships between the organization and its donors. Experienced trustees who have participated in capital or endowment campaigns for other not-for-profits may find that the fundraising sales points are different for the arts. Inexperienced board members may resist participating in solicitation meetings because they are uncomfortable asking directly for a contribution. Both groups will benefit through a willingness to step up to the task, rehearse and role-play and elicit the advice and expertise of others in the organization and the field.
- Are willing to be a partner with staff and board colleagues on solicitations. Few, if any, solicitations of a donor should be conducted solo. Forming a solicitation team with a trustee peer or a staff person will allow each of you to make different points, listen to the prospect's comments and questions with different ears (and each may hear the same comments very differently) and combine forces of enthusiasm, expertise and style.
- Are able and willing to do what you say you're going to do. Nothing will handicap a campaign as quickly as volunteers who procrastinate, commit to a schedule that their day job won't allow them to maintain or put off participating in the training and practice sessions that will enable them to feel comfortable with the process of cultivating and soliciting donors. Timing is essential to capital construction schedules and endowment investment programs. Your active involvement may well make the difference between success and failure for the campaign.
- Are prepared to share experiences, celebrate successes and debrief failures. Beyond an organized training session, the ongoing process of reporting and examining solicitation experiences will enable volunteers and staff to learn from campaign activities.
- Plan to make your own gift before you ask anyone else to support the campaign. Regardless of whether your contribution is above or below the level of those you plan to solicit, registering your own solid support of the campaign is the most important gesture that you can make to influence others in the community.

PHASE 2: THE QUIET STAGE

Armed with a plan, prospects and leadership, the substantive work of the campaign begins in earnest with the "quiet stage." Despite its name, the process of soliciting leadership gifts shouldn't be one of completely covert activity. It presents the opportunity for your campaign to be the worst kept secret in your community—one that creates a buzz in social and business circles and creates the image of a well-organized, emerging campaign that piques the interest of arts patrons across the spectrum.

Why, then, is it a "quiet stage"? Because before your campaign can be officially launched to the full public, at least sixty percent (some argue for as much as eighty percent) of the gifts and pledges necessary to meet the goal must be secured. With those commitments in place, the campaign has built strong momentum that will signal that success is within reach, and the public phase—in which a large number of gifts at much smaller levels will be raised from the broader community—can motivate donors to provide the final layer of support.

Begin with the Board

The top prospects in a capital or endowment campaign are trustees themselves. If you don't support the campaign, why should anyone outside the organization? By now, the preparation phase has kept the board fully informed of the process, and you and your colleagues have voted to proceed with the initiative. Along the way, each board member has had the opportunity to consider his or her commitment to the campaign. Still, each must be formally solicited for a specific gift. Surveying a roster of thirty to sixty names of trustees, the theater's board leaders and campaign chairs may be tempted to dismiss this formality: "They all know they're supposed to give, so we don't have to take the time to ask them. Let's just cut to the chase and mail out the pledge forms."

That's an efficient means of obtaining lukewarm support and handicapping a campaign at the outset. Granted, thirty to sixty meetings may present a time-consuming undertaking for campaign leaders. But sending the message that the campaign—or the individual—isn't worthy of an hour's dialogue and a thoughtful request for a targeted sum of money is unlikely to build enthusiasm, yield capacity gifts or engage trustees as members of the campaign team.

There are a couple of goals in the board solicitation process. Foremost among these is the imperative to secure one hundred percent participation from the full board. Nothing communicates as clearly to the community that the theater's trustees believe the capital or endowment initiative is essential to the organization's future success. Further, it is important to motivate each trustee to "stretch" to make a gift that, regardless of amount, reflects a willingness to set the standard for others. One of the most significant gifts made to one theater's campaign was at the $10,000 level. Although a modest amount, the contribution captured the attention of other trustees because it was made by a young professional whose resources were clearly limited. Impressed by his commitment, others were prompted to reevaluate their own giving plans—and to dig deeper to match the spirit of his gift.

A common question: "What percentage of the total goal for a capital campaign should come from the board?" The answer will vary with every organization. Trustee gifts have comprised anywhere from twenty-five percent to eighty percent of total funds raised for construction or endowment campaigns. While meeting a large proportion of the goal from trustee gifts has obvious advantages, your organization will need to set its board-giving at a level that is appropriate to your own situation.

Reaching Out to the Rest of the Family

From there, the campaign should build outward through the layers of patrons who are closest to the theater family—former trustees, current donors, subscribers who may not currently donate to the annual fund but who may respond to a request to support this special campaign, and so forth. The gift chart, developed during the campaign preparation phase, will provide a general illustration of the number of gifts that will be required at each level to meet the campaign goal. The sample chart on the next page summarizes a view of the gifts required to meet a goal of $20 million:

GIFT RANGE	GIFTS NEEDED	PROSPECTS NEEDED	TOTAL INCOME	TOTAL RAISED	PERCENT OF GOAL
$3,000,000	1	3–5	$3,000,000	$3,000,000	15%
$2,000,000	1	3–5	$2,000,000	$5,000,000	25%
$1,000,000	3	9–15	$3,000,000	$8,000,000	40%
$500,000	6	18–30	$3,000,000	$11,000,000	55%
$250,000	10	30–50	$2,500,000	$13,500,000	68%
$100,000	25	75–125	$2,500,000	$16,000,000	80%
$50,000	30	90–150	$1,500,000	$17,500,000	88%
$25,000	50	150–250	$1,250,000	$18,750,000	94%
$10,000	100	300–500	$1,000,000	$19,750,000	99%
< $10,000	Many	Many	$250,000	$20,000,000	100%

Gift charts are based on various bits of conventional wisdom, including:

- The lead or top gift required for a successful campaign must be equal to at least ten to fifteen percent of the total campaign goal. An anchor gift of this magnitude sends a clear signal to other donors that the capital or endowment project has captured the support of community leaders at the highest levels of capacity and influence and creates a benchmark for other donors.
- Solicit the lead—or largest—gifts first. Confidence and momentum is built most effectively by starting at the top of the giving pyramid, rather than working up from the bottom or the middle.
- On average, three to five prospects will be required in order to successfully secure one gift. The estimated twenty-to-thirty-three-percent success rate is based on the theory that, regardless of how good your prospect research is, there will always be factors that lead prospects to decline or delay the opportunity to make a gift. The sample gift chart (above) offers simple multiplication to show the range of prospects required at each level for this $20-million campaign. Although results will vary with each gift level, it's fair to say that if your organization cannot identify at least three prospects for each gift required, you'll need to expand your base of prospective donors before undertaking the campaign.

- Eighty percent of the funds needed will come from twenty percent of the donors. The illustration shows eighty percent (or $16 million) coming from forty-six (or roughly twenty percent) of the 226 donors at the $10,000+ gift levels.

Although useful to those who clamor for formulas for success, conventional wisdom (and the gift chart, for that matter) is best viewed as a guideline for your campaign, rather than as a set of hard-and-fast rules. You may be successful in securing a $5-million lead gift for your $20-million campaign and have no prospects at the $1-million and $2-million levels; or have twenty prospects for the $100,000 level and only five at the $250,000 level; or three prospects for $750,000 gifts—which aren't even reflected on the chart. In the end, these tools are references for preparation and planning, and you are best served by shaping the campaign and its strategies to fit the needs and resources available to your organization.

It is obviously important to begin soliciting these donors; however, it's even more crucial to prepare the way through an appropriate series of cultivation steps—a process analogous to "dating" the prospective donor before racing to "propose marriage." Some theories of major-gift development hold that the relationship-building process will require as many as twelve contacts, in the form of letters, events or meetings, before a donor is ready to respond favorably to a solicitation for major support. Earlier, the theater evaluated whether it had sufficient prospects with the capacity and readiness to make major gifts. While some of those donors may have been deemed ready for solicitation at the outset, others may be the focus of a continuing cultivation process. In that respect, capital and endowment campaigns—like annual fund programs—are models of multitasking. Campaign leadership and the corps of solicitors will be involved in parallel efforts to cultivate prospects, refine preliminary ratings, add new names to the pipeline of prospective donors, incorporate new volunteers into the structure and nurture and steward the donors and gifts that come in during this and all phases of the campaign. As momentum builds, mileposts are met and new information becomes available, participation of the trustees continues to be vital to the success of the campaign.

Peer Solicitation

As with annual fund solicitations, face-to-face meetings with a peer provide the most effective method of building a strong relationship between the prospect and the organization, providing an appropriate forum to make the case and securing the most generous gift for a capital campaign. Letters and telephone calls don't offer the forum for dialogue that is necessary to convey the importance of the campaign and the donor's involvement as effectively as a personal approach. And, in the end, it's simply harder for the prospect to resist your enthusiasm and say no to a well-made case presented on a personal basis.

While your theater's managing, artistic and development directors may be highly effective partners on a solicitation team, solicitation by a peer is essential to the process. No matter how impressive their vision, management skill and enthusiasm for the organization may be, the staff's role is strengthened and complemented by the presence of a civic volunteer who represents community investment and oversight in the organization and the project. Your willingness to participate conveys a message of credibility and support that may be as compelling as the particulars of the case statement.

Follow-up Issues

The solicitation steps outlined in Dawn Rains's "Annual Fund" article also apply to capital campaigns. Because of the magnitude of the gifts sought for capital and endowment campaigns, however, there are some additional things to consider. You will need to allow time to discuss multiyear payment options, naming opportunities, gift restrictions and similar issues that surround capital and endowment contributions more frequently than with gifts to the annual fund. One issue that takes on increasing importance is that of obtaining a written pledge summarizing the terms of the capital or endowment gift. Documentation is essential for auditing and gift-tracking purposes, and a pledge cannot be considered confirmed until the donor has signed an authorizing statement. In a capital campaign, donors may be restricting their gifts to a specific component of a construction project. In an endowment campaign, donors may require that investment income from an endowed fund be used only for a specific purpose or program. Both will need to be confirmed in writing to demonstrate the "donor intent" that is necessary to satisfy auditors' requirements during the campaign and in future years. Also, if your theater is financing a construction project with a bank loan, the bank will require evidence of donors' commitments and payment schedules as part of the loan application process.

Once all the details of a gift have been finalized, the solicitation process is complete—but the stewardship and relationship-building process continue. Successful campaigns are those that ensure that the donors who respond early in the process are not ignored in favor of the continuing pursuit of recalcitrant prospects who require more extensive cultivation. "I made my gift early in the campaign," observed one capital campaign patron, "and that was the last I heard from anyone. Meanwhile, others who resisted were wined and dined at various events for another year. What's wrong with this picture?" Rewarding those early donors with continuing recognition, progress reports and invitations to later events serves to nurture their long-term involvement with the organization. It may also foster a growing enthusiasm that will motivate others to move forward with their own decisions to support the campaign.

Once a donor has made a philanthropic investment in a capital or endowment campaign, he or she may be willing to offer suggestions of other potential donors. Whether these are prospects for top-tier gifts or more modest levels of support, those suggestions will assist the campaign to reach beyond the current members of the family and expand the sphere of influence for the capital or endowment project and for audience/donor development in general.

Just as the "pipeline" of prospective donors must be constantly replenished with new names, the leadership structure will benefit from the inclusion of new faces that have been identified during the campaign. Capital and endowment projects expand the possibilities for the theater's future and may create the opportunity for a new or long-standing subscriber to become inspired in ways beyond those created by past annual fund efforts. Well-managed campaigns and perceptive trustees will gather these new potential evangelists and advocates and find ways to engage them in the theater's work as candidates for the board, volunteers for the campaign, chairs for annual fundraising events or other opportunities.

Phase 3: The Public Stage

Reaching the milepost of sixty to eighty percent of the campaign goal is cause for celebration! Share the good news with the community through a formal, public announcement that the capital or endowment campaign is officially launched. A highly visible "kickoff" event is the traditional means of celebrating achievements to date and providing a compelling invitation for others to jump on the bandwagon of success as it heads for the finish line.

For construction projects, a groundbreaking ceremony and press conference have traditionally provided a photogenic, newsworthy option. For endowment campaigns, it may be appropriate to produce a press conference to announce newly established funds, recognize lead donors and highlight the artistic initiatives that will be supported. Similar public relations opportunities coordinated with the opening of a season, a major benefit fundraiser or an annual meeting may also garner the news coverage for the campaign kickoff, as well as the opportunity to interact with a range of the theater's audience members and community constituents.

While the focus during the "quiet stage" was on the small group of leadership donors who were crucial to transforming the capital or endowment project from a dream to a reality, the "public stage" has a much wider audience. The message now is that success is within reach, and every community member (and every dollar) can play a vital role in meeting the goal. This is the arts organization's opportunity to finish the campaign with a dramatic expansion of its donor base. The theater's campaign activities offer new donors and audience members the chance to see the organization in a new light and capture their attention and involvement in ways they may not have considered before.

All the elements of the campaign during the public stage should reflect these goals of expanding the donor base and engaging the broader community—from the larger corps of trustees and volunteers who will be engaged in reaching out to those donors, to the range of events offered to gather community members together to hear about the exciting future, to a highly visible "final stretch" campaign theme that will pervade the theater's print and electronic materials and on-site visual displays.

Although grassroots fundraising activities such as direct mail appeals and telephone solicitations will be introduced during the public stage, one-on-one solicitations should continue as well. Board members may be called upon to host private events, welcome and cultivate guests and deliver informal speeches or "pitches" to elicit support for the campaign. In both the grassroots efforts and group gatherings, a variety of leveraging tools may be used as incentives to spur prospective donors to participate in the campaign. Many theaters use challenge grants from individuals and organizational funders to generate matching funds from the community in order to meet campaign goals, underwrite elements of the construction project or increase the principal in permanently endowed funds that are designated for key programming initiatives. Your theater may also launch a campaign to "buy a seat" in the new theater or feature special "mini-campaigns" to endow actors' salaries, school performances, costumes or other featured components of your operations through restricted endowment funds. While the scale is smaller than naming opportunities offered to leadership donors, these mini-campaigns offer the full range of donors the chance to support a discernible element of the larger campaign—and provide trustees and other volunteers the tools to stimulate support from the broader community.

Phase 4: The Post-Campaign Stage

Even when the new building is opened, the capital or endowment goals have been reached and victory has been declared, the follow-up work continues well past the point at which visible campaign activities have concluded. A celebration event to open the new building or mark the conclusion of the endowment campaign will provide a forum for thanking both the donors and the many volunteers who have played a role in achieving the campaign victory. Recognition on donor walls or plaques and in commemorative publications will acknowledge those players as well. Meanwhile, campaign leadership and theater staff should provide a thorough debriefing of the campaign itself. An internal audit examining campaign procedures, structure, solicitation methods, materials, prospects and donors, and income and expenses will ensure that future campaigns will benefit from the lessons learned during this one.

Collection of outstanding pledges may continue for several years, annual reports on the use of donors' funds will continue in perpetuity and, most importantly, all campaign donors and volunteers will continue to be cultivated and engaged as part of the theater's ongoing stewardship process. Ideally, these people have been involved in a rewarding experience that has transformed them and their view of your organization. Though the campaign may have ended, the relationship between the theater and these stakeholders has moved to a new level that must continue to be nurtured.

Despite fears that capital or endowment projects will negatively impact annual funds, most organizations find that these campaigns have a dramatically positive effect on annual fundraising activities. Donors set their own sights higher for annual gifts, grow accustomed to maintaining a higher level of support and become more invested in the theater's work and potential. "We look back on the long-range projections we prepared for annual fund income at the outset of the campaign and now, four years later, we're finding that we were much too conservative," said one development director. "Even with setbacks in the economy, we're raising more for annual operations than we had predicted. Part of that is due to the capital and endowment campaigns that strengthened our donors' belief that our work is worthy of their increased support."

For many arts organizations, the first capital or endowment campaign is a defining process that leaves not only the legacy of a new facility or a permanent endowment but also a base of knowledge and experience that transforms the organization and its relationship with the community. The impact of the campaign will continue through ongoing major gifts programs, strategic planning, board development, etc. But the greatest impact of all will be on the art itself, through the opportunities and ambitions that are within reach as a result of the campaign's success.

Though the focus of your efforts is on the art and the "institution" that your organization has become, the anchoring force for capital and endowment campaigns comes from the board of trustees. No other single factor is more important to a campaign's success than an active, committed group of trustees to act as leaders, advocates and solicitors. Enjoy the challenge, the learning experience and the accomplishment of truly "making a difference" in your theater and your community.

LEADERSHIP SUCCESSION IN NOT-FOR-PROFIT ORGANIZATIONS:

A Board Member's Viewpoint

Prudence R. Beidler

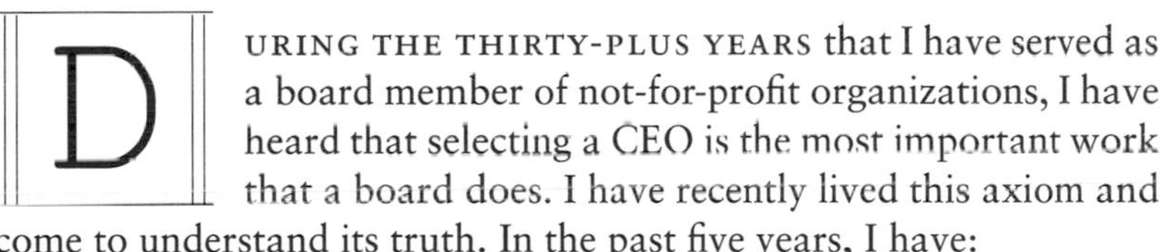

DURING THE THIRTY-PLUS YEARS that I have served as a board member of not-for-profit organizations, I have heard that selecting a CEO is the most important work that a board does. I have recently lived this axiom and come to understand its truth. In the past five years, I have:

- Chaired the search for a new head of school following the seventeen-year tenure of the outgoing head.
- Served on the search committee to select a new CEO at a community foundation following the twenty-seven-year tenure of the outgoing CEO.
- Served on a search committee to select a new CEO at a 110-year-old social service organization following the ten-year tenure of

the outgoing CEO (I had also served on the search committee during the previous search).

- Advised the search committee at a health-care organization that was replacing a CEO whose tenure had been more than ten years; I then rejoined the board in time to be a participant in the choice of the new CEO.
- Chaired the board of a children's museum and served as a member of the search committee to replace the retiring founding CEO of seventeen years.

Each search was different, and yet there were a great number of similarities among them. As much as I love stability in the organizations I serve, I have come to understand how important it is to see leadership transition as routine in the life of a healthy not-for-profit organization, just as it is seen in the for-profit sector. In addition, I now understand that such times of transition offer unique opportunities to engage, reflect and rebuild. A summary of some of my gleanings from my experiences with leadership succession follows.

Advance Planning

Ideally, it would be wonderful if all organizations had regular discussions about leadership succession. In my extensive board experience, most do not. Leadership succession is a scary subject because it implies change, and change is fraught with emotions that most individuals, let alone groups of individuals, would rather not tackle. Yet a good board has to think constantly of the organization's future and who will be leading it, and a good board chair must be aware of whether the organization's CEO is perceived as the right person to continue leading the organization and whether the CEO intends to continue in his or her present position. Some good ways to ensure that the discussion of succession is slightly less scary are:

1. Include leadership succession as a regular part of strategic planning. A good strategic plan is prepared and reviewed regularly by the staff and board together. This gives both groups an opportunity to talk about general views of succession and, hopefully, some specific issues related to the organization's current needs.
2. The board should do a periodic evaluation of the CEO—the board's only actual employee—matching the CEO's

accomplishments against specifically projected goals. A representative group of board members generally performs such a review—with input from the entire board—then prepares a written document to share with the CEO. It is smart to use this annual review as an opportunity for the CEO to update his or her job description and for the evaluation team to review it as well. (All senior employees should update their job descriptions annually.) This review process gives both the board team and the CEO a sense of how it is going in the organization and may offer some chance to discuss the CEO's intentions for the future.

3. IT IS A WISE PRACTICE TO INCLUDE A LINE ITEM IN THE BUDGET for transition expenses associated with changes in senior staff, including the CEO. One of the most difficult problems an organization faces at a transition point is meeting the generally larger than anticipated expenses associated with a search. Though I call this a wise practice, it is not a common one.
4. SCRUPULOUS RECORDS OF EACH CEO SEARCH SHOULD BE KEPT, so that organizations can look back over previous experiences to review the process and materials used during the previous search. Nothing is more frustrating than having to reinvent the wheel for your organization when lessons from the past could have been highly instructive.

Circumstances of the Transition

It is crucial that a board be clear about the circumstances surrounding a transition as they set off to find a replacement. The following questions should be considered:

1. WAS THE CHANGE IN LEADERSHIP DETERMINED BY MUTUAL agreement? Was it a board decision or a decision by the current CEO?
2. WHAT IS THE TENURE OF THE OUTGOING CEO? IN OTHER words, is there memory within the organization for leadership transition?
3. WHEN IS THE CURRENT CEO'S INTENDED DEPARTURE DATE? WILL it be necessary to have an interim CEO in place before a search can be realistically completed?
4. WHAT IS THE ORGANIZATION'S HISTORY IN TERMS OF LEADERSHIP succession? Have a number of CEOs left after a brief tenure?

If this is the case, it is imperative that the board see this as a sign of an organization in trouble and not as routine. Funders certainly see frequent CEO change as an indicator of an organization in disarray.

The board must understand that it owns the process of choosing a new CEO. This is not an opportunity for shared leadership of any sort. There are many ways of including other organizational stakeholders in the process of the search, but this is first and foremost a board responsibility and must be seen as such by all concerned parties.

Beginning the Search

The biggest problem associated with starting a search is simply facing the reality of the need for it. Once an organization does that, there is a lot of work to be done.

1. FIRST, DECIDE WHETHER OR NOT TO USE A SEARCH FIRM. I CANnot state strongly enough my belief that getting professional expertise is a wise investment to help secure an organization's future. There are several reasons:

    - Search firms can help demystify the search process; they know what to do and when to do it
    - Search firms have access to candidate pools in a way board or staff members do not
    - Search firms can ask hard questions during background checks
    - Good search firms operate as management consultants for a wide range of issues facing an organization at a transition point, such as its mission and its management structure.

    An issue frequently raised around using a search firm is expense. This is shortsighted; because an executive search is seen as such a critical process, it is often possible to get special funding from foundations or other donors. If you intend to use a firm, do not let the financial concerns deter you. Find a way; you will almost never regret it.

    There is also a question about whether to use a firm specializing in the not-for-profit sector or one with both for-profit and not-for-profit clients. My recommendation is to go with the one that seems like the right match. In making a choice, it's important to gather information about possible firms, interview several of them, and check references before making a decision. In many ways, the process of picking a search firm is practice for the process of selecting the CEO. Consider all the search firm candidates as consultants (whom you are not paying until you make a final choice) and ask meaningful questions, being sure to take careful notes. You will learn an enormous amount about leadership succession from all the search firm candidates, even those you do not select. Remember, however, that hiring a search firm does not abrogate a board's responsibility for the search process. It must be understood that while the firm guides the process, the board manages and directs it.

What if you simply cannot manage to fund a professional search or you choose not to use a firm for some other reason? It is possible to do your own search, of course, but be very cautious about your planning, timetable and homework in terms of reaching the broadest possible pool of candidates and checking references.

2. WHO SHOULD BE ON THE SEARCH COMMITTEE? GENERALLY, a search committee is composed of five to nine active members of the board. The following factors should be considered:

   - Board leadership: The board chair should be a member of the search committee. It is also good policy for the chair of the search committee to be the next likely chair of the board. In any case, it is not a good idea to put people on the committee who will not be around to work with the new CEO.
   - Board tenure: A mix of long-term and more recent board members is desirable.
   - Expertise: A variety of personal and professional expertise and points of view is also desirable.
   - Confidentiality: An understanding of the confidential nature of the search is crucial. If you doubt a board member's ability to meet this standard, do not add him or her to the committee.
   - Commitment: It is imperative that all committee members see this as their top volunteer priority. While it is a short-term task (hopefully complete in less than a year), a search is enormously time-consuming, and committee members must be realistic about the demands on their time that this responsibility will make.

- Staff representation: The current CEO should not serve on the committee. Another staff member chosen in a manner that is deemed fair and appropriate can add enormous value. Not only can such a person offer a fresh perspective on the organization's operational needs, but prospective candidates often appreciate the opportunity to ask knowledgeable staff about operational issues.

3. Review all organizational records and documents from previous searches. If possible, talk with some of the people who were involved in those searches and ask for their suggestions. Also talk to your current CEO about how the process went to see what he or she suggests. Be sure that your CEO's job description is in order, particularly if it is determined that you will need an interim CEO.
4. In the course of getting ideas for possible search consultants, you should talk with other organizations that have recently undergone transitions. Beyond asking whom they recommend to help with the search, ask for advice about the process in general. Invaluable observations may emerge from these conversations.
5. If you will be using an interim CEO, determine a process for deciding who that will be. There may be an appropriate person on your senior staff. If so, this person may become an internal candidate for the final position. It is possible to hire someone from outside your organization to become an interim, but this can be quite difficult and often exposes the staff to a double transition. Still, if there is a long time between the retirement of one CEO and the arrival of another, it may be your best option. Another option, which I have personally experienced, is to run the organization as an office of the chair, with volunteers and staff working together. I would not advise this as a long-term management model, but it can serve in the interim.

   I believe that the best leadership transition model is one in which the current CEO gives a year's notice of his or her intention, a committee is formed, and the new CEO is chosen before the current one leaves.
6. Determine how you will communicate—both internally and externally—with your organization's stakeholders. I cannot stress enough how important it is, during this period, to keep in touch with the people who work for and care about your organization. Change does not have to equal crisis, and transition

can be a crucial point of opportunity for organizations. But if you fail to communicate adequately about what is going on, you will raise concerns about your organization's health. Even if everything is going smoothly, if only a small group knows exactly what is happening, there may well be a perception of trouble.

The information you need to communicate and the ways of doing so include:

- An announcement of the CEO's retirement (internally first, then externally to a broad group of stakeholders); this letter usually comes from the CEO and can be followed by a press release.
- A letter to stakeholders noting which search firm has been chosen and describing the planned process for the search and the expected timetable; this letter should be upbeat, noting all the other operations taking place during the search, so that the search, while important, doesn't seem all-consuming (internally and externally).
- A letter with the vitae of the new CEO and details about his or her arrival (internally first, then externally).

Additionally, the board and search committee chairs should be available to meet with staff at several points during the search to answer questions. Please note that these meetings are distinct from sessions with staff that specifically address what the staff sees as the organization's needs and desirable personal traits in a new CEO. The board chair should also be available to meet with key funders to discuss how the search is going.

I would like, in particular, to make a note about communication between the search committee and other board members. Although the full board has to vote to accept the search committee's recommendation for a new CEO, the full board cannot actively participate in the process. This is problematic because it creates some incredibly active and engaged board members and others who feel marginalized. There will always be board members who wish they had been invited to serve on the search committee. It is critical that the full board be kept informed on all aspects of the process, but it is also important that members be engaged in discussions about desirable traits in CEO candidates, their views on the institution's needs, and their hopes for its future. This may add time to the search, but will be well worth it when there is a greater feeling of engagement by the full board.

The Search Underway

At the beginning of the actual search process, the task at hand may seem overwhelming. But if you are deliberate about the process you use, there's a very good chance that you will have satisfying results.

1. Be sure your search timetable is realistic. Searches using search firms seldom take less than six months and sometimes take longer. Generally, a year from the announcement of one CEO's retirement to the arrival of another is enough time. If you try to compress the timetable, you may regret it later. Also, suggesting that a shorter timetable is possible often creates false expectations by staff and other stakeholders.
2. If you have hired a search firm, be very clear about what you expect from the firm and its method of operation before any actual work begins. Most search firms have a pretty clear process that they normally follow, but will be flexible if you want some modifications for your organization. Generally, firms will:

    - Conduct initial meetings with board and staff to outline how they see the search proceeding.
    - Conduct planning sessions with the search committee and other key stakeholders to consider the institution's needs and the desired traits in CEO candidates; there will also be discussion about whether the search should be national or local and where the firm usually finds its pool of candidates.
    - Prepare a document describing the position and the institution; this document must be approved by the search committee and may be reviewed by others if the search committee feels that it is desirable.
    - Collect résumés (usually fifteen to twenty) for the committee's perusal; often the booklet of résumés is sent ahead to committee members for them to review as a group, with input from the search consultant, before interview candidates are selected.
    - Prepare the group for interviews by suggesting appropriate questions, desirable formats for discussions, etc.

- Arrange interviews and guide committee members during the interview process, though committee members will be the actual discussants.
- Guide the committee as candidates are discussed, and assist with reference checks, additional interviews and visits to the institution.
- Work with the committee and final candidate to arrange terms for hiring.

Whether handled by a search firm or the search committee itself, it is crucial that there be a point person to act as calendar coordinator and secretary during the process. This can be a staff member at the institution or someone associated with one of the committee members, but it must be a professional person who works in a timely manner.

Also, it is crucial that meeting and interview dates be established as far in advance as possible to ensure maximum committee participation.

3. THROUGHOUT THE SEARCH, THE BOARD CHAIR IN PARTICULAR IS responsible for staying tuned in to staff feelings. From the staff viewpoint, the loss of a CEO can seem devastating, especially when there is no institutional memory of a time when the CEO was not present. Further, staff who were hired by the outgoing CEO may worry that their own positions are vulnerable because a new CEO might not retain them. A good board chair listens, reassures staff that an appropriate process is in place, and communicates that the board feels strongly about maintaining stability.
4. ALL STAKEHOLDERS NEED TO BE ASSURED THAT THE ORGANIZATION will continue to fulfill its mission during the search process. This can be done in a variety of ways, but it underscores the importance of regular communication. The institution must treat the transition as a time to reflect on past successes, ensure that the present mission is being met, and think about the future. While a transition requires some caution, there should also be a sense of the organization moving forward and excitement associated with this movement.
5. WHILE THERE ARE OPPORTUNITIES TO CANDIDLY ASSESS THE organization's strengths and weaknesses during the transition, this is the wrong time to radically change the organization's mission. Nor would I recommend using this time to radically change the management structure, or any other major operational aspect of the institution. A good question to use as a

screen in determining what not to do during a transition is to ask how a new CEO would feel upon learning about something that had been changed or undertaken just prior to his or her arrival.

Candidates

A diverse pool of candidates will always yield the strongest result. On several occasions I have been part of searches in which the candidate we fell in love with was not one we would have expected to love, whether by background, résumé or some other criteria. It's important not to prejudge people, and a good search firm will persuade you to consider candidates who may not seem ideal when first considered. Keeping an open mind is very important.

1. Just as prospective search firms operate as consultants for your organization, so will all the candidates you interview. A difference here is that you will be footing the bill for travel expenses, but other than that you can expect to learn a lot from all the candidates you interview, even if it is clear fairly early in the process that you will not choose a given candidate. Because you will have sent a complete set of materials about your organization to all the candidates you plan to interview, they should be prepared with questions and comments specific to your organization. You should also expect to gain a sense from them about how they see your organization fitting into the broader context of the world within which you operate. You may not be interviewing candidates whose backgrounds exactly match your institution, but you should be able to ascertain whether they would be a good fit for you.

   In the interview process, it is important to note that as a group, you are "selling as well as buying." Your search committee reflects your organization. If you are gracious, courteous and friendly, you are more likely to attract a candidate's interest. Additionally, your level of candor in responding to questions about your organization will be of critical importance to candidates. Candidates will also watch to see how the members of the committee interact with each other.
2. In my comments about interim leadership, I noted the possibility of internal candidates. Internal candidates need to be

treated with special care for a variety of reasons, the most important of which is that the entire organization may be judging your treatment of this person. As a known quantity, the internal candidate is often the staff favorite.

In many cases, an internal candidate will be strongly viable for the position of CEO, though a full search will lend credibility to the choice of this person. If it is clear, however, that this person is not of the caliber that you wish to have for CEO, you must not treat the candidate as if he or she might be the possible successor. Never entertain the idea of a "straw" candidate whom you know you will not hire; this will compromise the process and the results of the search. If an internal candidate expresses interest but is not viable, it is the responsibility of the search committee chair or the board chair to speak privately with the individual and let him or her know the sense of the group.

3. References must be checked. This is another area where search firms add enormous value because they are able to ask questions in a way that elicits important information. If you are doing the search without a firm, it is even more critical to have a few members of the search committee call and check all references. Asking, "Is there something I should have asked?" sometimes elicits desirable information. Further, asking, "Can you recommend this person without qualification?" may reveal any reservations the reference might have about the candidate. I recommend that only a few committee members do the checking, so that they are better able to ensure consistency in the process.
4. I always look for information about volunteer work in a candidate's résumé. This is because the candidate will be working with a volunteer board as well as with other volunteers in the organization. The relationship with volunteers is likely to be smoother, in my experience, if a CEO has volunteered in his or her own life.
5. Generally the search firm talks to candidates about the salary and benefits associated with the job, but you should be prepared to answer questions about these things if they come up, even at initial interviews. You may also get a sense of how long a candidate would be prepared to stay in the job. It is unrealistic to expect lengths of tenure in not-for-profit organizations that were traditional in the past, but if someone says they usually remain in jobs for three or so years, I would see that as a red flag.

6. OTHER RED FLAGS CAN COME FROM A RANGE OF ISSUES. Sometimes a candidate will note his wife's reluctance to leave her family in the area where they are now living, or a particular need of a child that is being met in the hometown. Sometimes a candidate will just not "get" your mission. Sometimes a candidate is more reluctant to leave his or her current position than they had initially seemed. You may love a candidate who simply wants a much higher salary than your organization can afford. Your committee has to feel a sense of fit with the candidate you choose. You have to be able to think, Yes, I would really like to work with this person! If you don't feel excitement about the candidate, he or she is probably not the right person for you.

   If no candidate is chosen after the initial interview process, either the search firm or the search committee will have to come up with a new pool of candidates. I have had this experience on a search, and while it was discouraging, the second round yielded what I consider an even stronger pool than the first. The important thing is to keep your eye on selecting the best person to lead your organization. A couple of extra months is a sound investment in your organization's future.
7. WHEN THE SEARCH COMMITTEE AGREES ON A FINAL CANDIDATE, that person is recommended to the full board for approval. It is customary for the board to have an opportunity to meet with the candidate or, in some cases, two finalists. This is not always possible but helps with board engagement when it can be arranged. It is also common for the candidate to wish to meet with senior staff or even a broader group of staff representing the organization.
8. WHEN YOU FIND A CANDIDATE WHOM YOU ARE READY TO HIRE, there will be a period of negotiation, as start date, salary, vacation, benefits and other terms are agreed upon. This is another area in which the search firm adds value. There may be some real persuasion required; you shouldn't leave that completely to the search firm, but you should let the firm's consultants advise you. On one occasion, I wrote a personal note to the prospective CEO saying how impressed I was by him and telling him that I thought he could bring something quite remarkable to our organization. Was this a "begging letter"? More or less. But I don't think it hurt our cause and maybe it helped—he joined us and served for ten years. It's fine to be passionate, but never make a commitment you can't fulfill.

The Outgoing CEO

I have already mentioned how much emotion may be associated with the retiring CEO. It is critical to honor this person's history with your organization, to celebrate his or her commitment to your mission, and to ensure that he or she feels valued at the time of departure.

In terms of the outgoing CEO's role during the search, a wise search consultant once told me that the role of the retiring CEO is to be like the "mother of the groom—wear beige and keep your mouth shut." That being said, the retiring CEO has a huge fount of knowledge about the organization and would probably very much like to share it. It is common for finalist candidates to want to talk with this person and that should be fine with you. Presumably the retiring CEO is a terrific advocate for your mission and your organization.

I do not recommend overlapping terms, but some organizations find it very helpful. I think you have to determine what will work best in your organization. Letting go may be very hard for your retiring CEO, so if he or she is available to meet with the new CEO after the first few weeks of the new tenure, that might be the best approach. Clearly a cordial relationship between the two is the best for the health of the organization.

After the Contract Is Signed

Hooray, you say—and phew! But the transition work is not over and there are points of enormous vulnerability here. Communication with internal and external stakeholders remains extremely important. In some cases you will hire someone with a very different background than that of the outgoing CEO, and people will say, "What were they thinking?" Your stakeholder materials must make clear why you chose the candidate and the excitement you feel about his or her leadership of your organization. Knowing what he or she is bringing to the table, you can't wait for your new CEO to prove his or her worth.

If there is a considerable gap in time before the new CEO arrives, the board chair should determine how best to keep in regular touch. There should be a real effort to determine what the new CEO will need to know right away and whom he or she should meet first. Planning a low-key social event for the staff to meet the CEO and another for the full board to welcome him or her is highly desirable. There should be a sense of celebration around the arrival of the new

CEO, just as there should be appropriate celebratory events for the departure of the outgoing CEO.

Though the CEO may love his or her new job, if the spouse and/or children are having trouble adjusting, it will affect job performance. Be ready to be supportive of all the issues families face when they move.

There are critical ways the board continues to support the CEO even as he or she settles in to the job:

1. Someone, preferably the board chair, needs to check in with the CEO regularly to see how everything is going. This should be an informal conversation but be candid enough to allow the CEO to talk about any real problems he or she is facing. Some organizations refer to this as a wellness check, and in some cases, it is the responsibility of several people.
2. The new CEO should be encouraged to reach beyond the organization's board and staff for support. There may be local organizations that he or she can join, or executive coaching courses that he or she would like to take. The CEO should be encouraged to go to workshops and conferences to hone his or her skills and knowledge about the field within which the organization operates.
3. If possible, the new CEO and board chair should attend a conference together that specifically addresses the issues of their partnership.
4. The CEO should expect regular evaluations. A new CEO usually has a six-month evaluation and then another at the end of the first year. It is at these evaluation points that goals are discussed.
5. The board should regularly assess its own performance in supporting the CEO. A board that is open to assessing its own performance is much more likely to establish a healthy relationship with staff.

The period of a CEO search is one of the most dynamic and unsettling times in an organization's life. Once the search is over, everyone wants the organization to feel calm and stable. Realistically, there will be an adjustment period for the new leader as he or she assesses the organization's needs. At this point, the new CEO will be anxious to share his or her vision and goals for the organization. For the board-CEO partnership to thrive, the board will have to offer renewed energy to match that of the CEO. The board will be expected to clearly demonstrate commitment to face the challenge of achieving these goals. The wise board, hopefully no longer weary from the search, will feel enormous pride in the leader it has chosen and excitement about the work ahead. My experience is that boards work best when they have real work to do, and this period of leadership succession provides just such meaningful work.

Originally published in Succession: Arts Leadership for the 21st Century, *Illinois Arts Alliance Foundation, Chicago, 2003.*

ADDITIONAL PERSPECTIVES: Small Theaters, Artist Trustees and Alternative Models

Jaan Whitehead

THE UNITED STATES has the greatest diversity of theaters in the world, from large theaters like Lincoln Center to small start-up theaters Off-Off Broadway, from traditional theaters like the Guthrie to experimental theaters like The Wooster Group, from urban theaters like Steppenwolf to rural ensembles like Roadside Theater of Kentucky. No one, two or even three approaches to governing could fit them all. Each theater has its own history, geography and mission, and each develops its own style of governing. However, a general set of ideas has evolved over the years that is the basis for most theater governance.

In this article, I want to explore three issues that reach beyond traditional discussions of governance to address some of the concerns of less mainstream theaters or theaters looking for different ways of thinking about their governing needs. First is a discussion of some of the challenges affecting small theaters that, at a different stage of their life cycle, face different governing needs than more established theaters. Next are some thoughts on how artists can—and do—serve on the boards of theater organizations and what they can contribute to these organizations. And third is an exploration of some alternative models of governance that can open up more ways of thinking about how theaters construct and organize their boards.

Small and Emerging Theaters

As theaters grow, they go through identifiable stages of development, including a founding stage, an emerging or growth stage and a mature, institutional stage. What we often don't recognize or give enough credence to is that the boards of these theaters also need to go through their own stages of development. We tend to think of a board as something already formed, a developed structure with established roles and responsibilities. This is the familiar image of boards we talk about at conferences, read about in books and take as our blueprint for success. But this image reflects a mature board that is part of an established organization. Boards don't start out fully formed. Usually they start out as a few people full of enthusiasm for an artist or a mission, often having little understanding of what a board is or what it should do. It is a long journey from there to the complexity and sophistication of a mature board, a journey too often characterized by struggle and mishaps.

One of the best things a small theater can do to smooth this journey is to have a realistic understanding of the kinds of change its board needs to go through as it develops. Too often emphasis is placed on *whether* a board needs to change when the emphasis should be on *how* it needs to change. At each stage of a theater's growth, it doesn't just need a larger board or even a better board; it needs a *different* kind of board, one with different responsibilities, a different understanding of itself and often a different membership. Boards need to keep reinventing themselves as they grow, adding new dimensions of governing at each step while leaving old ones behind.

Understanding this process of development can help a theater in a number of ways. One is that such understanding can become a rich diagnostic tool. You can ask: "What stage is my board in now? Where does it need to go next? What does it need to get there?" There is something to compare the board to that puts it in perspective and points the way forward.

Understanding the development process also helps a theater avoid building up unrealistic expectations of what its board can do. It is easy to look at established theaters and see the many resources, particularly financial resources, that their boards provide. The sheer magnitude of the money can be blinding, making it difficult to see how much work is involved in getting to that level of support. It becomes tempting to think that a theater can jump over the intervening stages: "Two rich board members and all our problems will be solved!" But it doesn't work that way, and thinking it does can undermine the very efforts needed to produce more resources.

Unrealistic expectations can also become very frustrating for a theater, creating the kind of finger-pointing and guilt that can enervate a small organization. But, if a theater sees that what it is going through is a normal process, it can depersonalize that process. Then this negative energy—a negative energy too costly in a situation of scarce resources—can be rechanneled into positive steps of action. Rather than, "What am I doing wrong?" or, "What are you doing wrong?" the question can be, "What should we be doing to move forward?"

But by far the most important reason small theaters should understand the stages of development is that it helps them see that a point of change is also a point of choice. There are many decisions a small theater makes, such as whether to incorporate, establish a regular season, go equity, have its own space, or create a subscription or education program. Each decision impacts how the theater develops and, eventually, what it needs from its board. But these decisions can be made in different ways. There isn't just one path, and a theater doesn't have to go forward in only one way. It can choose to stay small if staying small best suits its needs and possibilities. Or it can choose to go out of business altogether if the changes associated with growth are too contrary to its values. Or it can see points of change as opportunities to try other models of governance, like the possibilities described later in this article. Realizing that there are choices, not just fixed paths to follow, can be a liberating discovery. And, these choices can be made deliberately rather than being forced by circumstances. A theater can choose whom it wants to come on its board just as it can choose how it wants to define success. The template we think of as a mature board is more malleable than it appears, for the kind of board a theater ends up with depends on the steps taken along the way. Understanding that these steps are steps of choice can help a theater shape its own process of growth.

> I think too often change is seen as growth and growth is automatically assumed to mean getting larger. But with dance, growth happens in all directions, it doesn't imply only becoming larger. A movement can grow into itself, it can grow more subtle, it can grow to be more still and reflective, it can grow horizontally and even back on itself like a wave. The growth must remain supple in order to be able to change again, for once the form becomes rigid we know the potential for authentic change is severely limited.
>
> —KAREN BAMONTE
> CHOREOGRAPHER

A FOUNDING BOARD

Each theater follows its own path of development, but the story of a typical theater goes something like this. At the beginning, the theater is usually dominated by a founding artist with a compelling artistic vision. There is little or no staff, and the board is created to fulfill the legal requirement that a not-for-profit organization must have a board with at least three members. The original board members might be relatives or friends of the founder or other people who share his passion and want to support him. Often the board members do the staff work on a volunteer basis; it is a small, close-knit group charged with the energy of the new enterprise. The concept of "governing" rarely enters the discussion, and pressures on time and resources tend to push attention to longer-range issues to the back burner. Survival comes first.

If the art connects with an audience and the theater starts to grow, strains appear as more resources are needed to finance and support the work. At this point, the first, paid professional staff is hired to free the founder from the expanding day-to-day administrative work of the theater and to take on the demands of marketing and fundraising. The first expansion of the board also takes place as the theater begins to look for people with legal, financial and other specialized skills that it needs but cannot afford to hire. Now the theater is starting to move past its founding stage; it has paid staff and a somewhat larger board that provides technical support. The budget is increasing, and priorities have shifted as administrative costs grow in relation to artistic costs. But issues of governance tend to remain rather obscure. The locus of power and control remain with the founding artists, and the board remains mainly a satellite of the theater.

> Originally, it was not clear to me what I wanted the board to be, so I could not communicate to them what they should be doing or what their relationship with the theater should be. How can the board be clear about their role in the theater if I am not clear?
>
> —JASON NEULANDER
> FOUNDER AND ARTISTIC DIRECTOR,
> SALVAGE VANGUARD THEATER, AUSTIN, TEXAS

A WORKING BOARD

If a theater continues to grow, particularly if it starts to grow rapidly, it eventually reaches a point where its resources are so inadequate that both the art and the young institution become starved for support. Now a theater needs a very different kind of board, one that is more fully developed and one that has new skills and probably new members. Having grown past its founding stage, it needs what is usually called a "working" board. And, as the name implies, one of the characteristics of a working board is that it takes responsibility for itself; it develops its own identity separate from the rest of the theater, it takes ownership of its own work and it takes responsibility for more aspects of governing. This is the biggest change that takes place in the governing life of a theater; no longer just a satellite, the board takes on its own form and independence and begins to become a partner to the theater.

> I want my board to be a partner who sees the practicalities of the dream, who can think big and help make the dream happen.
>
> —JEREMY COHEN
> ARTISTIC DIRECTOR, NAKED EYE THEATRE COMPANY, CHICAGO

One of the first things that happens as a board establishes its own identity is that board roles become separated from staff roles. When a theater is emerging from its founding stage, board members are usually still doing much of the staff work. As the theater matures and hires its own professional staff, board members need to move out of the everyday work of the theater and take on more traditional board roles. But this may not be easy. One of the most delicate problems theaters face is that many of their original board members may not be the people needed for the next stage of development. Board members who have been devoted to their volunteer work and are now supplanted by paid staff often lose their sense of identity, and being asked to raise money or develop other governing skills may not be comfortable for them. Also, when new board members are brought on who have needed skills, they may come from different social and economic parts of the community. And they may be more aggressive in pushing for change or less attuned to the theater's artistic spirit. If these changes aren't handled carefully, schisms can emerge between "new" and "old" board members, seriously hampering further development. And, if a board is unable to separate itself successfully from staff responsibilities, a legacy of board micromanagement can be created that will plague a theater for a long time. One of the unexpected dynamics of board development is that what is a strength in one stage can become a liability in a later stage. Board members acting as staff is such a case, very valuable early on but often a problem later.

Another change that takes place as a board develops is that its loyalty shifts from the founder to the mission of the theater, and that loyalty continues beyond the tenure of the founder. In fact, when a founder leaves, it is the board that chooses the new leader and is responsible for the institution's continuity. No longer just cheerleaders and supporters, board members become "trustees," holding the institution in trust as the leadership changes. What was once a personal role for board members now becomes a professional one.

A further part of a board's growing independence is that the board's leadership becomes separate from the theater's leadership. Where a founder usually chose his own board, including the leadership, the board now takes responsibility for reproducing itself. Through its nominating and election process, it begins to make its own choices. And it starts to take ownership of its own work. It develops a clear understanding of its responsibilities and creates an effective committee and leadership structure to carry them out. The board is now active rather than passive, developing its own internal momentum. And it takes on the job of educating, nourishing and evaluating its own membership. As its independence and capabilities grow, the board develops into a real working board.

Of course, creating such a board is not easy, and it does not happen all at once. Both the board and the theater's professional leaders have to invest considerable time and energy in the process—for a small theater, both are scarce resources. Immediate demands always appear more important. Board development can also be frustrating; results can be slow in coming and often the payoff is not readily apparent. And even with good efforts, there seems to be a continual lag between the board a theater needs and the board it has at any point in time. The art always seems to be ahead of the board's ability to support it. But when a board does find its own life, you can almost feel it quicken with new energy. Then new balances are established, and a board begins to provide real benefits for the theater. When this happens, the board moves out of the theater's shadows and begins to take its place beside it as a partner.

> My greatest desire is to empower my board, to have them understand that they are important and that they have agency. I want them to see their board service as a vocation, and I want them to see that our theater is part of a national theater movement and that their work is part of this bigger picture.
>
> —AARON DAVIDMAN
> ARTISTIC DIRECTOR, TRAVELING JEWISH THEATRE, SAN FRANCISCO

A GOVERNING BOARD

After a working board finds its feet and starts to take responsibility for itself, a further change needs to take place for it to mature into a full governing board. The board's structure is now in place, and that doesn't change much. But what does need to keep changing is how trustees use that structure. In order to become a mature board, trustees need a more sophisticated understanding of what it means to govern. By law and custom, the roles and responsibilities of a board always exist, even when a board is made up of only three friends of the founder, but the reality is that boards grow into these roles and responsibilities over time. As a board approaches maturity, it begins to see that fundraising means more than raising money; it means taking deeper responsibility for the fiscal stability of the theater and being accountable for the resources needed by the theater to operate. Similarly, it begins to understand that financial oversight means more than passing a budget or reading financial statements. It also means meeting established financial standards and accepting the risk that, if the theater fails, it is the board that is ultimately responsible.

But the most difficult thing a board needs to learn as it matures is how to share power in judicious and creative ways. People often don't understand that a board always has the legal powers of governance. In the founding stage, these powers are rarely felt. But, when a board starts to develop, they become evident. This can be threatening to theater leaders who now see that they can be fired by the board and that the board can have significant budgetary control over the theater's resources. The fear of losing power and control is one of the very real reasons many founders resist the development of a strong board even when its contributions are needed. And this fear is always intensified by horror stories about how some boards have fired leaders in peremptory and even demeaning ways or shifted resources too far from the artistic mission. It can also be exacerbated when new board members lack experience in handling this kind of power and are precipitous or clumsy in how they act. Using power well is a learned skill like any other skill. After understanding they have it, trustees have to learn how to use it with restraint and balance. A wise board knows that power should be a diffuse phenomenon. It may reside legally in the board, but it will be ineffective unless it is shared with the theater's staff, for it is the staff that holds the information and resources needed to effect and carry out decisions. When a board governs well, it rarely needs to show its power because it has established the relationships and trust needed to be a real partner with the theater. But during the process of development, power can be a divisive issue, one that never really goes away but one that a board and staff can learn to manage.

Finally, there is one other, more subtle, accomplishment that marks a mature governing board, which is that it takes ownership of its own creativity and imagination. A theater's artistry doesn't have to stop at the edge of the stage. Boards have their own artistry, and they can conduct their business with their own creativity and imagination. A board meeting should never be just a recitation of reports; it should include carefully planned opportunities for everyone to participate in stimulating discussion and clearly defined decision-making. And a board meeting, no matter how small or poor the theater, should never be held in a dingy basement. It should be held on the stage or at someone's home or at an interesting site in the area. And there should be props and potluck dinners and visiting artists and other ways of bringing board members together as creative human beings. Board members can be asked to share their own first experiences with theater, whether acting in a school play or trying to write their own scripts. Or perhaps they play an instrument or paint or dance. Everything about a board should have the same creative attention given to it that the theater gives to its art.

THINGS THAT CAN HELP

When a board reaches a mature stage of development, it can become a source of real support for a theater. But as anyone working with theaters knows, the evolution from a founding board to a working board to a mature governing board seldom happens smoothly. It is a complex and very human process. Upheaval, crisis, new breakthroughs, new people, lost people, joy and pain are all part of the story of growth. Negotiating this rocky path—and each theater will have its own version of it—can be difficult. But there are some things that can help.

At a practical level, one of the most constructive things a young theater can do is to ask one or two experienced board members who have worked with other arts organizations to join its board. At this point, board experience is as valuable an asset as fundraising or financial experience. Experienced board members can help educate the board—and the staff—about the changing needs of the theater, being sensitive to and even anticipating schisms that develop over personalities or power as changes start to happen. They can also be helpful in recognizing that many original board members do have the ability to move forward with the theater if they are given sufficient support and training. And they can begin to provide some of the internal leadership a board needs to start taking responsibility for its own work.

Consultants can also be useful at this point, providing insight into the changes that are taking place and how to meet them. Consultants can guide a theater in its board development efforts, and they can be helpful in "taking the heat" when specific board members need to be asked to leave or when all board members need to be asked to reevaluate their commitment. They can also provide leadership in planning retreats and ongoing education programs for trustees on issues of governance such as those discussed in other parts of this book. And, perhaps most important, they can help theaters understand the need to find ways to recognize and reward trustees for the important work they do.

Small theaters can also help themselves by sharing resources and ideas with other theaters. Board members can talk to other theaters that have been through these changes and take advantage of their learning curve, gaining not only counsel but emotional and moral support. Or board members can ask one or two trustees of a larger, more established theater to "buddy" or "mentor" them to provide experienced help. A local arts service organization might facilitate such a program by developing a pool of experienced trustees willing to work with small theaters. A theater can also partner with other small theaters. Many savvy founders of today's theaters are acting in entrepreneurial ways to share overhead costs, apply for joint grants, develop medical insurance programs and in other ways reduce the pressures facing them as they grow. By extending this kind of partnering to board development, small theaters could create joint efforts to identify and recruit new trustees or even share consultants.

It will never be easy to attract and keep dedicated board members when a theater is not well established and does not have long arms into its community. And it will never be easy to find the time and energy to devote to board development or to make the internal adjustments needed to allow space for a governing board and accept the sharing of power that implies. But if a theater has a better understanding of what to expect, it can begin to make more informed choices about how it wants to create its own future.

Artist Trustees

A second issue that seems to fall outside most discussions of governance is the role that artists can play on boards. It is surprising how rarely the issue of having artists serve as theater trustees is raised, much less discussed. In fact, most theaters have very few, if any, artists on their boards. In the most recent TCG Board Survey (2004), of the 111 theaters surveyed, only fifty-eight percent had any artists at all on their boards and the average for these theaters was between two and three artists. If the artistic director is one of these artists, which is most likely, then there were only one or two other artists serving as trustees on these boards. And, on forty-two percent of the boards, there were no artists at all, not even the artistic director. Although these are averages and only cover 111 theaters, it seems clear that, with the exception of artistic directors, artists play a small role in the governance of our theaters.

When you stop to think about it, this is puzzling. On corporate boards, which in many ways are the models on which not-for-profit boards are based, most board members have fairly extensive experience with the business world. They may be corporate lawyers or investment bankers but they share much of the mindset and values of the companies they govern. The number of directors with little or no business experience is small, and even many of these directors, such as university presidents and foundation heads, have led large, complex organizations. But, in the art world, governance is delegated mainly to people who have little direct experience in the work of the organizations they govern. Although most board members have valuable and much needed knowledge about the financial, fundraising and administrative procedures that support the art, few have a working knowledge of the art itself. Does this matter? What difference would it make if there were more artists on our boards? What prevents it?

PRECONCEPTIONS ABOUT ARTIST TRUSTEES

Artists can be remarkable board members but the potential of their contribution is missed when people hold negative preconceptions about having artists serve as trustees. Board members can be seen as playing two kinds of roles for a theater: internal roles and external roles. The external roles are those connecting the theater to the wider community, such as fundraising and advocacy. The internal roles are those mainly handled within the theater, such as selecting and hiring the theater's leaders, planning and budgeting. When artists are considered for board membership, it is usually to play one of the external roles, using the artist's cachet to enhance a theater's standing in the community. For small theaters, gaining the support of a known and respected artist can help them "break out" of the pack in terms of visibility and funding. For large theaters, attracting "stars" to their board gives them the advantage of using these highly visible people to cultivate major donors or access political power. Representing a theater to the external world is an accepted role for artist trustees, and many distinguished artists have played this role with great benefit for their theaters.

It is when boards start thinking about including artists in the internal governing of the theater, in areas such as budgeting and leadership change, that objections arise. I have often heard trustees, managers, and even artistic directors say they think it isn't appropriate to have artists directly involved in the governing process. The most common reason given is that artists lack the skills boards seek for themselves, particularly financial and governing skills. The skills they do have—artistic expertise and sensibility—aren't seen as qualities needed for governing, and so aren't considered important by nominating or board development committees. Rather, the belief is that a board's artistic input should come from the artistic director and his staff or from outside advisory boards or guest speakers. In other words, artist trustees just are not needed.

The corollary to this is that, if working artists are added to the board, they will need to be educated to have the skills of traditional board members. They will have to understand budgets and balance sheets, and they will have to learn the give-and-take of running a theater with fiscal discipline. And they will have to learn the procedures and sensibilities of a board. All this takes time and effort, so the obvious question is: Why do it unless there is something artists can contribute that is genuinely needed?

A more subtle objection that floats around discussions of artist trustees is whether artists would "fit in" with the social, intellectual and decision-making environment of a board. Artists tend to be concerned with different issues and have different priorities and values than traditional board members. And they tend to think differently, approaching decision-making in ways that are more elliptical and intuitive than linear and analytical. Would these differences divert board conversations into areas not directly relevant to the issues at hand, using valuable time and possibly creating frictions or miscommunication among board members? And an even more difficult question: Would artistic directors want their influence with the board diluted by having other artists at the table who may have different views of artistic issues as well as voting power to affect decisions on these issues? And do board members themselves want artists to have voting power if it means introducing different values and budget priorities into their decision-making?

Finally, practical arguments are often raised when theaters consider adding artists to their boards. One is that it would complicate a board's own giving policies because exceptions would have to be made for most working artists whose incomes don't allow for modest, much less substantial, financial contributions. Another is that boards might be unsure about conflict-of-interest problems if an artist trustee might be hired by the theater in the future. Finally, there is the obvious question of whether artists would want to serve on boards even if they were asked. Given their busy lives, would they want to take the time to invest in becoming a trustee? And would they believe that their contribution would make a difference?

CONTRIBUTIONS ARTISTS CAN MAKE

If you look at these objections carefully, every one can be turned around to become a strong argument for having more, rather than fewer, artists involved in governing. For example, although artists may not have traditional board skills, they do have knowledge and expertise that can be very relevant to a board's work. Specifically, their knowledge of the practical issues of artists' lives (salaries, benefits and working conditions, for example) can be a valuable input to budget discussions, just as knowledge of fundraising and marketing can. Artists can help articulate and even advocate for the artistic needs of a theater as other board members do for the administrative needs with which they are more familiar, putting more balance into the budget decision-making process. And artists can tie budgetary discussions more directly to the artistic mission.

More fundamentally, artists have a deep understanding of the process of creating art, how it encompasses a series of steps involving points of human creativity, each point carrying the possibility of something going wrong. Deepening board members' understanding of this process helps them see that a production of a play cannot simply be viewed as a product that can be adjusted or perfected. It needs to be seen as the end result of a complex and risky process. When trustees recognize this, it changes the way they evaluate plays and helps them defend the theater when a production does go badly. And, even more broadly, artists can help place the work of a theater in the wider context of what is happening in the industry nationally, how the work fits in and what the problems and trends are, all part of the larger framework of governing. So artists can bring valuable expertise to the board table if their input is recognized and wanted.

Similarly, the different values, sensibilities and modes of thought that artists bring to the table can enrich board discussions rather than divert them. Most board work is geared toward end-state decision-making: setting goals, analyzing information, monitoring progress and evaluating results. There seems to be a "right" way to proceed. Bringing artists into the discussion can lead to different questions being asked and different goals being suggested. And it can show different connections among issues and introduce different values for consideration. Although the conversation may be diverted for a while, such diversions can be avenues to new solutions, not poor uses of time. And they can challenge a board's thinking and perhaps expand its definition of stewardship.

Finally, there are the practical arguments against having artist trustees. However, with a little imagination, many ways can be found to accommodate artist trustees within a board's giving policies, particularly in light of the potential artists actually have to raise money, and certainly there are ways to monitor conflicts of interest. I think the real problem is convincing artists to want to serve on boards and making their experience worthwhile. Their lives are as busy and over-committed as those of other important people boards try to attract. But, from listening to artists who have served on boards, a number of things can be done to support artist trustees.

What Theaters Can Do

First, a theater needs to be clear about what it expects from an artist trustee. Many artists who serve on boards really don't know why they are there and often the theaters don't either. The nature of the time commitment, the role the theater expects the artists to play and any financial commitment all need to be spelled out. Although this is true in recruiting any board member, additional efforts may be needed for artists. And potential artist trustees need to be asked the same questions that are asked of other prospective trustees to see if they are a "fit" with the theater: Do they support the theater's artistic mission? Its long-term plan? Its values and way of working? Any particular artist can be a bad fit with a theater just as any particular non-artist can.

Second, a theater does need to give artists the necessary skills for governing, such as understanding financial statements and learning about the structure and operations of a board. Holding the same fiduciary responsibilities as other board members, they need to understand these responsibilities and be prepared to carry them out. And a theater needs to think carefully about how to use an artist's time, just as it would with a corporate CEO who is busy and often out of town. Notifying artists in advance when they are needed and briefing them on the issues enables them to contribute to the work of the board much more effectively.

Finally, and probably most important, for the experience to be a success, a board has to genuinely want to include artists in substantive ways and then work hard to make it happen. In many ways, the arguments against having artists on boards are remarkably similar to the arguments that have been raised whenever efforts have been made to diversify boards, whether racially or sexually or by social or economic status. But what these other experiences have shown is that, to be successful, new types of board members can't be brought on in token ways just for the sake of appearances. And they can't be brought on with the expectation that they will be absorbed and transformed into traditional board members who will maintain the status quo. Successfully including a more diverse group of people means the board itself has to change; it has to include a broader range of ideas

THEATRE FOR A NEW AUDIENCE

We are a small theater in New York known for our work in the classics, particularly Shakespeare. Some years ago, our board chair, Ted Rogers, led an effort to create an Artistic Council for the theater that included actors, directors, designers and a number of highly respected and seasoned artists from other fields. Ted insisted that these artists be actual members of the theater's governing board, not just part of an advisory council, so today about a third of our board are artists.

For me, it makes a difference having artists at the board table. They can speak to their own areas of expertise but they can also bring to life the world of the artist; the conditions under which he works, what it means to live on the road and what the special joys are when he feels welcome and the work goes well. All this expands the understanding and knowledge of the other board members. I also think it matters that the artists are actually fellow board members. They are respected because they know and understand the theater, plus there is a feeling that we are all in this together. They enhance my work by giving more credibility to artistic concerns.

But I have learned that, if you really want artist trustees to be involved in decision-making, you have to make the effort to inform them and ask for their specific help. Artists are not going to meetings on their own; you have to facilitate this. You have to tell them there is a special issue that needs their attention and their input. And you have to bring them in at the level that the decision is actually being made, which may be at the Executive Committee level rather than the board level. So, if you need the actress Dana Ivey to speak about artists' salaries or the set designer Doug Stein to speak about plans for a new space, you need to tell them ahead of time so they can be there. You also need to give support to artists to speak up since sometimes the language and tenor of board discussions can seem unfamiliar and even intimidating to them. The challenge is how to really use artists well, how to get them in the process early and engage them to make a difference.

—JEFFREY HOROWITZ
FOUNDING ARTISTIC DIRECTOR

and be attuned to a wider range of voices. It is a two-way process; the new board members and the old board members learn from each other. One of the most frequently voiced complaints from artist trustees is that they joined a board so they could make a difference but found that their ideas and expertise were not really wanted. They were there either to enhance the letterhead or provide access to particular resources and were expected to rubber-stamp decisions that, in reality, had already been made. In these cases, boards really didn't go through the process of determining why they wanted artists on their boards and didn't make the changes necessary to make the experience a success, either for the artist or for the theater.

Alternative Models of Governance

A third issue not often explored in discussions of governance is whether there are alternative ways theaters can think about their governing needs. Many new theaters just becoming involved in board issues are curious about what options they may have, while many nontraditional theaters are searching for modes of governance that better fit how they actually operate. And even many traditional theaters today are looking for more flexibility in their governing structure.

The Traditional Approach

The board model most familiar to theaters is the traditional model that was carried over from the corporate sector to the not-for-profit world, including the performing arts. Although there are many variations of this model, typically it is structured like a pyramid with a chair at the top, an executive committee next, then the full board and finally a series of specialized committees and subcommittees (see the "Models of Board Structures" diagram on page 287). Theaters also often create temporary committees, such as search committees or special ad hoc task forces, to meet particular needs not covered by the standing committees. And many theaters have auxiliary boards, such as Patron or Honorary Boards, as a way of keeping major donors and former board members close to the theater.

A complex board like this is usually found in large theaters; smaller theaters would have simplified versions. But in all cases, a traditional board is not only hierarchal in its own internal structure but hierarchal in its relation to the theater. Sitting above the theater, the board is responsible for hiring the theater's leadership, setting or validating its policies and ensuring its financial integrity. The theater, itself, becomes encompassed within this governing structure.

The question is whether this model, even in its many variations, works well for any particular theater, whether it meets a theater's needs in a coherent way. Usually, because it is the one known and traditionally used, the corporate model is accepted without a great deal of question. But this may be imposing a governing structure on a theater whose mission or way of working just doesn't fit it. When this happens, a theater often experiences struggles over power and intensifying conflicts between board and staff. A lack of congruence exists between the theater and its board that, over time, can become increasingly stressful.

A More Organic Approach

But there is another way of looking at boards that can open up alternative possibilities, which is to actually invert how we think about creating a governing structure; to turn the process upside down. Rather than imposing a board structure from outside and expecting a theater to adjust to it, the governing structure can be designed to flow out of the artistic and institutional nature of the theater itself. Then the structure of governing is adjusted to meet the needs of the theater rather than adjusting the needs of the theater to meet the governing structure. This replaces the hierarchal view of boards with a more organic approach in which the theater and the board feed into and nurture each other.

This organic approach can be illustrated by looking at three aspects of governing where problems often arise with traditional boards. The first is a theater's relationship to its community; the second, its relationship to how it creates its art; and the third, its relationship to power. Obviously there are other areas that could be explored, but these three are interesting because they suggest different ways of reorganizing traditional boards. And it is instructive that in exploring these three cases one of the main things revealed is that it is *who* serves on a board that really makes the difference. If the governing structure is designed to place the right people in the right places, many of the problems disappear.

A Theater and Its Community

A theater's relationship with its community often becomes an issue when a theater wants to diversify its board to better reflect the community but is afraid this will conflict with the board's ability to give and raise money. In fact, wanting to maintain the board's fundraising capability often becomes the reason for not bringing more community members onto a board. But using the distinction between internal and external board functions suggested earlier, not all functions have to be included on the governing board. Although the internal functions of governing such as finance and board development must be included, some of the external functions such as fundraising or education can be placed in working auxiliary groups that have clear connections to the board but not governing power.

For example, one way of addressing a perceived conflict between the diversity and fundraising goals of a board is to separate them. Rather than keeping both on the governing board, the fundraising responsibilities could be moved to a separate Development Board. Made up of patrons and experienced fundraisers, this new board could retain its high "give or get" requirement while the now more community-centered governing board could develop other giving policies, such as requiring one hundred percent participation or making the theater one of a board member's top three giving priorities. Not only would reorganizing board functions this way allow the theater to diversify its governing structure; often, top fundraising people would prefer not to take on the everyday work of a regular board. Of course, a fundraising board like this would have to have prestige both in the theater and in the community to make it work, but that could be created under the right leadership just as theaters often create capital campaign committees with distinguished outside members and leaders. Although a simple example, this shows how a board structure doesn't have to accommodate all of its functions on the governing board. Its structure can be adjusted to allocate some of these functions elsewhere so that the people a theater wants to hold governing power, in this case more representative community leaders, are placed in the right positions. Reorganizing the structure reallocates the people.

An actual but more complex example of how reorganizing board functions can help a theater connect with its community was developed for Living Stage, an inner-city theater company affiliated with Arena Stage, which used theatrical techniques to help disadvantaged children and adults recognize their own creative potential and

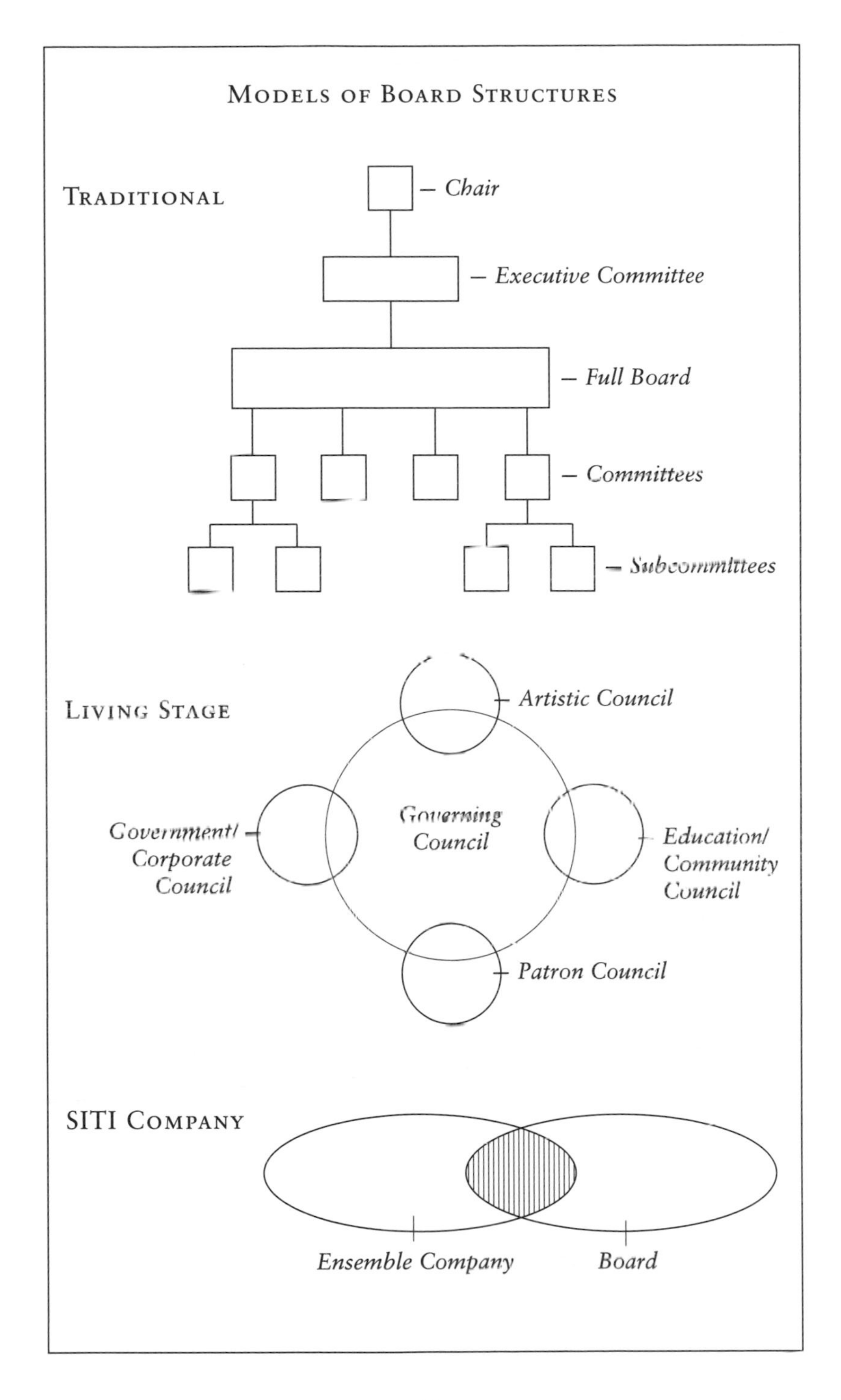
Models of Board Structures
Traditional
Chair
Executive Committee
Full Board
Committees
Subcommittees
Living Stage
Artistic Council
Governing Council
Government/ Corporate Council
Education/ Community Council
Patron Council
SITI Company
Ensemble Company
Board

take more control over their lives. The theater worked in a number of different ways: contracting with the city government in Washington, D.C., partnering with other community organizations and developing patrons who supported its work. A small theater, it did not have the resources to support a large, traditional board, nor did a traditional board fit the way it actually interacted with the community.

To meet its needs, the theater proposed an alternative board structure centered on a small Governing Council that functioned as a Committee of the Whole. Surrounding this central council but attached to it were four working councils extending into the communities that represented the theater's constituencies and major sources of support. As shown in the "Models of Board Structures" diagram, the board included a Government/Corporate Council of people who could help develop contracts for the theater's work; an Education/Community Council of people who partnered with the theater; a Patron Council of major donors; and an Artistic Council that advised the theater on artistic matters. The chair of each council sat on the central Governing Council, connecting these volunteer groups directly to the governing process. By simplifying the structure this way, the theater not only recognized its limited staff resources but, more importantly, created a structure more in tune with the way it actually operated. And it placed the right people in the right places in the governing process—the people most concerned with internal governing in the center and those more concerned with external needs around the edges.

A THEATER AND ITS ART

A second, often problematical, aspect of governing is the relationship of a board to its theater's artistic process. Often this becomes a problem for nontraditional theaters (particularly ensemble theaters) if the way they create their art is not in harmony with a traditional board. An example is the SITI Company of New York, an ensemble company of artists, founded by Anne Bogart in 1992 as an alternative way for artists to work. The artists of the SITI Company create plays together over extended periods of time, building a repertory that tours both in this country and abroad. The company has no building and no established season, and, in many ways, operates more like a modern dance company or European theater than our more familiar American theaters.

Almost all of the original SITI ensemble members are still with the theater, and their professional and personal lives are deeply entwined with it. Because most of their livelihood comes from the theater, the artists have a strong stake in governing decisions, particularly budget decisions. Although always evolving, the SITI Company is creating an approach to governing that can be described as two intersecting ovals. One oval represents the ensemble company, including not only the actors but designers, playwrights and other people who work closely with the company on an ongoing basis. The other oval represents the board. Where the two ovals intersect represents company members who also sit on the board: the artistic director, the associate artistic director and three or four company members nominated by the ensemble on a rotating basis. Also on the board are distinguished outside artists who support the company's work. At this point, of a board of eighteen members, six are company members, two are outside artists and ten are outside non-artists. This arrangement allows company members significant input into the governing process and also reflects the collaborative nature of the theater. In many ways, the goal of the board is to work like an ensemble with sensibilities similar to the company, so the two intersecting ovals can also be seen as two intersecting ensembles.

In the Living Stage approach, the governing process is restructured by reallocating some of the board's external functions to groups acting as satellites around a central governing core. In the SITI approach, the governing process is restructured by including ensemble members in the process and by creating a board structure more in harmony with the theater's collaborative sensibilities. These are both examples I know personally and have worked with.

A THEATER AND POWER

The third issue, the relationship of a theater to power, is more elusive. But since it lurks behind so many questions of governance, it is also worth exploring, even in a preliminary way. Power is a complex and opaque phenomenon. It makes us uneasy, and we generally don't like to think about it, much less talk about it. But ignoring how power is structured and used in a theater makes it difficult to understand some of the conflicts that occur not only between a theater and its board but within a board itself. And, without this understanding, it is difficult to look for ways to resolve such conflicts.

One way to explore issues of power is to take a cue from the Living Stage and SITI Company examples, because what these examples reveal is that *who* sits on a board becomes the defining question. They also reveal that *who* sits on a board is closely related to *how* a board is structured. A board's structure and membership go together. In the case of a traditional theater, the board is organized around functional areas, such as finance, fundraising, marketing, board development and advocacy, so it calls for people with those skills to be on its board. The Living Stage board, on the other hand, is structured to emphasize relationships with the theater's various communities and constituents, so it draws a wider range of people, from patrons to artists to government and community leaders, into its governing structure. And the SITI board is organized to include members of the ensemble company, so a high proportion of artists are part of its governing structure. In each case, different board structures call for different kinds of members.

But, looking at this from a different angle, it is also true that whoever is chosen to sit on the board is the person who will hold governing power. It is the people sitting around the board table who have power. So they all go together; the structure creates the membership and the membership determines who has power. If a theater wants to place more power in the hands of artists or community members or patrons, it needs to create a governing structure that, as much as possible, calls for such people to be included.

But there is a further dimension that needs to be added to any understanding of power, for it is not only who sits on the board but whether these individuals have the skills to use power well. As the earlier discussion of small theaters showed, trustees, whoever they are, have to have the wisdom and experience to use power in balanced and constructive ways. They have to understand that power is only effective if shared, and they have to build the kind of trust between a board and staff that makes such sharing possible. Unless this trust is established, a staff can effectively "take" power by controlling what information a board has and when it has it, while a board can be tempted to "overuse" power by peremptorily making policies or personnel changes that are at odds with the rest of the theater. Trust is the bond that stabilizes power in an organization. So, in addition to having the right members in the right places on a board, experience and wisdom are also necessary. There is much that is intangible in the mechanisms of good governance, which, in many ways, is what the "spirit" of governing is all about.

Putting this together, a theater's relationship to power can be seen as the interaction of three dimensions of governing—a board's structure, its membership and its behavior. If a theater wants to explore its own relationship to power, it can ask itself the following questions: First, is its board structure designed to be in congruence with the theater's needs; does it have an organic relationship to the theater? Then, will this structure bring to the board the kinds of people the theater wants to have in power; will the right people be in the right places within the governing process? And finally, do these people have the skills to use power wisely? Will they create the necessary bonds of trust? If all three of these dimensions of governing—structure, membership and behavior—are in harmony, a theater has a good chance of having an environment in which power becomes a creative rather than a destructive force. Achieving this is not only the hallmark of a healthy theater; it is at the heart of the art of governing.

CONTRIBUTORS

PRUDENCE R. BEIDLER is Chair of the Chicago Children's Museum and serves on the executive committee of the Chicago Community Trust. In addition, she is working on two book projects, one about leadership succession in not-for-profit organizations and the other, a guidebook for volunteers. She is past Chair of the board of Jane Addams Hull House, Planned Parenthood/Chicago Area, the Chicago Wellesley Club, the Lake Forest College Women's Board and the YWCA of Lake Forest. Educated at Wellesley College and the University of Chicago, she was formerly a teacher in the Chicago public schools. She has been a volunteer since junior high school and has served on boards of not-for-profit organizations for more than thirty years.

GIGI BRADFORD has worked in arts and culture for more than twenty-five years. Her areas of interest and expertise include contemporary literature, the not-for-profit arts, intellectual property issues for artists and scholars, and philanthropy for the cultural sector.

From 1997–2001 she was Executive Director of the Center for Arts and Culture, America's first think tank for arts and cultural issues. At the National Endowment for the Arts from 1991–1997, she managed the Literature Program, the Heritage and Preservation Division and the Millennium Projects, designed to showcase the best of the agency's programs and projects. Additionally, she directed the Folger Poetry Program from 1984–1991 and was Executive Director of the Academy of American Poets. She is the recipient of the first Elizabeth Kray Award for service to the field of literature. She received an M.F.A. in poetry from the University of Iowa Writers' Workshop.

Ronnie Brooks is Director of the James P. Shannon Leadership Institute, a program of the Amherst H. Wilder Foundation's Center for Communities that provides a year-long renewal experience for foundation and not-for-profit organization leaders. She is also a consultant specializing in strategic planning, leadership development and not-for-profit organization governance and management.

She has extensive experience in both the public and private sectors in Minnesota. She served as Special Assistant to the Governor of Minnesota and as Director of Majority Research for the Minnesota State Senate, and has managed development projects for the mayors of both Minneapolis and Saint Paul. She was also Vice President of the Keystone Center, a Colorado-based public policy organization; Executive Director of the St. Paul Downtown Council; and Manager of Community Development and Policy Planning for the Dayton-Hudson (now Target) Corporation. She has played a leadership role in several Minnesota civic and professional organizations. She was President of both the Citizens League and the Mediation Center and a board member of the Voyager Outward Bound School, the David Preus Leadership Council, the Civic Leadership Foundation and MAP for Nonprofits.

She is on the faculty of the Legislative Staff Management Institute of the University of Minnesota's Hubert H. Humphrey Institute of Public Affairs, where she focuses on issues of leadership and management in the not-for-profit sector. She is a recipient of the Lloyd Short Award for Distinguished Public Service and the YWCA Outstanding Leadership Award. She is a graduate of the University of Michigan and received her M.A. in political science from Michigan State University.

James Bundy serves as Dean of the Yale School of Drama and Artistic Director of Yale Repertory Theatre. He directed the New England premiere of Amy Freed's *The Psychic Life of Savages* as part of Yale Rep's 2003–2004 season. From 1998–2002, he was Artistic Director of Great Lakes Theater Festival in Cleveland, Ohio. He was formerly Associate Producing Director of The Acting Company, one of the nation's foremost touring repertory theaters, and Managing Director of Cornerstone Theater Company, known for its innovative, community-based productions of new and classic plays. In addition to productions at Great Lakes Theater Festival, he has directed at The Acting Company, California Shakespeare Festival, Alabama Shakespeare Festival and The Juilliard School's Drama Division. He has been a Drama League fellow and a member of the Lincoln Center Theater Directors Lab. He received his degree from Harvard University and trained in acting at The London Academy of Music and Dramatic Art. He also received an M.F.A. in directing from Yale School of Drama in 1995.

Richard P. Chait has been Professor of Higher Education at the Harvard Graduate School of Education since 1996. From 1985–1996, he was Professor of Higher Education and Management at the University of Maryland. Previously, he was Mandel Professor of Nonprofit Management at Case Western Reserve University, Associate Provost of Penn State and Director and later Educational Chairman of the Institute for Educational Management at Harvard.

As a teacher, he has a special interest in the case-study method of instruction. His research has focused on academic administration and campus governance. In addition to writing numerous articles about the academy, he is the coauthor of four books, including *Beyond Traditional Tenure* (Jossey-Bass, San Francisco, 1982), *The Effective Board of Trustees* (the American Council on Education/Oryx Press, Phoenix, 1991), *Improving the Performance of Governing Boards* (the American Council on Education/Oryx Press, Phoenix, 1996) and *Governance as Leadership: Reframing the Work of Nonprofit Boards* (BoardSource, Washington, D.C., 2004). He currently serves as Principal Investigator for the Project on Faculty Appointments, a three-year, $1.9 million grant funded by The Pew Charitable Trusts. The Fulbright New Zealand Board of Directors selected him as a Fulbright U.S. Distinguished American Scholar.

He was a trustee and member of the executive committee of the governing boards of Goucher College in Maryland and Maryville College in Tennessee, and is a director of the National Center for Nonprofit Boards. He is past Chair of the American Association for Higher Education board. He earned a B.A. from Rutgers University and an M.A. and Ph.D. from the University of Wisconsin.

KATHLEEN CHALFANT is an actor with a long career of notable roles on and Off-Broadway and in film and television. Stage productions include *Angels in America* (Tony and Drama Desk nominations), *Racing Demon*, *Five by Tenn*, *Guantanamo*, *Wit* (Drama Desk, OBIE, Lucille Lortel and Outer Critics awards) and *Nine Armenians* (Drama Desk nomination). Film credits include *Murder and Murder*, *Bob Roberts*, *The Last Days of Disco*, *Dream Work* and *Kinsey*. TV work includes a recurring role on *Prince Street*, *The Guardian* and *A Death in the Family* and various roles on *Law & Order*. Other awards include the 1996 OBIE award for Sustained Excellence of Performance and the Drama League and Sidney Kingsley awards for her body of work. She received a 1998 Connecticut Critics Circle Award and the 2000 Ovation, Garland and Los Angeles Drama Critics Circle awards for *Wit*. She is a founding member of the Women's Project and serves on the boards of the Vineyard Theatre, Broadway Cares/Equity Fights Aids and the Screen Actors Guild.

JOAN CHANNICK is Deputy Director of Theatre Communications Group and Director of the U.S. Center of the International Theatre Institute. She worked previously as Associate Managing Director of CENTERSTAGE in

Baltimore and as Marketing Director of the Yale Repertory Theatre. Preceding her theater career, she practiced securities litigation with the Boston law firm of Gaston Snow & Ely Bartlett. She serves on the U.S. National Commission for UNESCO, the International Theatre Institute executive council, and the boards of the Literary Managers and Dramaturgs of the Americas and the League of Professional Theatre Women. She teaches a course on legal issues in the arts at the Yale School of Drama.

PETER CULMAN retired from CENTERSTAGE in Baltimore in 2000 after thirty-four years as its Managing Director. During his tenure and with the help of the theater's trustees and staff, CENTERSTAGE balanced its budget for twenty-three seasons and purchased and renovated a 110,000-square-foot facility with two theaters as well as fifty living units for visiting artists and interns. Under his leadership, CENTERSTAGE was awarded three NEA Challenge Grants and completed three endowment/capital campaigns totaling more than $30 million, building an endowment close to $20 million. His national involvement in theater includes two terms as President of the League of Resident Theatres (LORT) and service as a board member of Theatre Communications Group (TCG), as Treasurer and board member of the American Arts Alliance and as a member of the National Endowment for the Arts Theatre Overview, Companies and Special Project panels. In 1991, he received the Zeisler Award from TCG for distinguished service to not-for-profit professional theater. In 1992, the Maryland Institute College of Art awarded him an honorary Doctorate of Fine Arts. Currently, he is Adjunct Professor of Homiletics at St. Mary's Seminary and University, a trustee of the Institute for Christian-Jewish Studies and a consultant to theaters and other not-for-profit organizations.

PATRICIA EGAN is a principal of Cool Spring Analytics, which provides consulting services to arts organizations, other not-for-profits and funders in the areas of governance, strategic planning, financial management and financial analysis. She has eighteen years of experience in not-for-profit theater management at Portland Stage Company, Yale Repertory Theatre/Yale School of Drama, CENTERSTAGE and, most recently, as Managing Director of Trinity Repertory Company. She has consulted with National Arts Stabilization (now National Arts Strategies), working with arts organizations in Baltimore and Arizona on planning, financial management and governance issues, and serving as interim President of NAS during 2000. Other consulting experience includes work with the NEA, state arts councils, and arts and environmental organizations on strategic and organizational planning, fundraising and financial management. She has a degree in mathematics from Tufts University. She serves on the advisory committee for Theatre Communication Group's Fiscal Survey and on the board of Everyman Theatre in Baltimore. She teaches courses in financial management at the Yale School of Drama.

ZELDA FICHANDLER is one of the pioneer founders of the American regional theater, creating Arena Stage in Washington, D.C., in 1950 and serving as its artistic leader until 1991. Her history-making example, force of personality and eloquence as a speaker and writer have made her a leading national figure in the performing arts, and her personal vision for theater has had a transforming effect on the entire field. As Producing Artistic Director of Arena Stage, she directed many of Arena's productions including *Mrs. Klein*, *Uncle Vanya*, *The Three Sisters*, *Death of a Salesman*, *An Enemy of the People*, *Six Characters in Search of an Author*, *A Doll House* and the American premieres of new Eastern European works, *Duck Hunting*, *The Ascent of Mt. Fuji* and *Screenplay*. Arena Stage was the first American theater company, sponsored by the State Department, to tour the Soviet Union. As a producer, she nurtured all of Arena's plays, making a home for important European playwrights like Brecht, Frisch, Ionesco, Mrozek and Orkeny, alongside significant American revivals of works by Albee, Miller, Williams, O'Neill, Wilder, Kaufman and Hart, and classics by Shakespeare, Shaw, Molière, Ibsen and others. Broadway hits *The Great White Hope* and *K2* also started at Arena Stage.

In 1984, her concern for the development of young actors led her to take on the additional role of Chair of the Graduate Acting Program at New York University's Tisch School of the Arts, a position which she continues to fill. Graduates of this program now occupy leading positions in film, television and the stage, winning top awards in the various media. From 1991–1994, she also served as the Artistic Director of The Acting Company, a young company of actors that tours a classical repertory throughout America.

She has received the National Medal of the Arts, awarded in 1997 by President Clinton; the Commonwealth Award for distinguished service to the dramatic arts; The Brandeis University Creative Arts Award; The Acting Company's John Houseman Award for commitment to the development of young American actors; the Margo Jones Award for the production of new plays; Washingtonian of the Year Award; the Ortho 21st Century Women Trailblazer Award and the Society for Stage Directors and Choreographers's George Abbott Award. The New York commercial theater world awarded Fichandler and Arena Stage the Tony Award in 1976, the first to be given to a company outside New York. In 1999 she was inducted into the Theater Hall of Fame, making her the first artistic leader outside of New York to receive this honor. In 2003, she received the Lifetime Achievement Award from PlayMakers Repertory Company in North Carolina.

GWEN COCHRAN HADDEN, President of Cochran Hadden Royston Associates, has provided consulting services to major performing arts organizations and performing arts service groups since 1990, specializing in the areas of cultural diversity, diversity in the arts, arts management, human resources development, organizational development, culture change and crisis management. Her client list includes the Alabama Shakespeare Festival, Americans for the Arts, the Association of Performing Arts Presenters, Atlanta Symphony Orchestra, Cape Ann Symphony Orchestra, CENTERSTAGE of Baltimore, North Shore Music Theatre, Peabody Essex Museum, Seattle Repertory Theatre and Theatre Communications Group. She has served as an officer of the board of overseers of the Boston Symphony Orchestra and the board of trustees of the American Symphony Orchestra League. She has authored several articles for national arts publications and is currently working on a book entitled *The Crazy Quilt of Cultural Identity.*

THOMAS P. HOLLAND is Professor and Director of the Doctoral Program in the School of Social Work, University of Georgia, Athens. Previously, he was Associate Dean and Chair of the Doctoral Program at the Mandel School of Applied Social Sciences, Case Western Reserve University, Cleveland, Ohio. Holland has published extensively on management and governance of not-for-profit organizations and consults nationally in this field. He is the co-author of *Improving the Performance of Governing Boards* (the American Council on Education/Oryx Press, Phoenix,1996) and *The Effective Board of Trustees* (the American Council on Education/ Oryx Press, Phoenix, 1991).

JIM HOUGHTON is Founding Artistic Director of Signature Theatre Company in New York, the first not-for-profit theater company in the U.S. to devote each season of productions to the work of a single living playwright. Signature's Playwrights-in-Residence have included Edward Albee, Lee Blessing, Horton Foote, Maria Irene Fornes, John Guare, Bill Irwin, Adrienne Kennedy, Romulus Linney, Arthur Miller, Sam Shepard, Paula Vogel and Lanford Wilson. August Wilson will join the company in 2005–06 as Playwright-in-Residence. Since the theater's founding in 1991, Signature and its artists have received many honors including the Pulitzer Prize and OBIE, Drama Desk, Lucille Lortel and Outer Critics Circle awards, as well as the William Inge Theatre Festival's 1998 Margo Jones Medal, presented to Mr. Houghton for an outstanding contribution to the American theater. In 2003, Signature was named "Theatre of the Year" by the National Theatre Conference.

His directing credits for Signature Theatre Company include Lanford Wilson's *Burn This* (nominated for a Lucille Lortel Award for Outstanding Revival and a Drama League Award for Distinguished Revival); Arthur Miller's *The American Clock* (nominated for a Drama Desk for Direction); Miller's radio play *The Pussycat and the Expert Plumber Who Was a Man* (broadcast on National Public Radio); Sam Shepard's *Curse of the Starving Class*; Romulus Linney's *Heathen Valley* and *Ambrosio* (world premiere), both co-directed with Mr. Linney; Adrienne Kennedy's OBIE Award–winning *June and Jean in Concert* (world premiere); Bill Irwin's *Mr. Fox: A Rumination* (world premiere); Horton Foote's *The Last of the Thorntons* and *Laura Dennis* (both world premieres); and the New York premieres of Edward Albee's *Fragments* and *Marriage Play* and Lee Blessing's *Two Rooms*. In the fall of 1999 he directed the regional premiere of Arthur Miller's *Mr. Peters' Connection* at the Guthrie Theater.

He serves as Artistic Advisor to the Guthrie Theater, where he acts as a consultant on all artistic planning, and is implementing new programming featuring work by living playwrights. In 1999, he was named Artistic Director of the renowned O'Neill Playwrights Conference, and took over in the fall of that year as the organization's second Artistic Director in its thirty-five-year history. He served in this capacity through the 2003 Conference. From 1996–1999, he also served as Artistic Director of the New Harmony Project, a national conference for theater, film and television writers.

DOUG HUGHES, director, has been represented on and Off-Broadway by numerous productions including John Patrick Shanley's *Doubt*, for which he received Drama Desk, Outer Critics Circle and Lucille Lortel awards and a Tony nomination for best director; and Bryony Lavery's *Frozen*, for which he received Tony, Lortel and Outer Critics Circle nominations for best director. Other New York productions include *Flesh and Blood*, which was awarded the Society of Stage Directors and Choreographers Foundation's award for most distinguished production in the New York season; *The Beard of Avon*, *Embedded*, *Othello* and *Henry V* all for the New York Shakespeare Festival; *A Question of Mercy* and *Lake Hollywood*. His work as a director has been equally divided between classics and new work and has been seen at most of America's leading resident theaters including the McCarter Theatre Center, the Guthrie Theater, The Shakespeare Theatre in Washington, D.C., LaJolla Playhouse, Seattle Repertory Theatre, Hartford Stage, Steppenwolf Theatre Company, Yale Rep, Playwrights Horizons and Actors Theatre of Louisville.

From 1997–2001, he served as Artistic Director of the Long Wharf Theatre in New Haven, Connecticut, where he produced the premiere production of Margaret Edson's *Wit* in 1997, which later transferred to New York and went on to win the Pulitzer Prize and the New York Critics Circle and Drama Desk awards. His other posts have included Associate Artistic Director of Manhattan Theatre Club (1980–83), Associate Artistic Director of Seattle Repertory Theatre (1984–1996) and Director of Artistic Planning for the Guthrie Theater (1996–1997). He is a visiting lecturer in the directing program of the Yale School of Drama. He is a graduate of Harvard University.

PETER FRANCIS JAMES, actor, has extensive credits on Broadway and in not-for-profit theater, including *On Golden Pond* with James Earl Jones at the Kennedy Center and on Broadway, *Much Ado About Nothing* and *Hamlet* (The Public Theater's Shakespeare in the Park), and *Drowning Crow* and *Judgment at Nuremberg* on Broadway. His work in film and on TV includes roles in *Oz*, *The Rosa Parks Story*, *Law & Order*, *Third Watch* and *Simple Justice* (as Thurgood Marshall). For the last five years he has taught Shakespeare in the Acting Program at Yale School of Drama.

CHRISTINE JONES, scenic designer, has been designing sets for plays in New York as well as regional theaters across the country for more than a decade. On Broadway she designed Julie Taymor's production of *The Green Bird*. Favorite productions include *True Love*, for which she created an installation in an old zipper factory and turned car seats into audience seating, and *Flesh and Blood* at New York Theatre Workshop, for which she and the crew used eighteen-foot tree trunks to create a forest onstage. Recently she has been designing for opera, including productions of *Lucia di Lammermoor* at New York City Opera and *Giulio Cesare* at Houston Grand Opera. Since November 2002, she has been developing Theatre for One: a booth designed for one actor and one audience member. She is a graduate of NYU's Tisch School of the Arts and Lecturer at Princeton University.

LIZ LERMAN, co-author and originator of the *Critical Response Process*, is a performer, writer, educator, choreographer and Founding Artistic Director of Liz Lerman Dance Exchange, based in Takoma Park, Maryland. Her innovative work has been seen throughout the United States and abroad. Recognized in 2002 as a MacArthur Genius, she has also received an American Choreographer Award, the American Jewish Congress "Golda" Award, the first annual Pola Nirenska Award, the D.C. Mayor's Art Award and *Washingtonian* magazine's Washingtonian of the Year Award. Her work has been commissioned by Lincoln Center, American Dance Festival, Dancing in the Streets, BalletMet and the Kennedy Center. From 1994–1996, she directed and collaborated with The Music Hall in creating *The Shipyard Project* in Portsmouth, New Hampshire. She conceived and directed the *Hallelujah Project*, a national initiative in which the Dance Exchange created a series of celebratory dances through collaborations in fifteen communities from Maine to California between 1999 and 2002. She is a frequent keynote speaker and panelist for arts, community, religious and educational organizations, both nationally and internationally, and has consulted with such diverse organizations as Synagogue 2000, Harvard's Saguaro Seminar and the Juilliard School of Music. In addition to the *Critical Response Process*, she is the author of *Teaching Dance to Senior Adults* (Charles C. Thomas Books, Springfield, IL, 1984).

TODD LONDON is entering his ninth season as Artistic Director of New Dramatists, the nation's oldest center for the support and development of playwrights. He is former Managing Editor of *American Theatre* magazine and the author of *The Artistic Home* (Theatre Communications Group, New York, 1988). His essays and articles, blending arts journalism and advocacy, have appeared regularly in publications across the country and around the world, and have been translated for publication in Russia, North and South Africa, Scandinavia and, most recently, Serbia. He won the prestigious George Jean Nathan Award for Dramatic Criticism in 1997 for his essays in *American Theatre*, and a Milestone Award in 2001 for his first novel, *The World's Room* (Steerforth Press, Hanover, NH, 2001). That same year he accepted a special Tony Award honor on behalf of New Dramatists. In 1995 he was Guest Literary Director of the American Repertory Theatre and Visiting Lecturer of Dramatic Arts at Harvard. Former Chair of the New York State Council on the Arts Theater Panel and National Endowment for the Arts panelist, he serves on the board of Theatre Communications Group. He holds an M.F.A. in directing from Boston University and a Ph.D. in Literary Studies from American University.

DIANE MORRISON was on the board of New York's Signature Theatre Company from 1994–2001, serving as President and Chairman. During these formative years at Signature, she worked closely with Founding Artistic Director, Jim Houghton, to develop the board and the organization. She has been a founding member of TCG's National Council for the American Theatre. In 2001 Diane became the Executive Director of the Laura Pels Foundation, a major funder of theater in New York.

CHRISTINE FIEDLER O'CONNOR has twenty-five years of experience in not-for-profit management with a focus on organizational planning and capacity-building, revenue expansion, board-staff training, capital and endowment campaigns and relationship-building with diversified constituencies. She has held senior development positions with Seattle Repertory Theatre, American Conservatory Theater, Center Theatre Group/Mark Taper Forum and San Francisco Opera. Currently a consultant to not-for-profit organizations, both independently and through AlbertHall& Associates, LLC, she provides a wide range of services to performing arts, literary and other not-for-profit organizations. She helped design the University of Washington's Arts Management Certificate Program and teaches two courses in addition to serving on the program's advisory board. She previously taught at the University of Washington's Evans School of Public Affairs and San Francisco State University. She serves on the board of St. Joseph School in Seattle and is a member of the Washington Women's Foundation and its Cultural Grants Committee. She holds a B.A. from Chatham College.

TONEN SARA O'CONNOR became Managing Director of the Milwaukee Repertory Theater in 1974, after serving as Managing Director of the Cincinnati Playhouse in the Park, Producer of Theatre Company of Boston and Associate Producer of Company of the Four in Chicago, as well as serving variously as director, actress, stage manager, box office treasurer, wardrobe mistress and public relations director at other theaters. In October 1995, she completed her twenty-one year tenure as Managing Director with the Rep's successful "Campaign to Create the Future," a $10 million capital campaign.

She served as President of both Theatre Communications Group and the League of Resident Theatres, and, at various times, on the boards of the International Theatre Institute/U.S., American Arts Alliance, Theatre X, Milwaukee Chamber Theatre, First Stage Milwaukee, Milwaukee Artists Foundation, the Non-Traditional Casting Project, Milwaukee Arts Board and Ko-Thi Dance Company. She received the Zeisler Award from Theatre Communications Group for outstanding contributions to the administration of American theater, a lifetime service award from the Wisconsin Theatre Association, the Thomas DeGaetani Award from USITT and the Sacagawea Award from Professional Dimensions. Her book, *Working Space: The Milwaukee Repertory Theater Builds a Home* (Theatre Communications Group, New York, 1992), chronicles the eight-year saga of the Rep's leadership role in a $100 million downtown development in Milwaukee, which included the conversion of power plant structures into a three-theater complex.

She holds a B.A. with High Honors in Fine Arts from Swarthmore College and an M.A. in Drama from Tufts University, and was awarded the honorary degree of Doctor of Humane Letters by Mt. Mary College. She is the translator of a dozen French plays that have been produced by numerous U.S. regional theaters.

She began studying Zen Buddhism in 1982, has practiced in the Soto Zen tradition since 1986 and was ordained as a priest in 1994. Her Buddhist (and legal) name is Tonen. In addition to carrying out the administrative affairs of the Zen Center and editing and writing for its newsletter, she represents the Zen Center with the Milwaukee Association for Interfaith Relations, is active with the local chapter of the Buddhist Peace Fellowship, and serves on the Department of Corrections Religious Practices Advisory Committee, in recognition of her work with approximately seventy inmates in seven state prisons.

JIM O'QUINN has served as Editor-in-Chief of *American Theatre* since the monthly national arts magazine was founded in 1984. He has also been Editor of the biannual *Journal* of the Stage Directors and Choreographers Foundation, Managing Editor of *The Drama Review* and Editor and Publisher of *The DeQuincy Journal*, an award-winning weekly newspaper in southwest Louisiana. He reviewed theater regularly for the now-defunct

Manhattan weekly, *7 Days*, and his articles and reviews have appeared in *Stagebill*, *Theatre Heute*, *Tatler*, *High Performance* and other publications. He has also worked as a city-desk reporter for New Orleans's *Times-Picayune*, and as a composer and music arranger for theater. His children's opera *The Littlest Emperor* was produced in 1978 at New Orleans's Contemporary Arts Center.

DAWN RAINS has served as Director of Development for Seattle Repertory Theatre since 1999. Together with a sixty-five-member board of trustees and an eight-member staff, she is responsible for Seattle Rep's $3.2 million annual fund as well as completing a $15 million endowment campaign. She recently led a strategic planning process for the National Corporate Theatre Fund. She curates Theatre Communications Group's *Centerpiece* series on development. Prior to her tenure at Seattle Rep, she served as development and volunteer coordinator for the Council for Prevention of Child Abuse and Neglect. She has a Masters in Public Administration degree from the University of Washington's Daniel J. Evans School of Public Affairs, a Certificate in Fundraising Management from the University of Washington Extension and a B.A. from The Evergreen State College. She also serves on the board of Women's Funding Alliance.

NANCY ROCHE has been a trustee of CENTERSTAGE in Baltimore since 1987, serving as President of the Board for seven years and as interim Managing Director for one year. She has been a consultant on governance for National Arts Stabilization (now National Arts Strategies), was a councilor of the Maryland State Arts Commission from 1992–99, and has twice served as lay panelist for the NEA. In the summer of 2000, she participated as a theater trustee in the National Critics' Institute at the Eugene O'Neill Theater Center in Waterford, Connecticut, returning the following summer as a founding member of their week-long Trustees Program. She is a founding member of the National Council for the American Theatre and serves as a trustee and Treasurer of the board of Theatre Communications Group. In addition, she serves on the boards of the Roland Park Country School, the Institute for Christian-Jewish Studies and the Baltimore School for the Arts. She is a graduate of Dominican University and received an M.A. in Teaching and a Master of Liberal Arts, both from The Johns Hopkins University.

JUDITH O. RUBIN is Chairman of the Board of Playwrights Horizons, a distinguished thirty-three-year-old Off-Broadway theater in New York City. She served for eight years as a member of the National Council on the Arts of the NEA, six years as a member of the board of Theatre Communications Group, and has chaired the National Council for the American Theatre since its inception. She is a member of the Tony Awards nominating committee. She is Vice-Chairman of the board of Public Radio

International, and since 1989 has been a member of the New York State Council on the Arts. In 2003, she was named to the Cultural Affairs Advisory Commission of the New York City Department of Cultural Affairs, and in 2004 she was named to the Yale University Council Committee on Theatre at Yale. From 2002–2004 she served as a member of the Board of Regents of the State of New York, representing the First Judicial District (Manhattan). She is a trustee of the Mount Sinai Health System in New York and its School of Medicine. She is a former trustee of the Center for Arts and Culture, a cultural policy think tank in Washington, D.C. She was Commissioner for Protocol for the City of New York during the four years of the Dinkins administration, and is former President and Chairman of the 92nd Street Y, a large cultural center in New York. She is a graduate of Wellesley College.

NANCY SASSER is a principal of Cool Spring Analytics, which provides consulting services to arts organizations, other not-for-profits and funders in the areas of governance, strategic planning, financial management and financial analysis. She was a consultant to National Arts Stabilization (now National Arts Strategies), assumed the presidency of the organization in 1995 and served in that role until 2000, when she returned to consulting. In addition to working one-on-one with organizations and communities of funders on planning, financial management and governance issues, she conceptualized and oversaw development of a series of executive education programs designed to address key needs of today's arts and culture managers. Her career has intertwined business and the arts, including her work as a CPA, as Chief Financial Officer of American Oil Change Corporation (a Jiffy Lube franchise) and as Assistant Director of Houston Grand Opera. She holds a degree in art, an M.B.A. and an M.S. in Health Services Administration, all from Stanford University. She serves on the boards of the Maryland Institute and The Walters Art Museum. Past professional affiliations include the Advisory Council of Stanford Business School and numerous other not-for-profit organizations.

ROCHE SCHULFER is in his twenty-fourth season as Executive Director of Chicago's Goodman Theatre. He has supervised more than three hundred productions, including more than one hundred world or American premieres. In 1978, he inaugurated the Goodman's annual production of *A Christmas Carol*, which recently celebrated its twenty-fifth anniversary as a Chicago holiday tradition. With Artistic Director Robert Falls, he accepted the 1992 Tony Award for Outstanding Regional Theatre on behalf of the Goodman, and the 1999 Tony Award for Best Revival of a Play for *Death of a Salesman*, a production that originated at the Goodman. In June 2003, *Time* magazine named the Goodman the number one regional theater in the country. He has negotiated the transfer of dozens of Goodman productions to many different cities, including New York, Los Angeles, London, Dublin and Paris. He was responsible for supervising the development and construction of the new Goodman Theatre facility in downtown Chicago.

He has served in leadership roles with the American Arts Alliance (the national advocacy organization for museums, theaters, dance and opera companies), the Illinois Arts Alliance, Theatre Communications Group, the League of Resident Theatres and the Illinois Arts Council. He is a founder, past President and board member of the League of Chicago Theatres. He has served on grant panels for the National Endowment for the Arts, the Illinois Arts Council and the Department of Cultural Affairs. He has been recognized for his work as a national leader in arts advocacy by the city of Chicago, the *Chicago Tribune*, *Chicago* magazine, the Illinois Arts Alliance, the Chicago Jaycees, the Arts and Business Council, Columbia College, Lawyers for the Creative Arts, the League of Chicago Theatres and the American Arts Alliance. He consults with many arts organizations and has lectured at a number of colleges and universities. He currently teaches at DePaul Theatre School. He is a graduate of the University of Notre Dame and was Chairman of its Cultural Arts Commission.

BARBARA E. TAYLOR is Senior Consultant at the Academic Search Consultation Service, Washington, D.C. Prior to joining Academic Search, she served for twelve years as Director and then as Vice President for Programs and Research at the Association of Governing Boards of Universities and Colleges. She is a trustee of Wittenberg University, Springfield, Ohio; a senior fellow of the Cheswick Center, Rockville, Maryland; a fellow of the Stanford Forum for Higher Education Futures, Stanford, California; and a member of the board of directors of *In Trust* magazine. She is the co-author of *Improving the Performance of Governing Boards* (the American Council on Education/Oryx Press, Phoenix, 1996) and *The Effective Board of Trustees* (the American Council on Education/Oryx Press, Phoenix, 1991).

PAULA VOGEL, playwright, received the Pulitzer Prize for her play *How I Learned to Drive*, as well as the Lortel, Drama Desk, Outer Critics Circle and New York Drama Critics awards for best play and her second OBIE. The play has been produced all over the world, and her screenplay is in development for HBO. Her other plays include *The Long Christmas Ride Home*, *The Mineola Twins*, *The Baltimore Waltz*, *Hot 'N' Throbbing*, *Desdemona*, *And Baby Makes Seven* and *The Oldest Profession*. Theatre Communications Group has published two anthologies of her work, *The Mammary Plays* and *The Baltimore Waltz and Other Plays*, as well as *The Long Christmas Ride Home*. She has received the Rhode Island Pell Award in the Arts, the Hull-Warriner Award, the PEN/Laura Pels Foundation Award, The Pew Charitable Trust Senior Award, an AT&T New Plays Award, a Fund for New American Plays Grant, a Rockefeller Foundation

Bellagio Center Fellowship, several National Endowment for the Arts fellowships, a McKnight Fellowship, MacDowell Colony residencies, the Susan Smith Blackburn Award and the American Academy of Arts and Letters Prize in Literature. She is the Adele Kellenberg Seaver Professor of Creative Writing at Brown University, where she directs the M.F.A. Playwriting program. She was Signature Theatre's 2004–05 Playwright-in-Residence.

JAAN WHITEHEAD currently chairs the board of the SITI Company, an ensemble theater in New York led by Anne Bogart. She has served on the boards of The Acting Company, Arena Stage, Living Stage and the Whole Theatre Company, where her particular interests have been board development and institutional change. She has also been a trustee of Theatre Communications Group and the National Cultural Alliance (an arts advocacy group in Washington), and is a founding member of the National Council for the American Theatre. In addition to her work as a trustee, she has been Executive Director of Theatre for a New Audience in New York and Development Director of CENTERSTAGE in Baltimore.

She graduated from Wellesley College, holds an M.A. in economics from the University of Michigan, and early in her career worked as an economist for private industry and the Federal Reserve Board. She received her Ph.D. in political theory from Princeton in 1988. She taught at Georgetown University for several years but, as her involvement in theater deepened, she made the arts her main work while retaining her interests in economic and political theory. She has recently drawn on this background in writing a series of essays on the challenges facing the arts in a commercial society.

RESOURCE GUIDE

Listed here are suggestions of books, articles, websites and service organizations that readers can consult for further information about the performing arts, boards and the particular topics covered in each article. The listings are a selection of the growing literature on governance and additional resources can be found either in the books and articles cited here or by following the links on the various websites.

General Background

Books

Robert C. Andringa and Ted W. Engstrom, *Nonprofit Board Answer Book: Practical Guide for Board Members and Chief Executives*, BoardSource (formerly Center for Nonprofit Boards), Washington, D.C., 2002.

Robert C. Andringa with Outi Flynn and Sandra R. Sabo, *Nonprofit Board Answer Book II: Beyond the Basics*, BoardSource, Washington, D.C., 2002.

Stephen R. Block, *Why Nonprofits Fail*, Jossey-Bass Inc., San Francisco, 2004.

Marla J. Bobowick, Sandra R. Hughes and Berit M. Lakey, *Transforming Board Structure* (first in a series of six booklets on board committees), BoardSource, Washington, D.C., 2004.

William G. Bowen, *Inside the Boardroom*, John Wiley & Sons, Inc., New York, 1994.

John Carver, *Boards That Make a Difference*, Second Edition, Jossey-Bass Inc., San Francisco, 1997.

John Carver and Miriam Mayhew Carver, *Reinventing Your Board: A Step-by-Step Guide to Implementing Policy Governance*, Jossey-Bass Inc., San Francisco, 1997.

Richard P. Chait, Thomas P. Holland and Barbara E. Taylor, *Improving the Performance of Governing Boards*, The Oryx Press, Phoenix, 1996.

Richard P. Chait, William P. Ryan and Barbara Taylor, *Governance as Leadership: Reframing the Work of Nonprofit Boards*, BoardSource, Washington, D.C., 2004.

Diane J. Duca, *Nonprofit Boards: Roles, Responsibilities and Performance*, John Wiley & Sons, Inc., New York, 1996.

Peter Dobkin Hall, *A History of Nonprofit Boards in the United States*, BoardSource, Washington, D.C., 1997.

Cyril O. Houle, *Governing Boards*, Jossey-Bass Inc., San Francisco, 1989.

Richard T. Ingram, *Ten Responsibilities of Nonprofit Boards* (first in series of nine booklets on basic governance), BoardSource, Washington, D.C., 2003.

Sabrina Klein, *The Art of Serving on a Performing Arts Board*, Theatre Bay Area and National Center for Nonprofit Boards, 1999.

Paul C. Light, *Sustaining Nonprofit Performance: The Case for Capacity Building and the Evidence to Support It*, Brookings Institution Press, Washington, D.C., 2004.

Nello McDaniel and George Thorn, *Arts Boards: Creating a New Community Equation*, ARTS Action Issues, New York, 1994 (www.artsaction.com).

Nello McDaniel and George Thorn, *Leading Arts Boards—An Arts Professional's Guide*, ARTS Action Issues, New York, 2005 (www.artsaction.com).

Elizabeth Mills and R. Christopher Baker, "Finding Governance Resources: A Roadmap to the Web," *Centerpiece*: February 2000, Theatre Communications Group, Management Programs Archives (www.tcg.org).

Maureen K. Robinson, *Nonprofit Boards That Work*, John Wiley & Sons, Inc., New York, 2001.

Susan Kenny Stevens, *Nonprofit Lifecycles: Stage-based Wisdom for Nonprofit Capacity*, distributed by LarsonAllen Public Service Group, Minneapolis, 2001 (www.larsonallen.com).

D. Benson Tesdahl, *The Nonprofit Board's Guide to Bylaws*, BoardSource, Washington D.C., 2003.

Periodicals

Chronicle of Philanthropy: Key resource for not-for-profit fundraising (www.philanthropy.com).

The Nonprofit Quarterly: Articles on boards, fundraising and not-for-profits (www.nonprofitquarterly.org).

Reader: Ideas and Information on Arts and Culture: In-depth articles on arts and culture, book reviews and reprinted speeches and articles; Grantsmakers in the Arts (www.giarts.org).

Reports on the Performing Arts

Americans for the Arts, *Arts & Economic Prosperity: The Economic Impact of Nonprofit Arts Organizations and Their Audiences*, Americans for the Arts, Washington, D.C., 2002.

Mary Kopczynski and Mark Hager, *The Value of the Performing Arts in Ten Communities: A Summary Report*, Performing Arts Research Coalition and the Urban Institute, Washington, D.C., 2004.

Richard Kushner and Thomas Pollak, *The Finance and Operations of Nonprofit Performing Arts Organizations in 2001 and 2002*, Performing Arts Research Coalition and the Urban Institute, Washington, D.C., 2004.

Kevin McCarthy, Arthur Brooks, Julia Lowell and Laura Zakaras, *The Performing Arts in a New Era*, Rand Corporation, Santa Monica, CA, 2001.

Resources on Theater

American Theatre magazine, Theatre Communications Group, New York (www.tcg.org).

Dramatists Sourcebook, 23rd Edition (updated biennially), Theatre Communications Group, New York, New York, 2004 (www.tcg.org).

Jeremy Gerard, *Act II: Creating Partnerships and Setting Agendas for the Future of the American Theater*, The League of American Theatres and Producers and Theatre Communications Group, New York, 2002 (www.tcg.org).

Theatre Directory 2004–05 (updated annually), Theatre Communications Group, New York, New York, 2004 (www.tcg.org).

Zannie Giraud Voss and Glenn Voss with Christopher Shuff and Katie Tabor, *In Whom We Trust III: Theatre Governing Boards in 2004*, *Cenetrpiece*:

November, 2004, Theatre Communications Group, Management Program Archives (www.tcg.org).

Zannie Giraud Voss and Glenn Voss with Christopher Shuff and Katie Tabor, "Theatre Facts 2003," Theatre Communications Group, New York, 2004.

Academic Theater Journals

The Drama Review (TDR), The MIT Press, Cambridge, Massachusetts (mitpress.mit.edu/tdr).

A Journal of Performance and Art (PAJ), The MIT Press, Cambridge, Massachusetts (muse.jhu.edu/).

New Theatre Quarterly, Cambridge University Press, Cambridge, England (journals.cambridge.org).

Theater, Duke University Press (for Yale School of Drama), Durham, North Carolina (www.yale.edu).

Theatre Topics, Johns Hopkins University Press, Baltimore (www.press.jhu.edu/journals).

Websites

Americans for the Arts (www.americansforthearts.org): Main lobbying organization for the arts; publications on the arts such as economic impact statements, advocacy manuals and studies on community-based arts.

BoardSource (www.boardsource.org): Most extensive collection of publications on governance (formerly Center for Nonprofit Boards).

The Center for Arts and Culture (www.culturalpolicy.org): Arts policy research institute in Washington, D.C., various studies and publications.

The Foundation Center (www.fdncenter.org): Directories and information on fundraising as well as books on management and governance.

National Arts Strategies (www.artstabilization.org): Planning, financial and management material (formerly National Arts Stabilization).

National Endowment for the Arts (www.nea.gov): Extensive publications on the arts.

Nonprofit Genie (www.genie.org): Publications, newsletters and other information on not-for-profit organizations.

The President's Committee on the Arts and the Humanities (www.pcah.gov): Works to incorporate the arts and humanities into White House objectives and provides a bridge between federal agencies and the private sector. It provides recognition of cultural excellence, engages in research, initiates special projects and stimulates private funding.

Arts Service Organizations

American Association of Museums (www.aam-us.org): Promotes excellence within the museum community through advocacy, professional education, information exchange, accreditation and guidance on professional standards.

The American Symphony Orchestra League (www.symphony.org): Provides leadership and service to American orchestras while communicating to the public the value and importance of orchestras and the music they perform.

The Association of Art Museum Directors (www.aamd.org): Supports its members by establishing professional standards, serving as a forum for the exchange of information and ideas, acting as an advocate for its member art museums and being a leader in shaping public discourse about the arts community and the role of art in society.

The Association of Performing Arts Presenters (www.artspresenters.org): With a membership of 1,600 arts presenters, including large performing arts centers as well as small presenters, APAP brings performing artists and audiences together.

Chorus America (www.chorusamerica.org): Serves the spectrum of professional, volunteer, children/youth and symphony/opera choruses by providing information, publications, conferences, consulting and other programs to support choruses in North America.

Dance/USA (www.danceusa.org): Advances dance by addressing the needs, concerns and interests of the professional dance community.

National Alliance for Musical Theatre (www.namt.net): The only national service organization dedicated to musical theater, NAMT is committed to preserving and enhancing the American musical art form. Its membership includes theater institutions, universities and independent producers.

OPERA America (www.operaam.org): Serves and strengthens the field of opera by providing a variety of information and technical and administrative resources to the greater opera community with the mission of promoting opera as exciting and accessible to individuals from all walks of life.

THEATRE COMMUNICATIONS GROUP (www.tcg.org): The national service organization for the not-for-profit theater serves to strengthen, nurture and promote the professional not-for-profit American theater. Publisher of *American Theatre* magazine, the *Centerpiece* series on governance, and plays and books on theater.

The Art of Theater

Peter Brook, *The Empty Space*, Atheneum, New York, 1984.

Peter Brook, *The Shifting Point*, Theatre Communications Group, New York, 1987.

Martin Esslin, *An Anatomy of Drama*, Hill and Wang, New York, 1976.

Peter Hall, *The Necessary Theatre*, Theatre Communications Group, New York, 1999.

Paul Kuritz, *The Making of Theatre History*, Prentice Hall, Englewood Cliffs, NJ, 1988.

Todd London, *The Artistic Home: Discussions with Artistic Directors of America's Institutional Theatres*, Theatre Communications Group, New York, 1988.

Jonnie Patricia Mobley, *Dictionary of Theatre and Drama Terms*, NTC Publishing Group, Chicago, 1992.

Going National: A Nutshell History of the Regional Theater Movement

Theatre Communications Group, *Preserving the Legacy: Voices of the American Theatre*, Volumes 1–3 (DVD), New York, 2003.

Joseph Wesley Zeigler, *Regional Theatre: The Revolutionary Stage*, Da Capo Press, New York, 1973.

Whither (or Wither) Art?

Lenora Inez Brown, "The Real World," *American Theatre*: November 2002.

Polly Carl, "Creating the Swell," *American Theatre*: November 2002.

Todd London, "The Shape of Things," *American Theatre*: November 2002.

Cynthia Mayeda, moderator, "Is Art the Bottom Line," *American Theatre*: May/June 2003.

Jaan Whitehead, "Art Will Out," *American Theatre*: October 2002.

National Arts Policy: What Trustees Need to Know

Americans for the Arts, *The Nancy Hanks Lecture on Arts and Public Policy, 10th Anniversary Compendium*, Washington, D.C., 1997 (more current lectures available by individual years from American for the Arts).

Livingston Biddle, *Our Government and the Arts: A Perspective from the Inside*, ACA Books, New York, 1988 (contains story on the founding of the NEA).

Gigi Bradford, Michael Gary and Glenn Wallach, editors, *The Politics of Culture: Policy Perspectives for Individuals, Institutions, and Communities*, The Center for Arts and Culture, The New Press, New York, 2000.

Joni M. Cherbo and Margaret J. Wyszomirski, editors, *The Public Life of the Arts in America*, Rutgers University Press, New Brunswick, New Jersey, 2000.

Hallie Flanagan, *Arena: The Story of the Federal Theatre*, Limelight Editions, New York, 1985.

Jerre Mangione, *The Dream and the Deal: The Federal Writers' Project, 1935–1943*, Syracuse University Press, Syracuse, New York, 1996.

Kevin F. McCarthy, Elizabeth H. Ondaatje, Laura Zakaras and Arthur Brooks, *Gifts of the Muse: Reframing the Debate about the Benefits of the Arts*, Rand Corporation, Santa Monica, CA, 2005. Commissioned by the Wallace Foundation (www.wallacefunds.org).

Arthur M. Melzer, Jerry Weinberger and M. Richard Zinman, editors, *Democracy and the Arts*, Cornell University Press, Ithaca, New York, 1999.

Kevin V. Mulcahy and Margaret Jane Wyszomirski, editors, *America's Commitment to Culture: Government and the Arts*, Westview Press, Inc., Boulder, Colorado, 1995.

The Role of Advocacy in Trustee Governance

NATIONAL ARTS ADVOCACY ORGANIZATIONS

THE AMERICAN ARTS ALLIANCE (www.americanartsalliance.org): Represents the interests of America's professional not-for-profit arts organizations before Congress and other branches of government. Website contains voting records and other advocacy tools.

AMERICANS FOR THE ARTS (www.americansforthearts.org): Works to advance the arts in America and is dedicated to representing and serving local communities and creating opportunities for every American to participate in and appreciate all forms of art. Website details voting records and lists committees and staff responsibilities for arts issues.

THE ARTS EDUCATION PARTNERSHIP (www.aep-arts.org): National coalition of arts, education, business, philanthropic and government organizations that promotes the essential role of the arts in the learning and development of every child and in the improvement of America's schools. The AEP was formed in 1995 through a cooperative agreement among the National Endowment for the Arts, the U.S. Department of Education, the National Assembly of State Arts Agencies and the Council of Chief State Schools Officers.

INDEPENDENT SECTOR (www.independentsector.org): Coalition of leading not-for-profit organizations, foundations and corporations whose goal is to strengthen not-for-profit initiatives, philanthropy and citizen action.

NATIONAL ASSEMBLY OF STATE ARTS AGENCIES (www.nasaa-arts.org): Membership organization of the nation's state arts agencies that empowers state arts agencies through strategic assistance that fosters leadership, enhances planning and decision-making, and increases resources.

NATIONAL ARTS SERVICE ORGANIZATIONS

Theatre Communications Group, "Grassroots Kit" (www.tcg.org/frames/advocacy/fs_advocacy_tools.htm). (See "Arts Service Organizations," under "General Background" for more information about TCG.)

FEDERAL GOVERNMENT LINKS

National Endowment for the Arts (www.nea.gov).

Thomas: Legislative information from the House and Senate, a service of the Library of Congress (http://thomas.loc.gov).

United States House of Representatives (www.house.gov).

United States Senate (www.senate.gov).

The Changing Legal Environment for the Arts

Better Business Bureau Wise Giving Alliance, *Standards for Charity Accountability*, 2003 (www.give.org/standards).

BoardSource and Independent Sector, *The Sarbanes-Oxley Act and Implications for Nonprofit Organizations*, 2003 (www.independentsector.org).

GuideStar (www.guidestar.org).

Bruce R. Hopkins, *Legal Responsibilities of Nonprofit Boards*, BoardSource, Washington, D.C., 2003.

Thomas K. Hyatt, editor, *The Nonprofit Legal Landscape*, BoardSource, Washington, D.C. 2005.

Independent Sector, *Statement of Values and Code of Ethics for Nonprofit and Philanthropic Organizations*, February 3, 2004 (www.independentsector.org).

Daniel L. Kurtz, *Board Liability: Guide for Nonprofit Directors*, Moyer Bell Ltd., New York, 1988.

Maryland Association of Nonprofit Organizations, *Standards for Excellence: An Ethics And Accountability Code for the Nonprofit Sector (1998–2004)* (www.marylandnonprofits.org).

The Nonprofit Quarterly, "Regulation and Accountability: The New Wave," Special Issue on the Regulatory Landscape, 2005 (www.nonprofitquarterly.org).

Panel on the Nonprofit Sector, *Interim Report Presented to the Senate Finance Committee*, March 1, 2005 (www.independentsector.org).

Senate Finance Committee Hearings, *Charity Oversight and Reform: Keeping Bad Things from Happening to Good Charities*, June 22, 2004.

Grant Thornton, *National Board Governance Survey for Not-for-Profit Organizations*, September 2004 (www.grantthornton.com/nfp).

The Artists Speak

Rob Austin and Lee Devin, *Artful Making: What Managers Need to Know about How Artists Work*, Prentice Hall, Englewood Cliffs, New Jersey, 2003.

Arthur Bartow, *The Director's Voice*, Theatre Communications Group, New York, 1988.

Helen Krich Chinoy and Linda Walsh Jenkins, editors, *Women in American Theatre*, Theatre Communications Group, New York, 2005.

Holly Hill, *Actors' Lives: On and Off the American Stage*, Theatre Communications Group, New York, 1993.

Todd London, *The Artistic Home: Discussions with Artistic Directors of America's Institutional Theatres*, Theatre Communications Group, New York, 1988.

David Savran, *In Their Own Words: Contemporary American Playwrights*, Theatre Communications Group, New York, 1988.

Urban Institute, *Investing in Creativity: A Study of the Support Structure for U.S. Artists*, Washington, D.C., 2003 (contains an extensive bibliography of resources on artists and creativity).

Jaan Whitehead, "To Have and Have Not," *American Theatre*: March 2001.

The Spirit of Governance: Six Interviews

Gwen Cochran Hadden, "Diversifying Our Boards," *Centerpiece*: July 2000, Theatre Communications Group, Management Programs Archives (www.tcg.org).

Liz Lerman and John Borstel, *Critical Response Process*, Dance Exchange, Inc., Takoma Park, Maryland, 2003 (www.danceexchange.org).

Board Development

Sandra R. Hughes, Berit M. Lakey and Marla J. Bobowick, *The Board Building Cycle*, BoardSource, Washington, D.C., 2000.

Management Consultants for the Arts, "The Chair: More than Just a Title," *Centerpiece*: March 2001, Theatre Communications Group, Management Programs Archives (www.tcg.org).

Nancy Roche, "Professional Development for Trustees," *Centerpiece*: April 2001, Theatre Communications Group, Management Programs Archives (www.tcg.org).

Katherine Tyler Scott, *Creating Caring and Capable Boards*, Jossey-Bass Inc., San Francisco, 2000.

Jennifer Sokolov, "Enduring Partnerships," *Centerpiece*: October 1999, Theatre Communications Group, Management Programs Archives (www.tcg.org).

(Most of the books under "General Background" have good chapters on board development.)

The New Work of the Nonprofit Board

Richard P. Chait, Thomas P. Holland and Barbara E. Taylor, *The Effective Board of Trustees*, The Oryx Press, Phoenix, 1993.

Richard P. Chait, Thomas P. Holland and Barbara E. Taylor, *Improving the Performance of Governing Boards*, The Oryx Press, Phoenix, 1996.

Richard P. Chait, William P. Ryan and Barbara E. Taylor, *Governance as Leadership: Reframing the Work of Nonprofit Boards*, BoardSource, Washington, D.C., 2004.

A Guide to Strategic Planning: Taking Aim Before You Fire

Michael Allison and Jude Kaye, *Strategic Planning for Nonprofit Organizations*, Support Center for Nonprofit Management, John Wiley & Sons, Inc., New York, 1997.

Bryan W. Berry, *Strategic Planning Workbook for Nonprofit Organizations*, BoardSource, Washington, D.C., 1997.

BoardSource, *Strategic Planning: Design for the Future*, Special Edition of *Board Member* magazine: Vol. 11, Issue 5, Washington, D.C.

John M. Bryson, *Strategic Planning for Public and Nonprofit Organizations*, Third Edition, Jossey-Bass Inc., San Francisco, 2004.

John M. Bryson and Farnum K. Alston, *Workbook: Creating and Implementing Your Strategic Plan*, Second Edition, Jossey-Bass Inc., San Francisco, 1995.

Sandra Hughes, *To Go Forward, Retreat! The Board Retreat Handbook*, BoardSource, Washington, D.C., 1999.

Deborah L. Kocsis and Susan A. Waechter, *Driving Strategic Planning*, BoardSource, Washington, D.C., 2003.

WEBSITES

Lessons Learned Toolsite (www.nea.org/resources/lessons): A compendium of planning advice from noted arts consultants, National Endowment for the Arts Publications.

National Arts Strategies (www.artstabilization.org).

Understanding Financial Statements

GUIDES FOR BOARD MEMBERS

Steven Berger, *Understanding Nonprofit Financial Statements*, BoardSource, Washington, D.C., 2003.

Andrew Lang, *Financial Responsibilities of Nonprofit Boards*, BoardSource, Washington, D.C., 2003.

Management Resources

Thomas A. McLaughlin, *Streetsmart Financial Basics for Nonprofit Managers*, John Wiley & Sons, Inc., New York, 2002.

Susan Kenny Stevens, *All the Way to the Bank: Smart Nonprofit Money Management*, Weishair & Co., LLP, Minneapolis, 2002.

Accounting Manuals

Richard F. Larkin and Marie DiTommasco, *Wiley Not-for-Profit Accounting Field Guide*, John Wiley & Sons, Inc., New York, 2003.

John A. Tracy, *Accounting for Dummies*, Hungry Minds, Inc., New York, 2001.

Websites

National Arts Strategies (www.artstabilization.org).

The Annual Fund

Kent E. Dove, Jeffrey A. Lindauer and Carolyn P. Madvig, *Conducting a Successful Annual Giving Program*, Jossey-Bass Inc., San Francisco, 2001.

Worth George, *Fearless Fundraising*, BoardSource, Washington, D.C., 2003.

Kay Sprinkel Grace, *Beyond Fundraising: New Strategies for Nonprofit Innovation and Investment*, John Wiley & Sons, Inc., New York, 2005.

Russ Alan Prince, *The Seven Faces of Philanthropy*, Jossey-Bass Inc., San Francisco, 1994.

Dawn Rains, "The Role of Trustees in Major Gifts Fundraising," *Centerpiece*: October 2003, Theatre Communications Group, Management Programs Archives (www.tcg.org).

Henry Rosso, *Achieving Excellence in Fundraising*, Jossey-Bass Inc., San Francisco, 2003.

Terry Schaff and Doug Schaff, *The Fundraising Planner: A Working Model for Raising Dollars You Need*, Jossey-Bass Inc., San Francisco, 1999.

Alan L. Wendroff and Kay Sprinkel Grace, *High Impact Philanthropy: How Donors, Boards, and Nonprofit Organizations Can Transform Communities*, John Wiley & Sons, Inc., New York, 2001.

WEBSITES

Association of Fundraising Professions (www.afpnet.org).

Board Café (www.boardcafe.org).

Center on Philanthropy at Indiana University (www.philanthropy.iupui.edu).

Charity Channel (www.charitychannel.com).

The Chronicle of Philanthropy (www.philanthropy.com).

The Foundation Center (www.fdncenter.org).

Grassroots Fundraising Journal (www.grassrootsfundraising.org).

Guidestar (www.guidestar.org).

Capital and Endowment Campaigns

Kent E. Dove, Conducting a Successful Capital Campaign and Planned Giving Program, Jossey-Bass, Inc., San Francisco, 2000.

Planned Giving Services, *Charitable Gift Annuities: The Complete Resource Manual* (www.plannedgivingservices.com).

Dawn Rains, "Endowments in a Changing Economy," *Centerpiece*: October 2002, Theater Communications Group, Management Programs Archives (www.tcg.org).

William J. Sturtevant, *The Artful Journey: Cultivating and Soliciting the Major Gift*, Bonus Books, Inc., Chicago, 1997.

Grant Thornton, *Planned Giving: A Board Member's Perspective*, BoardSource, Washington, D.C., 2003.

WEBSITES

NATIONAL COMMITTEE ON PLANNED GIVING (www.ncpg.org): A wide range of background information, resource materials, training programs, legislative updates and links to other organizations.

PLANNED GIVING TODAY (www.pgtoday.com): Practical resources for the gift planning professionals.

(Many national consulting firms' websites provide articles, sample gift charts and other background materials on capital campaigns.)

Leadership Succession in Not-for-Profit Organizations: A Board Member's Viewpoint

Illinois Arts Alliance Foundation, *Succession: Arts Leadership for the 21st Century*, Chicago, 2003.

Merianne Liteman, "The Board's Role in Succession Planning," *Centerpiece*: June 2003, Theatre Communications Group, Management Programs Archives (www.tcg.org).

Susan Kenny Stevens, "Helping Founders Succeed," *Centerpiece*: December 1999, Theater Communications Group, Management Programs Archives (www.tcg.org).

Websites

Transition Guides (www.transitionguides.com): Extensive information and articles on management transitions.

Additional Perspectives: Small Theaters, Artist Trustees and Alternative Models

Susan Gross, Karl Mathiasen and Nancy Franco, *Organizational Life Cycles: Revisited*, Management Assistant Group, MAG News, Summer 1998 (www.managementassistance.org).

Karl Mathiasen, *Board Passages: Three Key Stages in a Nonprofit Board's Life Cycle*, BoardSource, Fifth Printing, Washington D.C., 1998.

Nello McDaniel and George Thorn, *Arts Boards: Creating a New Community Equation*, ARTS Action Issues, New York, 1994 (www.artsaction.com).

Nello McDaniel and George Thorn, *Toward a New Arts Order: Process, Power, Change*, ARTS Action Issues, New York, 1993 (www.artsaction.com).

Susan Kenny Stevens, *Nonprofit Lifecycles: Stage-Based Wisdom for Nonprofit Capacity*, distributed by LarsonAllen Public Service Group, Minneapolis, 2001 (www.larsonallen.com).

Jaan Whitehead, "Art Will Out," *American Theatre*: October 2002.

NANCY ROCHE has been a trustee of CENTERSTAGE in Baltimore since 1987, serving as President of the Board for seven years and as interim Managing Director for one year. She has been a consultant on governance for the National Arts Stabilization (now National Arts Strategies), a councilor of the Maryland State Arts Commission from 1992–1999 and has twice served as lay panelist for the NEA. In the summer of 2000, she participated as a theater trustee in the National Critics' Institute at the Eugene O'Neill Theater Center in Waterford, CT, returning in the following summer as a founding member of their week-long Trustees Program. She is a founding member of the National Council for the American Theatre and serves as a trustee and treasurer of the board of Theatre Communications Group. In addition, she serves on the boards of the Roland Park Country School, the Institute for Christian-Jewish Studies and the Baltimore School for the Arts. She is a graduate of Dominican University and received an M.A. in Teaching and an M.L.A., both from The Johns Hopkins University.

JAAN WHITEHEAD currently chairs the board of the SITI Company, an ensemble theater in New York led by Anne Bogart. She has served on the boards of The Acting Company, Arena Stage, Living Stage and The Whole Theatre Company where her particular interests have been board development and institutional change. She has also been a trustee of Theatre Communications Group and the National Cultural Alliance, an arts advocacy group in Washington, and is a founding member of the National Council for the American Theatre. In addition to her work as a trustee, she has been Executive Director of Theatre for a New Audience in New York and Development Director of CENTERSTAGE in Baltimore.

Ms. Whitehead graduated from Wellesley College, holds an M.A. in economics from the University of Michigan and, early in her career, worked as an economist for private industry and the Federal Reserve Board. She received her Ph.D. in political theory from Princeton in 1988. She taught at Georgetown University for several years but, as her involvement in theater deepened, she made the arts her main work while retaining her interests in economic and political theory. Drawing on this background, she has recently been writing a series of essays on the challenges facing the arts in a commercial society.

THEATRE COMMUNICATIONS GROUP (TCG), the national organization for the American theater, offers a wide array of services in line with its mission: to strengthen, nurture and promote the professional not-for-profit American theater. Artistic programs support theaters and theater artists by awarding $3 million in grants annually, and offer career development programs for artists. Management programs provide professional development opportunities for theater leaders through workshops, conferences, forums and publications, as well as industry research on the finances and practices of the American not-for-profit theater. Advocacy, conducted in conjunction with the dance, presenting and opera fields, includes guiding lobbying efforts and providing theaters with timely alerts about legislative developments. The country's leading independent press specializing in dramatic literature, TCG's publications include *American Theatre* magazine, the *ArtSEARCH* employment bulletin, plays, translations and theater reference books. As the U.S. Center of UNESCO's International Theatre Institute, a worldwide network, TCG supports cross-cultural exchange through travel grants and other assistance to traveling theater professionals. Through these programs, TCG seeks to increase the organizational efficiency of its member theaters, cultivate and celebrate the artistic talent and achievements of the field, and promote a larger public understanding of and appreciation for the theater field. TCG serves more than 430 member theaters nationwide.